WOMEN
CHRISTIAN
MYSTICS

Speak to Our Times

Edited by DAVID B. PERRIN, o.m.i.

SHEED & WARD
FRANKLIN, WISCONSIN

As an apostolate of the Priests of the Sacred Heart, a Catholic religious congregation, the mission of Sheed & Ward is to publish books of contemporary impact and enduring merit in Catholic Christian thought and action. The books published, however, reflect the opinion of their authors and are not meant to represent the official position of the Priests of the Sacred Heart.

2001

Sheed & Ward
7373 South Lovers Lane Road
Franklin, Wisconsin 53132
1-800-266-5564

Printed in the United States of America

Cover and interior design by Madonna Gauding
Cover art used with permission from Freydoon Rassouli, (www.rassouli.com)

Library of Congress Cataloging-in-Publication Data

Women Christian mystics speak to our times / edited by David B. Perrin.
     p. cm.
  Includes bibliographical references.
  ISBN 1-58051-095-7 (pbk.)
     1. Women mystics—Biography. I. Perrin, David Brian, 1956–

BV5095.A1 W66 2001
248.2'2'0820902—dc21

2001031141

1 2 3 4 5 / 04 03 02 01

CONTENTS

ACKNOWLEDGMENTS

A significant number of people have been involved in the editorial process that has contributed to the realization of this book. I am grateful for their helpful guidance and insightful recommendations. In particular I would like to thank the following people who have contributed their precious time and talent to read and critically review one or more of the essays contained in this book. They are, in no particular order, Philip Sheldrake (Salisbury College); Élisabeth J. Lacelle (University of Ottawa); Keith J. Egan (Saint Mary's College); Margaret Laberge (University of Ottawa); Jill Raitt (University of Missouri); Steven Payne (Institute of Carmelite Studies); Richard Hardy (Pacific School of Religion); Mary Earle (Episcopal Theological Seminary); Andrew Quinlan (Saint Paul University); Peter Galadza (Saint Paul University); Michael Downey (Saint John's Seminary); Margaret Brennan (Regis College); Heather Eaton (Saint Paul University); John Russell (Brandsma Priory).

INTRODUCTION

Until recently, there has been a profound silence concerning the stories of Christian women mystics and, in general, Christian women. This has led to a quasi-intentional neglect of explicit discussion of the influence these women have had on Christian life with respect to its liturgical practices, belief systems and, in general, its overall culture. This negligible influence in the more immediate areas of church life has, in turn, lessened the impact of women on societal structures on many different levels as well. This can easily be seen when we acknowledge the fact that Christianity was, for a good number of centuries, the backbone of many political structures and movements in the Western world. Perhaps we could say that, in some ways, women have been a-politicized in both church and state circles. The *polis* is made up of the people but too often "the people" have excluded roughly half the potential membership!

As sad a situation as this has been in the past, the great strides made during recent decades, in both church and state circles, to recover the stories of the valiant and the victorious, the downtrodden and the defeated, have brought to our attention the enormous debt of gratitude we owe to so many women that have shaped and continue to shape our lives today; but they have not been recognized for doing so. However, the fact that both ecclesial and political structures have systematically deprived so many women of formal leadership roles did not stop countless numbers of women, some in quiet, others in more vociferous ways, of entering into the most complex and difficult church and state affairs over the centuries. Christian women mystics, far from being silent bystanders in shut-off monasteries, have dared enter into the toughest business affairs of church and state. It is here that they have left their mark for history to recover and assess for future generations.

Little does it matter that these women lived centuries ago, or during our own time; we find in many Christian women mystics' lives the material for great epic narratives because they often contributed their creativity and their wisdom against all odds to churches and societies that would rather have turned a deaf ear to them—and, in fact, often did! Indeed, how many countless women who lived admist the smothering oppression of patriarchal structures would never have dared hope that their lives could speak some meaning for people of their own time, let alone speak to foreign worlds in some distant future? Thus, this book is about recovery, the recovery of the stories of some Christian women mystics' lives that impacted their own time but whose stories cannot be left in a distant past because their stories still have something to offer us today.

We, in our technologically advanced society, need to hear their stories again and, in some cases, we have the privilege of hearing their stories for the first time. Women's stories, and as the stories of Christian women mystics being part of those stories, are of particular importance to us today because we are just beginning to realize how absent these stories have been from our own histories. A book such as this helps us recognize that these women have something to contribute to our own narratives, to the way we, too, must negotiate our way through the complexity of human life as these women did themselves. As Kirsi Stjerna indicates in her essay "Medieval Womans' Stories: Stories for Women Today," we are about the same task today as these women were in their own time: "connectedness, purpose and happiness." Life, love, death—all ring similiar regardless of the era in which humans undertake those perilous journeys.

But what does it mean to know the story of another? Ultimately we piece together the story of the other already according to our current self-understandings. But our current self-understandings cannot remain intact. In telling the story of the other, we interpret our own lives, tell our own stories as if through a glass darkly, and come to a *better* understanding of who we are with the God that governs our lives. In the end we are about right relationships with each other, ourselves, God, and our world. As Stjerna says of the ultimate goal of Birgitta of Sweden's spiritual journey, our task is "not only to learn to love God better, but to change the world." And so we are invited to listen again to women who have lived valiantly the drama of human life and who, to date, have not had the opportunity to teach us.

Listening again does not mean we sit back in our comfortable tightly knit intellectual dwelling places and sigh contently knowing we've done our part to heal past wounds by passively patronizing women's stories with albeit our attentive ears. No, listening again means to allow their stories to touch our stories, to let their lives enter into our lives such that we gain the hard-won wisdom they have to offer. Nor does listening again mean we laboriously try to fit their stories into our preconceived categories. Rather, we listen in order to allow their stories to *break open* the sealed containers within which we sometimes live. We need their stories to provide for us the grist for our own wisdom. They have walked treacherous and burdensome ways, as do we as individuals and as a collective body. Taking up their stories into our lives provides some wider context within which we can reflect and expand our own worlds outside the often times patriarchal or other limiting horizons against which we have come to know and define who we are as Christians and as human beings.

The paradox within which we live is that even though we have available to us more and more resources at the technological level, we seem to have fewer resources available to us at the human level; we are out of touch with who we are as creatures in the cosmos. We have exorcized the God of Abraham and Sarah, of Isaac, and of Ruth from our natural world in so many different ways. We no longer recognize God in the mystery of the universe, and the end result is a dehumanizing of the lives we live: we lose touch with our deep and profound emotional selves and we tend, instead, to function predominately on the level of the cerebral. In turn, this has resulted in the loss of the sense of the sacredness of our own lives. Recovering the stories of the "mystery of our world," the stories of Christian women mystics, may lead us back to contemplating the God who journeys with us in the mundane and in the ordinary. The stories of these women mystics can teach us how to humanize our lives and our world by bringing us to appreciate how God has and continues to be present in the minutist aspects of our lives. They have lived this reality and know it to be true from the inside out!

It has been acceptable, up to our own times, to allow men's stories to inform and educate us with respect to the deepest and most profound questions of life, questions that touch the deepest nature of our relationship with our world and with God. Men's stories have been woven far more integrally into the Christian culture over the centuries in almost an exclusive way. This is no longer acceptable—if it ever was. Men's contributions have been recognized and we want to continue to honor their contribution, but we must not stop there. There is so much work yet to be done in order to bring women's stories into our more immediate consciousness. We cannot continue to exclude half the population from engaging in the public spheres of meaning-making for our lives. As Ellen Ross points out for us in "Visions of Spirit: Prospects for Retrieving Medieval Spirituality," many of us are drawn to "women's mystical writings because these texts speak eloquently of the love between human persons and the Divine—they express the joy and exhilaration of human intimacy with the Sacred." In short, we can find through these writings glimpses of the way God has profoundly touched and humanized our world and continues to do so today. Ross's analysis of medieval women's spiritual writings also leads us to believe that it is time to revisit our ritual behaviors and the way we image God. Her analysis reminds us that mystical texts "consistently present images and rituals as critical to spiritual transformation." Human suffering, often witnessed to in Christian women's texts, is frequently the door that opens up spiritual transformation in the human story. Ross thus emphasizes the fact that suffering "is not an end in itself but a path toward greater intimacy with God," it is a "site of learning . . . a place where one may meet God."

Following the rise of feminist scholarship in the latter part of the twentieth century, as well as an increase of the availability of hereunto unattainable manuscripts and documents concerning women's stories and lives, we have witnessed a radical increase in our awareness of just how important the "silent" stories of women are for our current self-understanding, as individuals, as a Christian church, and as a society. We gain access to our humanity through listening to the rich diversity of both men's and women's stories. We find ourselves, at times, in the senseless ambiguity of life; our Christian legacy is frought with brokenness and violence. We do not want to replicate past mistakes. And so we listen to these women's stories because they were frequently socially engaged, they met head-on the social challenges of the times in which they lived. Through their genuine engagement in the worlds in which they lived, they model for us the possible in what seemed at times the impossible. Through their social involvement they embody the passionate and forgiving Jesus of the Gospels. Through their extreme self-giving, they remind us that it is not dogma that enlivens the Gospels but human action in the social and political spheres of the societies in which we live.

Jane Maynard delves into this point in "The Contribution of Julian of

Norwich's Revelations to Finding Religious and Spiritual Meaning in AIDS-Related Multiple Loss." Through her analysis of Julian of Norwich's traumatic loss experienced in Europe during the great plague in the fourteenth century, Maynard emphasizes that it is life that presents to us the greatest theological challenges, not textbooks or theological systems. In face of the incredible loss in Europe at the time of the plague—the level of loss that Maynard compares with the current crisis of those persons living and dying with AIDS—Maynard brings home the point that life challenges us to rethink so many of our theological categories, our language about God, and the way we talk about Christian mercy and forgiveness. Julian of Norwich is the backdrop against which Maynard develops these conclusions. Julian knew that, even in the face of great grief and enormous death, we may continue to find in the human heart a profound trust in the living God. God, indeed, journeys with us and continually makes all things new. The limitations of the human condition serve but as a pretext for the fullness of life with God as Julian of Norwich so well knew.

These Christian women mystics spoke to all segments of the societies in which they lived and often they placed themselves on the fringe of those societies. They often criticized the *status quo*, a *status quo* that had become so comfortable in itself and even at times oppressive toward others. Their purpose was to make things better for everybody. But these women mystics did not come from one strata of the society, the privileged or those not so favored. Ulrike Wiethaus, in her essay "Medieval Women Mystics: A Few Courtly Feasts, and Many Bag Lunches," emphasizes that Christian women mystics roamed the dung-filled streets of medieval Europe as well as frequented the pristine upper levels of society. In her essay she draws out the point that women Christian mystics came from all strata of society, the rich and the poor, but the one thing they had in common is that they spoke, and at times harshly, to the oppressive structures in which they lived in an attempt to make things better for everybody. They thus marginalized themselves from those structures in order to bring about newness to them from the outside. Wiethaus emphasizes that when the institutions become too strong, too controlling, as they did in medieval times, wild energies shoot off in the marketplace of life in order to bring renewal and develop spiritualities that reflect the necessities of the everyday life of God's people. Perhaps we could speak about the "ordinary mystic" here, the prophetess of the street that speaks the truth of God's presence in our world. Wiethaus, through her study of medieval women mystics, concludes that, indeed, street mysticism, a mysticism touching those who take bag lunches to work each day, is alive and well in our own time!

What must be recognized is that when we speak of mysticism in these pages we are not referring to the extraordinary and the sensational. Indeed, images of visions and unusual phenomenon often come to mind when we mention the word *mysticism*. But this is not the case for all mystics. It may not even be the norm. Mary Frohlich presents for us in her essay titled "Christian Mysticism in Postmodernity: Thérèse of Lisieux as a Case Study" four different ways of understanding the phenomenon of "mysticism." Frohlich's analysis suggests that the life of Thérèse of Lisieux may not satisfy the requirements of those who limit themselves to any single one of these approaches to mysticism, yet can still rightfully be termed "mystical." What comes out is that Thérèse of Lisieux lived a radical life of faith, a life that testifies to the fact that "the mystical is simply the gift of divine life that God freely shares with human beings." This "divine life" is exhibited in many different ways, in the ordinary as well as the extraordinary. But what could be "ordinary" about God's presence in our lives? To already know and sense that we are deeply loved by a personal God is already to be living one of the most spectacular adventures possible this side of eternity! Thérèse of Lisieux insisted that her path was not characterized by the extraordinary—and this gives each of us great hope. We need not look elsewhere for the sacred except for the everyday experiences of our life. Indeed, it is because we are united with God already that our life is possible. Union with God, at some level at least, is not the end point of our journey, as these Christian women mystics testify; rather, it is already a part of our reality as we set off to journey. As St. Paul indicates, along with so many holy men and women since, we live in God and God lives in us. This causes us to "perform" God's good works in the world. God's holy saving activity shines forth from under the cloud of what appears to be the "unholy" of everyday life.

The notion that mysticism is, indeed, "performative" is again revealed in the lowly life of Thérèse of Lisieux. Through her life story she has inspired countless number of men and women to actively participate in the redemptive work of God in the world. Frohlich emphasizes that these women mystics have drawn us, and continue to draw us, into God's act of redemption profoundly exhibited in the life of Jesus. Thérèse of Lisieux, as well as many other women mystics mentioned in these pages, has done this in an exemplary way. Thus these women offer us a way of organizing our lives around the unseen, the nonsense of our world, the mystery of the giveness of life that leads us along pathways that have no map to guide us. These women mystics provide for us the signposts of courage, trust, and deep faith. Perhaps we could say that these women mystics can teach us to look, essentially, to the relational and the sensual for the salvation of our world. It is in relationship, in the affective way we are alive with and for each other, that we come to find the great joy of life.

According to Annette Esser, in her essay "Marie d'Oignies: Female Visions of Strength," not all women Christian mystics can be applauded in this way. From the life of Marie d'Oignies, Esser notes that true "holiness has a dimension of sensual beauty and existential power as well." However, Marie d'Oignies practiced a certain extreme physical asceticism that Esser believes we should not follow now or in the future. By choosing to write an essay on Marie d'Oignies, Esser wanted to express the ambivalence she felt toward some women mystics that interpreted the Christian mystical tradition in a harsh and sometimes cruel way. The radical interpretation of the Christian tradition by Marie d'Oignies may have been counterproductive in Marie d'Oignies' time and, as Esser points out, may be in ours. Certainly the asceticism of Marie d'Oignies would be frowned upon today (or at least considered suspect). What Esser gains from the life of Marie d'Oignies is that we ought to examine what or who we are passionate about in life. The examination of our lives ought to include a hard look at our self-destructive tendencies and our negative attitudes toward others, our world, and our bodies. In short, an examination of the life of Marie d'Oignies calls us to critically examine our self-destructive attitudes and practices in order to creatively turn our woundedness in life toward the passionate engagement of the other such that we delve deeper and deeper into the joy of life. It is not the "fear of hell" that ought to compel us but the relational aspect of caring for others and giving our lives over for our brothers and sisters in gospel charity. Through looking at the life of Marie d'Oignies we can see and understand some of the neuroses we may have ourselves, neurosis based on a duality that splits the mind from the body or a neuroses based on a negative valuation of human sexuality.

The question of the role of suffering frequently surfaces in relationship to Christian mystics, and women Christian mystics are no exception.

During medieval times in a particular way, but also later and right up until our own time, physical suffering was seen as a way to achieve a certain holiness or saintliness. Since this was the case, some mystics subjected their bodies to what appeared to be harsh and cruel punishment; for example, they wore cords around their wrists or ankles that cut into their bodies, or fasted completely without food for great periods of time. The end result was meant to be a greater intimacy with the Divine that lived in the other "heavenly" world through a devaluation of the material, corporal reality of this "earthly" world. Happily today, Christians, for the most part, do not live in this dualistic framework, that is, a perspective on life that values the spiritual things of the other "heavenly" world while holding in disgust the material "earthly" realities such as our bodies. (Even though this split is not as prevalent in the practices of churchgoers today, we still see traces of the dualistic split in subtle but apparent ways, i.e., a negative evaluation of human sexuality.) Nonetheless it behooves us to try to make sense of the extreme measures that some women mystics took in order to achieve a greater degree of "holiness." It is also necessary to try to understand how suffering, which is naturally a part of the human condition, actually does contribute toward maturing us in our Christian journeys.

The difficult question of human suffering and the willingness of Christian medieval women mystics to suffer for their faith is scrutinized through an examination of the life of Catherine of Siena in Jane McAvoy's essay titled "Catherine of Siena: Contemplating the Fruitfulness of Christian Suffering." Granted, Catherine of Siena was and is an extreme case when it comes to the practice of bodily corporal "punishment" that I mention above, but her story continues to inspire many people today. Catherine, for example, undertook a fast that most likely led to her premature death at the young age of thirty-three.

McAvoy emphasizes the paradox of Christian suffering: that deep down, in and through our human suffering, we encounter the limits of our human condition. We realize who we are in a universe that exists not because we willed it so, but that exists through the gratuitous love of an "Other." Once cleared of our ego-centeredness, we are free to discover that mysterious "Other" *in* this very world. The mysterious "Other" is the God that conquers all through love. On our part, the desire for God and for God's deep compassion and love are the keys to understanding suffering in the Christian context. Human suffering, a suffering that cannot be avoided through the disappointments, ruptures, and limiting situations of life, brings us to realize that love will prevail and even now conquers all. Through suffering we come to discover that love is a dynamic, vibrant reality that releases incalculable human energy and drives us to accomplish the most extraordinary of human feats.

An analysis of Catherine of Siena's life leads us to insist that suffering is also an act of protest, that is, it acknowledges the fact that I refuse to attempt to take control, by violence or other means, of all the details of my own life as I interact and mix with others. By interacting with others, and thus encountering the difference of others, I will suffer that difference and discover in it my own limits. I will also discover, however, the pleasure and joy of the diversity of the human community and how much freedom there exists in willfully giving my life over to others. But through this willful giving over of my self (my life) to others, I cannot avoid suffering disappointment, unhappiness, or perhaps even betrayal. Christian suffering thus acknowledges the giveness of life; it accepts the fact that life comes with a certain wildness that we ought not to seek to control or deny. Jesus discovered this in his own journey.

The theme of suffering in relationship to Christian prayer is also taken up in Ann Astell's essay "NearDeath Experience and Julian of Norwich's Doctrine of Prayer." Julian of Norwich reminds us that it is through human suffering that we are led to cry out to God through our awareness of the poverty of our own lives and of our deep-rooted dependence upon others and upon God. Astell reminds us that "one cannot hope to live a truly Christian life without embracing the cross." Julian of Norwich reminds us, too, that our dependent cry to God becomes our "prayer" and we come to realize that God is the foundation of all our praying, that God is the "prayer" that moves us to pray and utter words of petition, praise, and lament. Prayer is not self-generated, not a complete act of the human will, but it comes first from God and leads us ever more intimately toward God.

Yet what is prayer if it is not also an act of love? Essentially our journey of prayer is one continuous act of love. We do this loving in the various moments of our lives, the joyful and the happy, as well as the sad and the despairing. It is God that sustains us through all of these moments, the God that can never be fully known but *who knows us* to the core of our beings and continues to love us even in our brokenness and sinfulness.

This is the teaching of the sixteenth-century mystic Teresa of Avila in her book *The Interior Castle,* and is the focus of the essay written by Roseanne McDougall: "From *The Cloud* (Unknown Author) to *The Castle* of Teresa of Avila." The fourteenth-century mystic/author of the book *The Cloud of Unknowing* essentially teaches us is that we cannot know God. What Teresa of Avila provides for us is a series of images or metaphors that give content to the "unknowing" of God. Teresa teaches us that *we can* struggle to describe the God that we cannot know by using images and symbols, as inadequate as they might be.

Through these images and symbols we come in touch with the *quality of relationship* that we are able to achieve with God. Describing God through images is essentially a task of describing the way the Divine interacts with the human and the way that we are in relationship with God in a very personal way. We cannot know God but we can describe the way we experience and are in relationship with God. What we come to in the end is the personal realization that the God of *The Cloud of Unknowing* is the personal God imaged in *The Interior Castle.* We come to know this in a *sure way* at a very deep level of our being. We are beings-known-by-God, and to be known by God is to be loved by God, absolutely and perfectly. Teresa of Avila, in *The Interior Castle,* thus gives shape and content to the formless experience of not-knowing God described in the text written a couple centuries before, *The Cloud of Unknowing.* For the sensory sensitive person of the twenty-first century, Teresa's rich imagery can assist us to locate and describe our own relationship with the God that defies all description.

With the essay by Sharon Elkins titled "The Virgin Mary in the Visions of Hildegard of Bingen," we are given a detailed description of how the Virgin Mary appeared in images in the visions of Hildegard recorded in her book, the *Scivias.* The image of the Virgin Mary has been a somewhat neglected topic in Hildegard's visions, as well known as they are. Elkins rectifies this situation in her careful analysis of the way Mary is, indeed, imaged in Hildegard's visions.

What is interesting to note is that in her visions, Hildegard attributes all of the wisdom and teachings to the visions themselves; she did not write reflections on them in her own voice. Hildegard was not about to risk speaking in her own name, thus her own authority, as a woman living in the patriarchal setting of the twelfth century! Was this, in fact, the reason she attributed all her wisdom and teachings to the visions that she both saw and heard? We will never have a clear answer to this question, but we can at least ask the question in contrast to a John of the Cross who, nearly four hundred years later, would write mystical poetry and risk writing extensive commentaries on them in his own name. John was a male cleric, and even though he was writing during the height of the terror of the Spanish Inquisition, which brought its own problems, he was part of the male hierarchal institution that would have protected him to some degree. John wrote in order to live out, in his own way, God's will for him, but he didn't live within the same constraining sphere as women would have lived during the same time.

But what is God's will? How are we, in our own time and place, to discern the will of the unknowable God? Is this not a contradiction? We often speak of the "will of God" in Christian conversations, but if God is unknowable, as I present above, how are we to be expected to know what God "wills" for us? Wendy Wright tackles this question in her essay "Elizabeth Ann Seton: 'Acquiescence to the Divine Will.'" What Wright brings home to us is that Elizabeth Ann Seton understood that the will of God "was manifest to one primarily through the responsibilities of one's state in life." How we take up our legitimate responsibilities and respond to the needs of our brothers and sisters according to the spirit of the story of Jesus *is* God's will for us.

Wright acknowledges that Elizabeth Seton may not be considered a mystic in the usual lists of persons in this category. However, as Mary Frohlich presents in her essay, there are at least four approaches to mysticism. In Frohlich's schema, we could place Seton in the discussion of mysticism as a "performance of a mystical drama": Seton's story has inspired countless numbers of lives and continues to draw men and women into new and authentic experiences of the paschal mystery. In this view mysticism is understood as a performance, an acting out, of the hiddenness of God made manifest in our lives, a manifestation that draws others into the deep mystery of God present in our world.

People such as Seton have experienced in a deep and profound way the personal God that, in the end, is unknowable. But they have put flesh on this God and have brought God's spirit to life in the way they lived their own lives. Seton knew that God's will, therefore, calls for pragmatic realism: in the unforeseen, unexpected, and sometimes tragic events of life, we choose to be flexible, to be supple, in an attempt to enflesh the spirit of the

Jesus of the Gospels. We come to understand through Seton's story that the construction of our lives, our very selves, is derived not from the loss, failures, or sins of our life, but rather from the deep-seeded hope derived by the Christian story that becomes, in a unique way, our personal story as Christian participants in it.

All the women Christian mystics presented in these pages struggled with the basic questions of human desire. Human desire, from many perspectives, is basically a religious question. This is true since human desire actively mediates the life of the human subject between the finite limits of the human situation within which we now live and the infinity toward which we move but already belong to in a primordial way. This is to say that we belong to God and live in God, yet we do not participate fully in the nature and life of God. The human subject experiences the force of the desire for God deep within, a desire that is insatiable, and it is this potency that initiates and sustains authentic human living.

The Christian promise is that one day we will live fully and completely in God because first God has shared Divine life with us. Women Christian mystics give us some glimpse into how this reality has taken on flesh: how Divine life spreads itself graciously and gratuitously around the globe and within the many different (ought I to say "messy") situations within which we live. We may not be able to understand the intricacy of all the complex human situations with which we are confronted, but the one thing that all these women Christian mystics affirm is that God is to be found dead-center in the heart of authentic human life! Authentic mysticism, far from nurturing an escape from "this world,"nurtures a profound desire to live within the struggles and joys of the everyday life of God's people. The revival of a healthy sense of mysticism has as its aim the development of strong and vibrant community that is based on a self-disinterested love, the kind of love that Jesus first shared with us.

At the heart of Christian mysticism, therefore, is the belief that God exists not as a distant Other, but as a Self that is very close to us in all we do and live. What the women in this collection have taught us is that mysticism cannot be understood as an act of *knowing* as much as it can be understood as an act of *feeling* the dynamic presence God's life in the world, this world, the only world that exists and which is shared both by the human and the Divine. The goal of Christian mysticism is not primarily an act of union with God or a particular moment of encounter with God;

rather, it is to live one's entire life *in the mystery* that we call God. These women strived to do just this.

These women lived a richly colored emotional life and consciousness that revealed the dynamic reality of God's mysteriousness embodied-in-the-world. Perhaps some of their expressions of this life are difficult for us to accept today, especially, for example, when it came to the sometimes-extreme bodily ascetic practices adopted by some of these women. But we must remember that these women lived in their own unique historical moments that nurtured certain values and expectations. We also live in our own unique historical moment with its own values and expectations, rituals and religious beliefs. It is sometimes too easy for us to look back and judge harshly what seems so foreign to us. Indeed, there is no reason to believe that some of our own religious practices, rituals, or beliefs will be judged just as harshly sometime in our own distant future!

What we can appreciate, in general, from the stories of the Christian women mystics presented in these pages is that the Christian past has a profound relevance for us today. This is especially true since it is these women's stories that have been neglected. We need to recover them and mine their stories to assist us to respond to our current living situations. Furthermore, we need to return to the equality of men and women in the earliest Christian stories in order to challenge the subsequent centuries of practice of exclusion and subordination of women to men. These pages give us a glimpse, a fleeting look, an exposure, to the wisdom and courage stored in the stories of Christian women mystics. These stories may enlighten our vision today.

We find in these women's stories beacons lighting the path to a greater inclusiveness, a broader and richer understanding, of the contribution past women, and in particular Christian women mystics, have made and continue to make to current situations within which we live. Perhaps history and our recording of it will always be distorted to some degree. However, we must attempt, through the re-reading and sometimes re-writing of the lives of those that have gone before us, ever more helpful and complete versions of the Word-made-flesh in the their faith-filled lives. We do this so that we too may become, in our own way, men and women that enflesh in a profound way the mystery of God alive in our world, as did these women Christian mystics.

PART I

Retrieving the Stories of Women Christian Mystics

1

MEDIEVAL WOMEN MYSTICS: A FEW COURTLY FEASTS AND MANY BAG LUNCHES

ULRIKE WIETHAUS

Introduction

Whether in the mystical systems of Judaism, Islam, or Christianity, the genius of medieval European people expressed itself poignantly in the bold innovations of their spiritual traditions. During the millennium that we now call the Middle Ages (ca. 500 to 1450 C.E.), all three religions developed mystical models centered on God as lover and human beings as beloved. All three can boast remarkable female mystics and a concomitant linguistic code acknowledging the presence of the feminine in spirituality. In the search for spiritual roots in medieval Europe, women thus have been astounded at the richness and sheer abundance of texts authored or dictated by female mystics.

As is true for this contemporary collection of essays, all surviving medieval texts by religious women were composed in and for specific communities. The rise of urban centers was a significant factor in the growth of such mystical literature, because a quickly expanding need for pastoral care in towns and cities encouraged the lay specialization in religious matters. Not only were priests, monks, and nuns recognized as caregivers of souls but, increasingly, religiously gifted lay women and men also organized themselves into loosely knit groups. Within the borders of Christendom, these groups ran the gamut from heretical rebels to communities of retired prostitutes to zealous reformers to radical mystics.

Eventually, some found recognition by the Church, adopted variations of already existent monastic rules that stressed poverty, chastity, and obedience, and attached themselves to any of the new reform orders such as the Cistercians, Franciscans, or Dominicans. Others remained comparatively independent and received various degrees of church sponsorship, such as the Beguines and Beghards. Still others were only recognized as spiritually legitimate by their immediate lay communities, but condemned as heretical by local church authorities, such as the Waldensians and Cathars.

Many characteristics distinguish these innovative movements from contemporary Western spirituality, but one difference is perhaps most noteworthy: the medieval penchant for community living. Although a strong part of Canadian and American religious history until the beginning of the twentieth century, the willingness to live according to spiritual ideals in a communal setting is now almost entirely confined to either monasteries or small apocalyptic fringe groups. The majority of spiritually interested women and men today tend to pursue their path individually, often with only fragile ties to a community, and try to fit it into an otherwise fully secular lifestyle. To understand medieval women's spirituality more deeply, then, we must imagine it as a communal effort, with intricate social obligations and relationships shaping the meaning of their spiritual texts—even if we credit only one particular individual as author.

Also bearing on medieval women's spirituality was the strong medieval sense of social status. In medieval society in general, firm distinctions were maintained between the rich and the poor, insiders and outsiders, foreigners and locals, Christians, Jews, and Muslims, members of the nobility and commoners, peasants and townspeople. These boundaries were enforced with violence and cruelty, supported with laws and religious practices. Culturally, these distinctions were conceptualized as divinely ordained, and were often endorsed with biologically framed arguments. The early modern theological debate about whether the inhabitants of the Americas were human had its roots in such medieval categorization of human difference, a tradition that lives on today in racist and sexist ideologies. Thus, medieval peasants and members of the nobility were thought to have different "natures," to the point that they were considered almost different species. Jewish men were believed to menstruate[1] and witches were seen as endowed with peculiar witches' teats that made them different from other women. Women as a group were consistently defined as inferior to men in all regards, whether intellectually, emotionally, or physically. The only exception was made for their spiritual equality before God, which could translate, in male regard, for a distinct female spirituality to which they, as men, had no or only little access.

As today's models of spirituality function in connection with secular value systems such as capitalism, individualism, Western hegemony, and militarism, so does medieval spirituality reflect the social realities of its time. The following contrast of two models of female medieval spirituality highlights two poles of medieval Christian society, divided by economic opportunity: the small class of noble and patrician people and the larger group of commoners, in particular ordinary townspeople. Although both models appear to be different in structure, they both thrived in a similar social milieu: the urban centers of Western Europe.

Courtly Feasts: Characteristics of Bridal Mysticism

The elite school of love or bridal mysticism, well known through medieval authors such as St. Bernard of Clairvaux (1090–1153), exemplifies some of the key aspirations of the nobility. Among these are the right to preferential treatment and respect, freedom of movement in all places and at all times, full membership among the privileged, refined manners, expensive personal property such as sumptuous clothing, jewelry, and books, and fine foods and entertainment as expressions of status. Ironically, these values found expression on the level of devotional texts only; the writers' actual lifestyles were marked by strict asceticism.

The paradigm of courtly love in itself is an expression of noble status and birthright, since peasants were deemed too coarse and brutish to play by its stylish rules. Its basic plot line can be quickly summarized, although it found remarkably complex treatment among a handful of medieval spiritual authors, whether female or male. For Christian mystics, the secular courtly love model becomes fused with elements of the Song of Songs: a "noble" soul, visualized as a young bride, is to be wedded to the "king" at the heavenly "court." Her yearning, adventures, courtship, and union with the bridegroom form the basis for psychological and theological explorations and are often expressed in a supremely poetic and literary manner. Coming into its own during the twelfth and thirteenth century, courtly love mysticism developed at a historical moment when the social structure based on a land-owning noble class and its contract with a larger peasant population began to give way to a more centralized, trade-and-city-oriented economy. This economic shift also necessitated the rise of a new class of bureaucrats, merchants, and burghers. Culturally speaking, the concept of courtly love mysticism was already in the medieval era in some way nostalgic and sentimental.

For one, it idealized a medieval social reality for a numerically small elite that was never quite as idyllic as it became imagined in the writings of medieval mystics, especially in its calculating marriage policies, rule of primogeniture, and the enforcement of gender inequalities. Second, it abstracted from the economic realities that allowed for the luxurious lifestyles of a few through the exploitation of many. In this context, we must consider that the key figure in the dissemination of courtly love mysticism, St. Bernard of Clairvaux, was of noble birth and a member of the Cistercian Order.

The Cistercian movement absorbed many of the adult sons of noble families, unable to inherit any land since they were not first born and offered them a dignified and socially respectable alternative. It also offered a livelihood and community, although less respect, to the lay brothers, poorer men faced with similar dilemmas of lack of access to inheritance and work. The Cistercian contribution to medieval culture lies not only in its prolific production of devotional texts but also in the massive clearing and cultivation of wooded and swampy areas across Europe. Away from the castles and seigniorial seats of their families, the monks who had visions of refined romances unfolding at the court of heaven no doubt evoked memories of the cultural life at home and thus sweetened the harsh lives of their rural same-sex communities.

We today are not immune from such spiritual migration of historical motifs and reminiscences. A comparable contemporary phenomenon of religious nostalgia is certainly the New Age emphasis on a golden age of Celtic paganism that preceded the Christianization of Old Europe.

Despite its lack of realism, however, the achievement of medieval mystical maps of a heavenly court for women lies in the fact that the figure of the noble bride afforded women writers a voice of dignity and impressive religious autonomy. No matter how restricted women's actual position in medieval society was, the heavenly court could signify a heterosexual utopia in which powerful men respected and honored women.

This model thus reflects both inclusion and exclusion—insofar as all human beings had a feminine noble soul, all could claim, at least spiritually, the dignity that it bestowed. In so far as the soul was conceptualized as noble and Christian, however, it invalidated the actual status of those who were not born noble or Christian. Nobility for all in the spiritual realm did not translate into a vision of equality in the social and economic realm. In so far as courtly love mysticism was a romance defined in heterosexual terms, it excluded persons of non-normative sexual orientation. Thus it should come as no surprise that the writings about courtly love mysticism contain anti-Semitic theological statements, denigrate peasants and servants and, to a lesser degree, condemn homosexuality.

Mystical Bag Lunches: Streets with a View

Complementing this rarefied spiritual model of courtly love is another type of female spirituality, less literary and more commonplace than courtly love mysticism, yet just as strongly charismatic and sophisticated in its own right. I have termed it "street mysticism," an expression of female spirituality that takes as its sacred space not the exclusionary court with its romantic intrigues, tournaments, minstrels, enclosed gardens, and female living quarters, but the open spaces of markets, churches, shrines dedicated to the saints, shops, apothecaries, roads, and hospitals. Although more diverse than a courtly environment, towns were still plagued by the medieval habit to draw strong social boundaries between "same" and "other." Not only Jews, but also prostitutes had to wear special markers and clothing that made them easily recognizable. Social roles allowed for little flexibility, and it took the efforts of an outsider to even recognize a holy woman as holy rather than mentally unstable. The moving story of Christina Mirabilis (d. 1224), for example, reveals the ambiguity that saintly behavior could evoke. Orphaned at an early age and living without a male head of the household, Christina and her two sisters subsisted at the margins of respectable town life outside of Liege in the Low Countries. After a dramatic near-death experience and concomitant visions of the afterlife, Christina displayed erratic behavior that was cruelly punished by the townsfolk, thus intensifying her and her sisters' social isolation. Her biographer accurately described her liminal status and the vulnerability it brought. His account, however, makes it difficult to decide what came first, Christina's persecution as a marginal young female, to which she responded with unusual behavior, or her behavior, which triggered cruel retribution by the townspeople.

> Christina ran from the presence of men with wondrous horror and fled into the deserts [uncultivated areas surrounding the town] and into trees and perched on the peaks of turrets or steeples and on other lofty places. The people thought she was possessed by demons and finally, with great effort, managed to capture her and bind her with iron chains. Thus bound, she suffered many pains and great privation (*The Life of Christina the Astonishing*, trans. King, 1999, p. 29).

It is only after the kind hospitality offered to her by Cistercian nuns, and the fancy the local count took to her, that the town's larger community began to define her not as a demoniac, but as a holy woman who could be of valuable service to her community, especially through the foretelling of future events and the fate of the dead. Her previous social marginalization became reinterpreted as a sign of divine guidance and, after much suffering, Christina finally found a safe and socially productive place in her community. In the words of her biographer,

> She had insight into many things with the spirit of prophecy and fore-warned many [multos praemonuit] to salvation and privately reprimanded many of their secret sins and recalled them to penance. When that unfortunate meeting at Stepes occurred in October 1213 between the duke of Brabant and his enemies where so many hundreds of men were killed, on that very day this blessed woman cried out as if in childbirth, "Alas! Alas! I see the air full of swords and blood! Hurry, sisters, hurry! Pray to the Lord! Shed tears lest from His wrath He re-press His mercy!" And she said to a nun at the monastery of St. Catherine's in St. Trond, "Run, sister, quickly run to prayer! Beg the Lord for your father because he is in great danger!" (*The Life of Christina the Astonishing*, trans. King, 1999, p. 53).

Although I treat street mysticism and courtly mysticism as somewhat separate systems, the social opportunities society offered to religiously gifted women cross any artificially set boundary. We find many examples of women and men who borrowed elements from both systems. The German Dominican nun Margarete Ebner (d. 1351) is a fine example of a female religious specialist who, although cloistered and of patrician background, offered cultural work much like a street mystic and drew repeatedly from the paradigm of courtly love in her devotional writings. Both systems thus bled into each other, especially so in the writings of the Beguines.

In 1994, two Austrian scholars published a recently rediscovered Latin manuscript on the life and revelations of a Viennese Beguine by the name of Agnes Blannbekin (d. 1315). Agnes Blannbekin can be characterized as a street mystic. A close study of the sometimes unwieldy text, composed by an anonymous Franciscan priest in close collaboration with Agnes Blannbekin, reveals fascinating glimpses into the daily religious lives of urban people, whether lay women and men, friars, priests, bishops, or holy women. For example, Agnes reports how people were trampled to death while attending a hugely popular outdoor sermon delivered by a bishop from out of town. She talks about bloodletting, witches, and the seduction of a town girl by a local priest. The anonymous scribe weaves into the text comments about his impatience with novices and his struggles with depression.

These vignettes of ordinary people's spiritual lives paint a picture very different from the courtly love mysticism propagated by Beguines of the patrician and noble classes during roughly the same time period, such as Hadewijch (no dates of birth or death are available; she lived during the first half of the thirteenth century), Mechthild of Magdeburg (ca. 1210–1282), and Marguerite Porete (d. 1310), or noble nuns such as Gertrude of Helfta (d. ca. 1301). Yet only if we see these models as complementary rather than oppositional can we move closer to an understanding of the richness of medieval women's spirituality.

Street mysticism worked with images to which most people had easy access. This included sacred symbols used during religious rituals, such as the Eucharist, relics, or the elevated role of the priest during Mass. However, street mysticism also sanctified the stuff of daily life, especially transactions and events that would ensure or jeopardize personal and communal well-being: mother and child relations; illnesses and death; abnormal behaviors that could be read as omens, whether of animals, people, or the weather; military events; and even actions such as cooking, maintaining a household, and the use of medicines. In her later years, the German Beguine Mechthild of Magdeburg even denounced a bridal mystical model and exclaimed mournfully that because she had lost her youthful beauty, she was better suited as the female head of the household, with God by her side as the *pater familias*. As her writing matured, more and more images from ordinary town life seeped into her writing, but also more descriptions of actual relationships among people.

Urban Communities, Religion, and Rituals of Healing

Viewed from a crosscultural perspective, it appears that altered states of consciousness are frequently, although not always, cultivated as a response to intense social or environmental stress. Collective experiences of episodic or structural liminality can be caused, for example, by harsh economic conditions such as famines, or by rapid and sometimes violent social transitions. For one recent example of the last decades of this century, we need only look to the Western feminist movement. It has comprised two seemingly contradictory wings: one political and economical, the other intensely mystical and spiritual. This bifurcation did not occur among more stable population groups, such as men in uncontested leadership positions, or the elderly who were generally little affected by feminist activism.

When traditional leadership structures and belief systems are breaking down during times of intense change, vulnerable groups may look for alternative sources of authority and new teachings about fundamental values in a changed environment. In the history of Christianity, mysticism rises and falls according to patterns of social stability and instability. The dramatic medieval shift from agrarian to urban settlement patterns, combined with the concomitant phenomena of social displacement, a rising population of urban poor, and new configurations of political power, certainly encouraged the emergence of several new types of charismatic religious leadership.

Among female populations, the mystical specialist rose to the forefront, the one who could offer pastoral care to an urban population, mostly geared toward assuring social cohesion within family networks. These services included care for the dying and the dead through prayers, funeral attendance, and communication with the dead. Note that Christina Mirabilis, for example, prophesied to a nun about her distant father who was in danger. The incident seems to take for granted that women like Christina not only had access to supernatural knowledge about worrisome quotidian matters but also were well acquainted with local families and knew their life stories and worries.

Beguines in particular served this important social function in towns, and were much sought after for their efforts. The nobility would often rely on cloistered members of their class for such cultural work: choir nuns, for example, whose task it was to remember the dead in purgatory through Masses and special prayers. Both a street mystic like Agnes Blannbekin and a courtly mystic like Mechthild of Magdeburg report on their presence during funerals, their visions of the dead in purgatory, and their heroic prayer work on the souls' behalf. The German Dominican nun Margarete Ebner (ca. 1291–1351) began her career as a mystic through intensive communication with the dead, who shared secret knowledge with her. Mystical states opened up supernatural spaces where the dead could be seen, talked to, and released from purgatory. Ebner shared numerous professional details in her autobiography, such as her difficulties to pray for stray souls. According to her experiences, not all the dead were equally accessible to intervention. One potential client in particular irked her. An unnamed out-of-town woman stole a eucharistic wafer to sell it to Jews, and was eventually executed by civil authorities. Her case seemed to have caused public turmoil, since the thief was pregnant, and her child was cut from her before the execution. The source does not tell us whether local people found this to be unusually cruel, since executions could be postponed until after the delivery of a child. In any case, Margarete decided to side with civic and ecclesiastical authorities in this matter and interpreted divine signals to mean that she should not pray for the woman's soul in purgatory. Obviously, the public was still so divided over this case that Margarete might have felt unsure as to her own responsibilities.

Specially gifted holy women were also recognized as healers of the living. As in the case of St. Elisabeth of Thuringia (1207–1231), one of the earliest and most dramatic models of urban female sanctity inspired by Franciscan ideals, even a holy woman's corpse was seen as charged with the ability to heal. Marie d'Oignies (1177–1213), stylized as the first officially recognized Beguine by her male biographer, helped women in difficult childbirth even after her death: parts of her clothing were wrapped around the woman in labor. The belief in a saint's curative powers has in numerous cases persisted until the present, as ongoing local and even transregional cults of their relics and gravesites demonstrate.

Finally, holy women participated in the production of devotional texts, whether as authors or informants with sometimes extensive control over the writing process. Only one medieval woman, however, the Dominican tertiary St. Catherine of Siena (1347–1380), has been elevated to the status of Doctor of the Church. Yet female-authored and female-informed texts circulated among both monastic and lay readers, were copied in full or excerpted liberally, and traveled near and far on the wings of a holy woman's reputation. It was not her learning that raised a holy woman into the ranks of male authors, however, but her perceived or real immersion into mysticism and the usefulness of the knowledge that she would garner from it. For example, although she was less prolific a scholar than her contemporary Hildegard of Bingen (1098–1179), Elisabeth of Schönau's (1129–1164) dictated writings were more widely circulated. The simple reason: Elisabeth was publicly recognized as a reliable visionary who could accurately convey supernatural knowledge.

In the daily life of a medieval urban community, the teachings of the Church on death, sin, and eternal life thus were experienced and validated through the cooperation between both male and female religious specialists. Certainly the priest was necessary and desired in administering pastoral care and the rites of the Church, but the community also expected holy women to help mend the fabric of affection and kinship ties torn by illness and death. Holy women's writings were supported and disseminated by their priests, confessors, and the male Church at large, if they were seen as supportive and illustrative of orthodox dogma.

In these networks of cooperation, street mystics such as Agnes Blannbekin, Marie d'Oignies, or Christina Mirabilis were best remembered through their active ministry to an urban population and remarkable mystical phenomena. Courtly mystics such as Hadewijch and Mechthild, on the other hand, left their mark as authors and teachers of a select group of spiritual seekers and as specially gifted supporters of the new orders. In several letters, the Beguine Hadewijch left us touching testimonies to the intensity of such communities, which included strong emotional attachments between a teacher and her female students, jealousy, rivalries, but also the transmission of sophisticated psychological insights in the dynamics of spiritual growth. Based on comments by Hadewijch and Mechthild, the groups that chose them as leaders and teachers must have operated with some sense of elitism and secrecy. Viewed from this perspective, the language of courtly love helped highlight the group's self-assigned special status. Mechthild, for example, understood her writings as a teaching tool to be used in her absence. Nonetheless, she intended it to be coded in some way. She exhorted her audience to read her books nine times in order to understand them fully. In Christian number symbolism, the numeral nine is most often associated with the nine angelic choirs. Mechthild's pedagogical program thus is contained in a number: she wanted her followers to manifest their inborn nobility by moving upward through the nine angelic choirs in a long and arduous spiritual process. In one of her letters, Hadewijch, for example, included a mysterious list of women and men across Western Europe whom she considered to have reached perfection, and whom she saw as paragons of her own spiritual program of achieving Christ-like perfection in its human and divine aspects.

Conclusion

Feminist historical research has taught us to name clearly the sexist exclusion of women from positions of teaching and ministry in the Church justified by social customs, but also by androcentric theologizing and biblical exegesis. When we follow medieval religious women into the public spaces of towns and the enclosures of life at court, however, we find that the distinctly medieval emphasis on social and gender status (always hierarchical) and clearly delineated gender roles (women as healers and caretakers of the dead) afforded a significant group of them a protected space of authority and autonomy that is perhaps unique to the Middle Ages, and that lasted for at least several centuries.

Scholars have amassed sufficient evidence to demonstrate the gradual cultural erosion of the special status granted to holy women during the late Middle Ages. Their increasing marginalization was caused by a host of factors, both secular and religious. Women's specialization in healing was gradually replaced by university-trained male doctors who rarely employed spiritual resources in their work. As new forms of government and economic exchange gained stability, mysticism gave way to other forms of collectively shared devotion and religious practice. Instead of relying on a holy woman, families depended increasingly on the institutionalized services of the Church, for example, local priests who would specialize in Masses for the dead, and charitable organizations. With an increase in general literacy and the invention of the printing press in the first half of the fifteenth century, more people had access to pamphlets and tractates. But the Church also contributed to these trends through theological efforts to minimize the validity of female mystical experience. Other factors include efforts to remove religious women from the streets and to enclose them behind gated walls; and finally, the tendency by both clerics and lay people of both genders to gradually associate religious specialists among the laity (both men and women) with witchcraft and heresy rather than mysticism.

Despite these efforts, the memory of female mystics from the Middle Ages has survived, even flourished in some communities, and inspired and encouraged female religious specialists in subsequent centuries. The current fascination with the Third Secret of Fatima demonstrates that even today's church hierarchy is not immune to spontaneous manifestations of teachings and healings derived through mystical cognition, whether in the streets, courts, or open fields.

NOTES

1. Peter Biller, "Views of Jews from Paris Around 1300: Christian or 'Scientific'?" in Diana Wood, ed., *Christianity and Judaism. Papers read at the 1991 Summer Meeting and the 1992 Winter Meeting of the Ecclesiastical History Society* (Oxford: Blackwell Publishers, 1992), 187–209.

REFERENCES

Caroline Walker Bynum, *The Resurrection of the Body in Western Christianity, 200–1336* (New York: Columbia University Press, 1995).

Albrecht Classen, "The Literary Treatment of the Ineffable. Mechthild of Magdeburg, Margaret Ebner, Agnes Blannbekin" in *Studies in Spirituality* 8: 1998, 162–187.

Thomas de Cantimpre, *The Life of Christina Mirabilis*, trans. by Margot King (Toronto: Peregrina, 1989).

Peter Dinzelbacher and Renate Vogeler, *Leben und Offenbarungen der Wiener Beguine Agnes Blannbekin (d. 1315)* (Göppingen: Kümmerle Verlag, 1994).

Peter Dinzelbacher, "Die'Vita et Revelationes' der Wiener Begine Agnes Blannbekin (d. 1315) im Rahmen der Viten-und Offenbarungsliteratur ihrer Zeit" in *Frauenmystik im Mittelalter*, edited by Peter Dinzelbacher and Dieter R. Bauer (Ostfildern bei Stuttgart: Schwabenverlag, 1985), 152–178.

_____. "Die Wiener Minoriten im ausgehenden 13. Jahrhundert nach dem Urteil der zeitgenössischen Begine Agnes Blannbekin" in Dieter Berg, editor, *Bettelorden und Stadt. Bettelorden und städtisches Leben im Mittelalter und in der Neuzeit* (Werl 1992),181–191.

Juliette Dor, Lesley Johnson, and Jocelyn Wogan-Browne, *New Trends in Feminine Spirituality: The Holy Women of Liege and their Impact* (Brepols: 1999).

Margarete Ebner, *Major Works*, trans., with an introduction by Leonard Hindsley (New York: Paulist Press, 1993).

Joan M. Ferrante, *To the Glory of Her Sex. Women's Roles in the Composition of Medieval Texts* (Bloomington and Indianapolis: Indiana University Press, 1997).

Andrew Kadel, *Matrology. A Bibliography of Writings by Christian Women from the First to the Fifteenth Centuries* (New York: Continuum, 1995).

Bernard McGinn, *The Flowering of Mysticism. Men and Women in the New Mysticism (1200–1350)* (New York: The Crossroad Publishing Company, 1998).

Roberta Agnes McKelvie, *Retrieving a Living Tradition. Angelina of Montegiove. Franciscan, Tertiary, Beguine* (St. Bonaventure: The Franciscan Institute, 1997).

Mechthild of Magdeburg, *Das fliessende Licht der Gottheit* (München und Zürich: Artemis Verlag, 1990).

_____. *The Flowing Light of the Godhead*, trans. with an introduction by Frank Tobin (New York: Paulist Press, 1998).

Catherine M. Mooney, "The Authorial Role of Brother A. in the Composition of Angela of Foligno's Revelations" in *Creative Women in Medieval and Early Modern Italy. A Religious and Artistic Renaissance*, edited by E. Ann Matter and John Coakley (Philadelphia: University of Pennsylvania Press, 1994), 34–64.

Barbara Newman, *From Virile Woman to WomanChrist. Studies in Medieval Religion and Literature* (Philadelphia: University of Pennsylvania Press, 1995).

Walter Simons, "The Beguine Movement in the Southern Low Countries: A Reassessment" (http://matrix.divinity.yale.edu/MatrixWebData/Simonse.txt).

Anneliese Stoklaska, "Die Revelationes der Agnes Blannbekin. Ein mystisches Unikat im Schrifttum des Wiener Mittelalters" in *Jahrbuch des Vereins für Geschichte der Stadt Wien* 43:1987 (7–34).

_____. "Weibliche Religiösität im mittelalterlichen Wien unter besonderer Berücksichtigung der Agnes Blannbekin" in Peter Dinzelbacher and Dieter Bauer, *Religiöse Frauenbewegung und mystische Frömmigkeit im Mittelalter* (Köln 1988): 165–184.

2

VISIONS OF SPIRIT: PROSPECTS FOR RETRIEVING MEDIEVAL SPIRITUALITY[1]

ELLEN ROSS

*M*edieval women's spiritual writings are living texts of vision and hope. While inviting us into the world of the Middle Ages, these narratives have the potential to inspire our own spirituality in these contemporary times. I believe that many of us are drawn to late medieval women's mystical writings because these texts speak eloquently of the love between human persons and the Divine—they express the joy and exhilaration of human intimacy with the Sacred. With extravagance, they name, nurture, and celebrate the relationship of God and humanity. In third-millennium American cultures, we hunger for resources that will enable productive journeys toward the Sacred. As such, medieval women's writings are essential aids in many practitioners' moves toward greater intimacy with God. These writings express the profundity of experiences of divine presence and absence that many of us glimpse and where many of us may even dwell in our own spiritual journeys. Thus, these spiritual narratives witness to the transformative possibilities of the reciprocal love that can exist between humankind and divinity.

Contemporary Anxiety about Medieval Mysticism: Violence, Suffering, and the Sacred

Yet many texts by medieval women make us profoundly uncomfortable. Such texts are, for example, rife with debilitating clericalism, anti-Judaism, and gender hierarchies that are highly inflammatory and deeply troubling to the sensibilities of twenty-first century audiences. These texts present a God who justifies and even sacralizes violence. At one point, the fourteenth-century Catherine of Siena urges the Queen of Naples to the crusading cause by saying: "I beg and urge you in the name of Christ crucified, to fire up your desire and get ready so that . . . [y]ou may give whatever aid or force is needed to deliver our gentle Savior's holy place from the unbelievers' hands and their souls from the devil's hand so that they may share in the blood of God's son as we do" (Catherine of Siena 1988, 112). This God wounds persons as a sign of divine love, as the thirteenth-century nun Gertrude of Helfta writes: "I had received the stigmata of your adorable and venerable wounds interiorly in my heart, just as they had been made on the natural places of my body. By these wounds you not only healed my soul, but you gave me to drink of the inebriating cup of love's nectar" (Gertrude of Helfta 1993, 100). This God is moved by persons' suffering to act mercifully, and yet is simultaneously portrayed as complicit in causing persons to suffer.

For some contemporary commentators like Sara Maitland, the focus on suffering and, in particular, on suffering women's bodies in late medieval religiosity renders this material a pernicious exercise in self-abnegation (1987). We fear that the implied divine violence or, at the very least, the divine *sanctioning* of violence and suffering may legitimate a spirituality that includes a volatile conflation of politics, religion, and the denigration of women's bodies. Understandably, we fear that texts in which believers understand or even cultivate pain as a means of spiritual transformation may lead persons to practice self-directed violence or endure violence as passive victims themselves.

In our own time, we know too well the dangers of a Christianity focused on the suffering Jesus and a model of imitative suffering in which persons endure violence directed against them because they believe they have been taught to "suffer as Jesus did." As Joy Bussert's research indicates: "Indeed, many battered women remain in violent relationships, many incest victims protect the secret, and many rape victims hesitate to report their assaults because of religious beliefs and values they have internalized from growing up in the church and in our culture" (1985, 2). The linking of language of violence and suffering so central to medieval mystical writings will surely, we fear, lead to the horrifying specter of the character Bess, in the Danish film "Breaking the Waves," whose brutal death at the hands of rapacious men is figured in the film as a Christ-like sacrifice—a sacrifice evoked by her "suffering love" as sanctioned by God and her husband. In medieval mystical texts, we confront once again the terrifying visage that the Christian heritage presents to us of a God immersed in the blood and suffering of humanity, not only as a healer, but, most hauntingly, as a perpetrator.

Yet the God present to us in these medieval texts is not unknown to us. It is the God of the biblical witness, that biblical witness that is the medium through which medieval women mystics experience the Sacred. This God who uses violence or painful experience to purify the believer, for example, is an old and venerable Christian tradition (Schwartz 1997; Wallace 1996)—this God is not a medieval mystical invention. The God who troubles us in these medieval texts—the God implicated in inflicting pain, or in being accessed through pain, or at the very least in permitting pain to function in a theological context—is the same God who allows the "righteous" Job to suffer, who tells the Hebrews to massacre their enemies in the Christian Old Testament, who strikes Ananias dead in the Book of Acts because he did not fully tithe, and who allows (or requires) God's own beloved Child to die in the New Testament. Here in these mystical texts, where we hope to find unparalleled joy, we also find ourselves once again in the muck and mire of the ambiguity of the Christian legacy. This is our struggle as Christians—our history is deeply ambiguous, marred by brokenness and violence, and by the unsettling claim that needless suffering can sometimes be redemptive.

We may dismiss these texts in our attempts to disown the Christian association of the Sacred and violence, but before we summarily do so, I urge us to explore more fully the nature of the suffering present in these writings. While I agree with scholars like Maitland that we do not want uncritically to replicate the medieval world in our retrievals of women's mystical thought, I want to suggest that studying these texts and appreciating the dynamics of theological and spiritual vision so central to them does not necessitate blanket approval of the medieval world or even our rough imitation of it. The point is not to read these medieval texts with an eye toward *replicating* them. Rather, the point is to *understand* these texts as testimonies to a complicated history of spiritual expression and to be open to the possibilities of a rich and potentially productive reflection on a world that may be very different from our own. Our understanding of the history of how women have practiced their faith may lead us to appreciate—and, perhaps, even be transformed by—the religious leadership and spiritual power of medieval women who practiced the religiosity recorded in these mystical texts.

Simultaneous attention to two distinct dimensions of contemporary Christian spirituality can help mediate the challenges and prospects of learning from writings by and about medieval women mystics. First, contemporary Christian spirituality asks of these texts, *What do they tell us about the world of medieval spirituality?* This question reflects the first task of spirituality: to familiarize contemporary persons with the history of how believers have cultivated, experienced, and responded to relationships of intimacy with God. Second, contemporary Christian spirituality asks, *What can these texts contribute to spirituality today?* This query reflects the second task of spirituality: to provide present-day Christian practitioners with images, rituals, and resources to nurture their own intimacy with God. Recognizing that these tasks of contemporary Christian spirituality are distinct provides a context for attending to the historical and social environments from which the medieval texts arise. We can appreciate both differences from and similarities to the contemporary context and seek to understand the integrity of these texts in their original settings; and also, while respectful of tradition and cognizant of differences, we can reflect upon the ways these texts can invigorate, challenge, and sustain contemporary spiritual practice.

A final caveat. It is important to affirm the fundamental importance of understanding medieval women's mystical texts in their own settings. This proviso keeps us from uncritically appropriating material that may not be productive or fitting for our contemporary setting. And, of equal importance, such an appreciation for the historical nature of these mystical writings keeps us from uncritically dismissing them as dead icons left over from a prior age. Consideration of the integrity of these texts teaches us about the creativity and wisdom of generations prior to our own, and may challenge us to think in new ways about our own religious practices and traditions.

Medieval Spirituality:
Female Inheritors of the Life and Work of Jesus Christ

Medieval mystics like Catherine of Siena, Gertrude of Helfta, and Angela of Foligno live out a trajectory within the history of Christianity. It is a trajectory of asceticism, spiritual transformation, prophecy, spiritual and physical healing, and advocacy. Here advocacy worked both ways: on behalf of people before God *and* on behalf of God before people. The fourteenth- and fifteenth-century texts I consider here emerge in a culture (from which there were detractors) that followed a unified, scripturally derived, and theologically consistent line of interpretation in understanding the economy of salvation. This trajectory is characterized by its focus on the significant role of the suffering Jesus who bodies forth the spiritual truth at the heart of medieval piety: the medieval God is not abstract and distant, but radically immanent in the suffering Savior whose wounds are an invitation to compassionate response and engaged relationship.

For these writers, the theological starting point is, first, that Jesus' suffering is integral to the offer of transformation he proffers to humans. Second, in this interpretive world, the suffering of Jesus stands as a plea to persons to imitate Jesus' suffering as a way of linking themselves to the reality of who Jesus Christ is. That is, the path of imitative suffering enables persons to participate in the spiritual power of the suffering Jesus. Furthermore, suffering leads persons to perceive the trinitarian God of love who is embodied in Jesus Christ. Some texts even claim that imitative suffering enables persons to achieve divinity and become what Jesus Christ is, namely God. Through the journey of imitative suffering, devotees enjoy a deeper encounter with God's love in Christ and, in some cases, experience divinization.

While this extraordinary call to religious suffering present in some mystical texts may seem strange and perhaps unhealthy to many of us now, I nevertheless urge us to attend to the *function* and *meaning* of this suffering in its medieval context. In general, ritualized identification of holy women with the suffering Jesus, in a world far removed from our own, did not foment in religious women a self-denigrating, agency-denying, body-hating, private agony, but rather enabled these women to function as public heralds and living embodiments of the Divine through their widely recognized works of preaching, prophecy, and healing. In their personal devotion, suffering erased the boundaries between the Divine and human persons, and invested medieval women with the very transformative power to teach and heal expressed by Christ himself.

This perception of imitative suffering is theologically sophisticated and grounded on a nuanced scriptural hermeneutic, one that reads the suffering Jesus as the key to understanding the typologically figured Christ in the Hebrew Bible and the New Testament. The central idea here is that in imitation of the suffering Christ, persons find the seeds of personal and corporate transformation. This foregrounding of Jesus' suffering and its implications for the lives of spiritual virtuosi was elaborated by the moral or tropological reading of Scripture that understands the Bible as God's personal address to humans and even as God's love letters to the human soul (Ross 1989). As James Marrow has demonstrated, that medieval iconography of the Passion is grounded in a subtle reading of the Bible (1979), I also suggest that the interpretation of the believer's suffering as integral to spiritual and social change is grounded upon a finely tuned scriptural hermeneutic.

The understanding of suffering as part of the process of spiritual purification is seen in numerous passages cited by medieval mystics: so for example, Isaiah 1:24–26:

> Therefore the Sovereign, the LORD of hosts, . . .
> > I will turn my hand against you;
> > I will smelt away your dross as with lye
> > and remove all your alloy. . . .
> Afterward you shall be called the city of righteousness,
> > the faithful city.

In the tropological reading in which Scripture is a personal address, persons are invited into a process of transformation to become faithful: it is a painful transformation of which God says: "I will turn my hand against you." Many twenty-first-century readers disregard such passages, but medieval mystics interpret their suffering through these scriptural lenses. The tropological reading gives rise to the idea that believers gain and express spiritual authority through their mimetic identification with Jesus Christ.

Catherine of Siena expresses this in her exegesis of Galatians 6:17 where Paul says: "I carry the marks of Jesus branded on my body." In interpreting this passage in its tropological or moral sense, Catherine urges readers of her own text to carry on the work of Paul, and says of those who do that "they want to be of service to their neighbors in pain and suffering, and to learn and preserve the virtues while bearing the marks of Christ in their bodies" (Catherine of Siena 1980, 144). Holy women are agents of reform in the spiritual lives of their contemporaries, and they are representatives of humanity to God. Mystics like Catherine of Siena, Gertrude of Helfta, and Margery Kempe, for example, advocate on humans' behalf and urge God to deal mercifully with the unrepentant living and the contrite dead. The power of these women's advocacy, at least in part, is often linked to their suffering. Like the biblical prophets Jeremiah, Ezekiel, and Isaiah, the fifteenth-century English laywoman Margery Kempe, for instance, rebels against her mission, saying that she does not want to weep and cry out at sermons anymore, bitterly lamenting the pain of her compassion for Christ's suffering (1944, 181). This work of weeping pains Margery to the point that she shouts out to God, "Lord, I am not your mother. Take this pain away from me, for I cannot bear it" (164). Christ tells her not to pray in this manner because her desire will not be fulfilled; he explains to her that her weeping will benefit the world (181–184), saying that through her "thousands of souls will be saved" (186). As well, Lidwina of Schiedam's (d. 1433) hagiographers explain that "the fevers [Lidwina] suffered almost daily for many years before her death released souls from Purgatory" (Bynum 1987, 127).[2] And Caroline Walker Bynum points to the "immoderate" nature of Mechtild of Magdeburg's confidence that her "suffering with Christ saves 70,000 souls from purgatory" (1987, 401, n.81). Immoderate though this claim may be, it is common in stories about and writings by medieval women.

At the very least, identification with the suffering Jesus leads to spiritual transformation, cultivation of compassion, and rigorous attempts to transform the world. For Catherine and others like her, the tradition of suffering was not finished with Christ, but was extended as an offering of transformation for persons: "I have been crucified with Christ; and it is no longer I who live, but Christ who lives in me" (Galatians 2:20). The offering to human persons here is that through suffering, human persons can experience and even become what Jesus Christ is.

I am not suggesting that we uncritically imitate the forms of suffering present in many medieval mystical texts, but rather that by frankly acknowledging the presence of suffering in these texts, we may study these sources with an appreciation for their thoughtful attention to scriptural and historical sources, and we may recognize how suffering functions in the religious lives and leadership of medieval mystics. What emerges from such study will both complicate and deepen our appreciation for medieval life and thought as well as challenge our assumptions about the role of pain and suffering in contemporary spirituality. As an example of this double benefit to understanding medieval writings, I point next to one often-overlooked accompaniment to suffering, namely, that imitation of or identification with the suffering Jesus is not an end in itself but a path toward greater intimacy with God—indeed, a path toward relationship with the *trinitarian* God who extends to persons the offer to participate in trinitarian life.[3]

Trinity and Deification in Women Mystics

In medieval mystical texts, the God Jesus Christ leads to is the triune God of Christianity. What often begins with a focus on Jesus and includes attention to and often identification with the suffering Jesus usually ends with a perception of the Trinity. At times, employing the traditional imagery of a soul imprinted with a seal, Gertrude of Helfta, for example, describes the intimacy of her union with God through the sign of the "resplendent and ever tranquil Trinity" being impressed upon her (Gertrude of Helfta 1993, 105). Other devotional texts also link trinitarian union with the experience of the suffering of Jesus Christ. The fourteenth-century Angela of Foligno's biographer Brother A. describes Angela's transformation in these terms:

> Moreover, we must ponder with great care what she also said, namely, that the elevations into the Uncreated and the transformation into the Crucified placed her in a continual state of being plunged into the fathomless depths of God and of being transformed into the Crucified (Angela of Foligno 1993, 247).

In most mystical texts, Christ and the Trinity are intimately inter-twined with each ohter because true understanding of life in Christ allows the devotee to plumb the depths of the meaning and experience of the Trinity itself.

Indeed, some medieval mystical authors like Angela of Foligno and

Gertrude of Helfta follow the thesis about the relationship of humans to Christ and the Trinity to its logical outcome. They claim at times that humans can be divinized—that the human person can merge with God and thereby become God or become so assimilated with God that observers or the devotees themselves cannot distinguish the person from God. Devotees are not only personally transfigured but also publicly transformed into purveyors of divine power. The God of medieval Christianity becomes visible through the sensual and the visual: devotees function as "texts" to be read by a world in need of spiritual transformation, offering the promise that human persons can be the site of divine presence, and even deified in the process.[4] Here we move through imitative suffering to a situation in which these mimetic devotees become through *grace* what God is by *nature*.

Throughout texts as diverse as those by or about Gertrude of Helfta, Mechthild of Magdeburg, Angela of Foligno, Meister Eckhart, Francis of Assisi, and Elizabeth of Spalbeck, among others, the boundaries between God and humankind break down. Divine and human merge as the distinctions between these two orders of being are consistently dissolved. The ways of describing this fusion of the human and the Divine orders are many.[5] Gertrude of Helfta, for instance, describes an experience that occurs on the second Sunday of Lent, traditionally the liturgical occasion for the reading of the narrative of Jesus' transfiguration, in which Gertrude is united with God by becoming, in body and soul, what God is:

> I saw the Lord face to face [Gen. 32:30,28] my soul was suddenly illuminated by a flash of indescribable and marvelous brightness . . . In this sweetest vision . . . [y]our eyes, shining like the sun, seemed to be gazing straight into mine . . . You, my dearest and sweetest, touched not only my soul but my heart and every limb. . . . I felt as though an ineffable light from your divine eyes [deifying eyes—deificis oculis] were entering through my eyes, softly penetrating, passing through all my interior being . . . [w]orking with marvelous power in every limb. At first it was as though my bones were being emptied of all the marrow, then even the bones with the flesh were dissolved so that nothing was felt to exist in all my substance save that divine splendor which, in a manner more delectable that I am able to say, playing within itself, showed my soul the inestimable bliss of utter serenity (cf. Wisd. 7:22, 23–26) (Gertrude of Helfta, 1993, 125–126, 152, n. 104).[6]

Gertrude describes her union as not only with Jesus Christ but as with the "mutual love of the ever adorable Trinity"(127). She says that she has been "given . . . [t]he grace to share with [God] on equal terms, like a queen with a king" (130). Through the process of transformation, Gertrude of Helfta becomes a purveyor of divine power and a spiritual advocate for the living and the dead. Gertrude becomes, in a phrase, the body of God to the world:

> I have deigned to join my heart so courteously and so inseparably with her soul that she is become one spirit with me . . . I have chosen to dwell in her in such a way that her will, and the works which stem from this good will, are so firmly fixed in my heart that she is, at it were, the right hand with which I work. Her understanding is like my own eye with which she perceives what pleases me; the movement of her spirit is like my own tongue . . . And her discretion is like my nostrils . . . I incline the ears of my mercy toward those to whom she is moved to compassion. And her attention is like feet for me, because she is always bent on going where it is fitting for me to follow (84).

The deified devotee embodies God and manifests divine presence and power in the world. So Gertrude makes extensive claims about her powers, including that if she promises pardon for anyone's faults, "God will respect her words as faithfully as if they had been spoken and solemnly promised by God's lips" (Gertrude of Helfta 1993). As Gertrude's biographer says, "she did not hesitate to play the part of an equal with God" (Gertrude of Helfta, 1993, 69). Likewise, God tells the thirteenth-century Franciscan tertiary Angela of Foligno, "You are I and I am you" (Angela of Foligno 1993, 205). Angela is "transformed into God" (253). Angela promises her followers that if they pursue the spiritual path she describes, they too may become God. Brother A., who records her teachings, and often says that he struggles to understand her correctly, begs her to tell him what will happen when the followers reach the highest stages of purification: "As I kept insisting, she finally told me: 'What do you want me to say? My sons seem to be so transformed in God that it is as if I see nothing but God in them, in both his glorified and suffering state, as if God had totally transubstantiated and absorbed them into the unfathomable depths of his life'" (249).

At times, human persons themselves become embodiments of Godself, sources of sacred power, and transfigured beings who share in the divine life. In the theologically nuanced reflection on the Trinity of the medieval mystics considered here, the lines of division between the divine realm and the human order finally blur and then are erased in christological ecstacy, trinitarian identity, and compassionate social engagement. Through the process of divinization, these texts celebrate the grandeur of the human condition. Humans, images of a trinitarian God, are invited, by following the path of the suffering child of God, to enter through that suffering into the realm of joyous intratrinitarian life. Believers may share in the power of God to heal and transform life, and at times, may even share, by grace, in the very being of God.

I have said that a first task of Christian spirituality is to cultivate understanding of the history of the spiritual traditions that are a central part of the Christian tradition. In this vein, these mystical texts suggest the type of intimacy that is possible between the Divine and humans. They also indicate that, at times, suffering is an integral part of the process of transformation. Studying these texts of theological and spiritual vision does not necessitate our mechanical replication of the medieval world. Rather, we seek to understand the spiritual expression in these texts and then to reflect on this richly textured world—a world very different from our own—as a possible world that we can inhabit and within which we discover a renewed sense of selfhood in relation to God and others.

Contemporary Spirituality:
Medieval Sources of Spiritual Wisdom and Theological Insight

I have noted that a second task of spirituality is to provide present-day Christian practitioners with potential images, rituals, and resources to nurture intimacy with God. Fundamentally for me, the most profound thing to learn from these texts is the joy and delight that accompanies believers in their journeys toward intimacy with the Sacred. This is why many of us turn to these narratives: they witness to spiritual transformation and companionship with the Sacred.

I suggest that we take from these works, however, neither a direct compilation of practices nor a complete and coherent worldview. For me, for example, the patriarchal structure of medieval Christianity renders it untenable as a metaview for our time. Yet, we can draw from these texts a witness to the intimacy possible between humans and the Sacred. These texts are visions of spirit: they are the works of women who express with spiritual wisdom and theological acumen the profound pleasures (both private and public) that await persons willing to risk the journey of spiritual transformation.

Let me conclude with three suggestions about how a dialogue with these texts may yield spiritual practices, spiritual wisdom, and theological insights that can contribute to our communion with the Sacred in our own time and culture.

First, we may learn from the *spiritual practices* in these texts. Medieval mystical texts consistently present images and rituals as critical to spiritual transformation. Medieval women's mystical texts offer a wide variety of ritualized practices for invoking divine presence through prayer, posture, singing, sacrament, and performance. The point is not that we should woodenly imitate the medieval rituals as such, but rather that we should reflect upon how a wide variety of contemporary, historically embedded rituals—alternately similar to and different from medieval practices—can function to nourish and cultivate spiritual transformation. In turn, these texts also call us to recognize the power of images to transform experience —that is, they call us to cultivate practices of image making and image contemplation as a means of expressing and deepening our spiritual realities. A comparison of traditional artistic depictions of the Trinity with, for example, Judy Chicago's rendering of the Birth Trinity as a portrayal of a woman giving birth, a person standing behind her to support her, and a third figure which is both the child being born and the midwife-figure (1985, 118–119) may be as spiritually thought-provoking to us now as was the portrayal of the cooperative action of three males in the common medieval depiction of trinitarian creation. But both the medieval depictions of Trinity and contemporary figurations of the same highlight the perichoretic intimacy between the three divine Persons that can serve as a model of genuine intersubjectivity in our own time. Attention to how statues, images, and physical spaces function in spiritual life calls attention to the variety of ways the Divine was manifest in medieval culture and, in turn, provides resources for reflecting on the ways spiritual persons can cultivate intimacy with God and access to the Sacred in the present.

Second, insofar as these texts witness to human transformation, we can learn from the profound *spiritual wisdom* so essential in these texts. While suffering is a critical part of the journey they describe, it is never figured as the goal. The goal, in a word, is joy. The taxonomy of joy is a necessary and crucial counterpoint to our fascination with suffering in these texts. The focus on suffering should be heeded, however. These texts observe that suffering is a part of the journey to transformation, an insight to which I think much spirituality, psychology, and theology in our own time attests. The pathos of the suffering prophetic voice in the world, the painful awareness of our own implication in the world of sin and persecution, the suffering of yearning for God, and the suffering borne of our awareness of our own resistance to transformation are among the great variety of sufferings witnessed to in medieval texts. While we may draw the lines about healthy and unhealthy suffering in very different ways from our medieval predecessors, we, with them, must acknowledge the presence of suffering—and, at times, the necessity of suffering—in the journey of spiritual transformation.

I am not suggesting, however, that we seek suffering in the journey to spiritual transformation in the way that, for example, the thirteenth-century Gertrude of Helfta asked God to wound her heart with the arrow of his love (Gertrude of Helfta, 1993, 102), or the way Julian of Norwich asked for suffering when she desired to have a sickness that would include "every kind of pain, bodily and spiritual, which I should have if I were dying" (Julian of Norwich, 1978, 125). Nor, by the same token, do we want to sustain the cosmological view of medieval thinkers like the twelfth-century Hildegard of Bingen, who suggested that God often afflicts those who experience intimacy with God with physical pain as a way of keeping them from becoming distracted by worldly matters (Silvas, 1999, 175). Yet, medieval women's testimony to the power of suffering as an essential aspect of the spiritual journey is a testimony that is still relevant today—not as a challenge to *seek* suffering, but as an invitation to acknowledge the *experience* of suffering as a possible site of potential spiritual transformation.

Reflection on the significance of suffering in the medieval context calls us to perceive the widespread presence of suffering in our own communities and, in particular, in the lives of persons who long for spiritual transformation. We are called to notice in our own lives the symptoms of suffering which may include anger, depression, rage, inaccessibility, and isolation. We are called to attend to the ways in which our culture encourages people to medicate suffering through alcohol, drugs, pornography, food, and work, among other strategies. The tradition of suffering in medieval spirituality urges us to acknowledge the inevitable role suffering plays in the human drama. Rather than teaching us to turn away from suffering, this tradition challenges us to acknowledge suffering as a site of learning and as a place where one may meet God. The witness of the historic Christian tradition is that the God of joy and healing may be experienced in the encounter with suffering.

Indeed, this medieval insight is not foreign to many healing contexts of the early twenty-first century; this insight is, for example, at the heart of the twelve-step recovery programs so prevalent today. This insight into the meaning of suffering is that dwelling for some time in the valley of suffering may be essential to the journey toward intimacy with God, self, and the world. There is a heritage for this insight, a lineage of many who have sought self-transformation of the world through and into love. These practioners know that not only is suffering inevitable, but that it is only by experiencing the depths of suffering, while neither denying nor medicating it, that the seeds of transformation into love can happen. This transformation through suffering further calls persons to become themselves purveyors of divine presence and public heralds of God's compassionate love to the world.

I am not suggesting, as do some of the medieval thinkers I study, that suffering in and of itself is to be sought after because it is salvific for oneself or others. Rather, I am saying that suffering is an inevitable consequence of being human; it *can* be a door through which one may journey to God—a God who made suffering a part of Godself in the person of Jesus Christ. Medieval Christians understood that the sins of the world were written onto the body of Christ; sometimes even, Christ's body was described as a book with the sins of the world inscribed on it in red ink (Ross 1997, 132). We, too, are invited to imagine ourselves in this lineage of Jesus Christ, as being Christ-like in our suffering and as inheritors of the brokenness that led Jesus' persecutors to torment him. That is, the sins, the hatred, and the sicknesses of this world wound our bodies and our psyches, our very beings, just as Jesus' body was wounded. And at the same time we may wound the bodies and psyches of others in our own alienation from the pain we carry within ourselves.

And yet the message of Jesus Christ as relayed by our medieval forbears is that although suffering is inevitable, it is joy that is the last word. Although evil dwells all around and even within us, the testimony of the

Christian heritage is, as Hildegard of Bingen put it, that "just as Lucifer for all his malice could not bring God to naught, so too, he shall not succeed in destroying the human race" (Silvas 1999, 179). Our cosmology may not be as literal or as apocalyptic as that of Hildegard of Bingen, but this heritage is a reminder to us to live always in the hope of the transformation of suffering to joy. This tradition calls us to acknowledge suffering for what it is, and even to dwell with suffering at times as a part of the journey to transformation of self and society through experiencing a God of love.

When I present my reflections on suffering someone always protests that perhaps I am legitimating oppressive suffering and suggesting that persons who are being victimized should suffer in silence. Neither I, nor most medievals, would ever make this claim, although as I previously noted, the history of Christianity is sadly ambiguous (and even horrifically unambiguous) at times about the meaning and function of suffering in spiritual life. I understand that what I am saying here may be perceived as dangerous—misunderstood, it could seem to lead to the world of the character Bess in "Breaking the Waves." I have no straightforward formula for separating suffering that can be construed as essential in the journey toward spiritual transformation from suffering that is utterly oppressive and suffocating of all life. As we know from stories we read in the newspaper everyday, as well as from the poignant testimony of writers like Elie Wiesel, there is incorrigible suffering *about* which we can make no sense (Wiesel 1999, 270) and *to* which we can perhaps respond only in the tradition of lament and by committing ourselves to keeping alive the memory of those who have suffered needlessly (Ricoeur 1995, 292).

In the face of the terrors of history and of our world today, there are some who have witnessed to the meeting of God in suffering and who have testified to the transformation into love through the path of suffering. In reflecting upon medieval spirituality I urge us to recognize the complexities of how suffering functions in spiritual transformation and to acknowledge the testimony of those who have gone before us—many of them athletes of God and intimates with God—who testify that the experience of suffering itself may be a significant aspect of spiritual transformation. The witness is that God took this suffering even into Godself in an affirmation of transformation and love. And God invites persons themselves to become living embodiments of God's love to a world in need of healing.

I reiterate, however, that in these medieval texts we also encounter what is unfathomable and reprehensible to us since these texts challenge us, as do biblical texts where we meet the disturbing association of God and suffering, to live within the ambiguous and at times disquieting world of the Christian heritage. These texts then remind us that our own constructions of the spiritual journey may be just as fraught with troubling distortions as are those of our predecessors.

Third, we may learn from the *theological insights* of these texts. When we ask how women understood God in the Middle Ages, scholarship often tends to focus on the Christ-centered nature of medieval texts. Indeed, Christ is central, but most medieval women's mystical texts are profoundly trinitarian. My sense in teaching and working in the area of contemporary spirituality is that many people are renewed and refreshed when they live toward the Divine as Trinity. For medieval Christians, the notion of God as Trinity is not an irrelevant dogmatic abstraction but a living testimony to the deep interdependence and interrelationality of each member of the Godhead with one another. Again, my point is not that we should simply repristinate the medieval world, but that while aware of its differences from our own world, we respond to the spiritual cosmos it sets before us as an occasion for a renewed understanding of the inward journey. The images and experiences that emerge from mystical traditions testify to how central the Trinity is to the lived spirituality of persons who devote their lives to loving the Sacred. The witness of mystical writings is that the experience of intimacy with Divinity is the experience of intimacy with a triune being (for example, Gertrude of Helfta 1993, 105). This is an argument for understanding sociality and community as both essential to what it is to be God and as essential to what it is to be human.

Many medieval mystics conjure the notion of a divine dance to express the manner in which the sacred partners of the Trinity turn and weave in interconnected harmony. This sense of the spiraling dynamic Trinity is brilliantly portrayed in medieval mystical texts like those of Gertrude of Helfta, where Gertrude seeks herself to be taken into the circle of the perichoretic divine dance:

> O love, you alone know this road of life and truth. In you are carried out dear contracts with the Holy Trinity. . . . In the love of the nuptial contract, [let me follow] where you reign and govern in the fullest majesty of your divinity, [where] in the most dulcet coupling of your living love

and in the living friendship of your fiery divinity, you lead with you in the most blessed circular dance in heaven thousands upon thousands of the very brightest virgins. They are adorned, at one with you, in snow-white robes, jubilantly singing the dulcet songs of everlasting marriage. (1989, 56)[7]

For Gertrude, the joy of everlasting life is the joy of dancing together with the Sacred for eternity. It is to enter into the divine dance, to become one with God in the jubilant celebration of spiralling, swirling trinitarian love. We may figure the dancers differently from the monastic world Gertrude inhabits, but the trinitarian vision of ludic divine harmony can still inspire our spiritual vision and engender strength for the contemporary journey.

Conclusion

The God of medieval mystical writings yearns for persons to become like God, even to become God in following the religious path. As Angela of Foligno expresses this divine longing: "God wants [God's children] to be totally transformed into God by love. . . . It is necessary that knowledge comes first, and the love follows which transforms the lover into the Beloved" (Angela of Foligno 1993, 295). At the same time that we may find the relentless construction of the suffering creature in the face of the Creator God disturbing in these texts, we may be jarred by the equally powerful assertion of the grandeur of human persons present in these writings. Persons are invited to become what God is, to share in the powers of transformation, and to share in the joy of the divine life. While the nature of the journey to this transformation into love is rife with the ambiguous legacy of Christianity's alliance with violence, it is important to appreciate the dynamics of transformation in medieval mystical texts in which holy women become advocates for persons with God and intimates with the Sacred. In this vein, I believe that the work of contemporary spirituality is, on the one hand, to familiarize contemporary persons with the historic ways believers have cultivated, experienced, and responded to relationships of intimacy with God and, on the other hand, to provide present-day Christian practitioners with images, rituals, and resources to nurture their own intimacy with God. Faith-centered texts that celebrate the God of love with sense-rich images and words undergird and sustain spiritual life. In reading medieval sources, we can appreciate both differences from and similarities to the contemporary context as we seek to understand the integrity of these texts in their original settings; and also, while cognizant of the differences, we will profit by reflecting upon the ways these texts can invigorate, challenge, and sustain contemporary spiritual practice.

Notes

1. I am grateful to the organizers, panelists, and audience participants at the November 1999 American Academy of Religion session on Women Mystics for their responses to the paper in which I originally presented the ideas I have further developed here. I am grateful to Mark Wallace, David Perrin, and two anonymous readers for their careful review of this article.

2. Accounts of the miraculous "death" and "resurrection" of Catherine of Siena say that "she agreed to continue living only because the Virgin Mary promised that God would free souls from Purgatory because of her pain" (Bynum, 1987, 171).

3. Among recent scholars who have attended to the significance of trinitarian traditions are Barbara Raw (1997) and Barbara Newman (1999).

4. Although I disagree with Edith Wyschogrod's assertion that "[s]elf-renunciation to the point of effacement is the mark or trace of saintly labor" (30), I find her notion of body as "text," or "surface of writing," to be helpful and important (30, 96, 204).

5. The concept of beatific vision so critical to late medieval thought is, I would argue, often closely connected to the theme of transfiguration. As Caroline Walker Bynum points out, "By the 1330s the faithful were required to believe that the beatific vision could come to the blessed before the end of time; and theologians held, although in different ways, that the gifts of the glorified body were in some sense a consequence of the soul's vision of God. Indeed, some theologians argued that a special miracle had been necessary to block the manifestation of God's glory in the human body of his son Jesus; the body Jesus displayed at the Transfiguration was, they held, his normal body, manifesting the beatific vision he constantly possessed. . . . But the notion that the beatific vision could spill over into bodily manifestations, such as beauty or agility, probably encouraged the extravagant claims of hagiographers, who described their holy subjects as rosy and beautiful despite flagellation and self-starvation, excruciating disease and death itself. Aquinas wrote that martyrs were enabled to bear up under pain exactly because the beatific vision flows over naturally into the body" (1991, 231). I am suggesting that while in some cases there is a difference between texts that focus on beatific vision and those that make claims to the divinization of devotees, in many other cases the language of beatific vision is more closely associated with deification than scholars often acknowledge.

6. God speaks to Gertrude about the transformation: "As I am the figure of the substance of the Father (Heb. 1:3) through my divine nature, in the same way, you shall be the figure of my substance through my human nature, receiving in your deified soul the brightness of my divinity, as the air receives the sun's rays and, penetrated to the very

marrow by this unifying light, you will become capable of an ever closer union with me" (Gertrude of Helfta, 1993, 104).

7. Gertrude of Helfta 1989, 56, note # 79: "The metaphor of the mystical dance, i.e., the dance in heaven (cf. also VI, 633), is often found in Mechthild of Magdeburg and other mystics describing the state of the soul in union with the divine. It goes back to patristic literature. . . ." An artistic vision of the sacred dance is magnificently portrayed in the fourteenth-century Rothschild Canticles (Hamburger 1990).

REFERENCES

Angela of Foligno. *Complete Works*. Trans. Paul LaChance (New York: Paulist Press, 1993).

Bussert, Joy, Helen McEvoy-Freese, and Mary Pellauer. "'To Set at Liberty Those Who Are Bruised': Violence Against Women." *Minnesota Impact* February, 1–16 (1985).

Bynum, Caroline Walker. *Holy Feast and Holy Fast: The Religious Significance of Food to Holy Women* (Berkeley and Los Angeles: University of California Press, 1987).

Bynum, Caroline Walker. *Fragmentation and Redemption: Esssays on Gender and the Human Body in Medieval Religion* (New York: Zone Books, 1991).

Catherine of Siena. *The Dialogue*. Trans. Suzanne Noffke (New York: Paulist Press, 1980).

Catherine of Siena. *The Letters of Catherine of Siena*. Medieval and Renaissance Texts and Studies, volume 52. Trans. Suzanne Noffke (New York: Binghamton, 1988).

Chicago, Judy. *The Birth Project* (New York: Doubleday and Company, 1985).

Gertrude of Helfta. *Spiritual Exercises*. Cistercian Fathers Series, no. 49. Trans. Gertrud Jaron Lewis and Jack Lewis (Kalamazoo: Cistercian Publications, 1989).

Gertrude of Helfta. *The Herald of Divine Love*. Trans. Margaret Winkworth (New York: Paulist Press, 1993).

Hamburger, Jeffrey. *The Rothschild Canticles: Art and Mysticism in Flanders and the Rhineland circa 1300* (New Haven: Yale University Press, 1990).

Julian of Norwich. *Showings*. Trans. Edmund Colledge and James Walsh (New York: Paulist Press, 1978).

Kempe, Margery. *The Book of Margery Kempe*. Ed. Sanford B. Meech and Hope E. Allen. Early English Text Society, no. 212 (New York: Oxford University Press, 1940).

Kempe, Margery. *The Book of Margery Kempe*. Trans. W. Butler-Bowden (New York: Devin-Adair, 1944).

Maitland, Sarah. "Passionate Prayer: Masochistic Images in Women's Experience." In *Sex and God: Some Varieties of Women's Religious Experience*. Ed. Linda Hurcombe, 125–140 (New York: Routledge and Kegan Paul, 1987).

Marrow, James. *Passion Iconography in Northern European Painting of the Late Middle Ages and Early Renaissance* (Kortrijk, Belg.: Van Ghemmert Publishing, 1979).

Newman, Barbara. "Intimate Pieties: Holy Trinity and Holy Family in the Late Middle Ages." *Religion and Literature* 31: 77–101 (1999).

Raw, Barbara. *Trinity and Incarnation in Anglo-Saxon Art and Thought.* Cambridge Studies in Anglo-Saxon England, number 21 (New York: Cambridge University Press, 1997).

Ricoeur, Paul. *Figuring the Sacred: Religion, Narrative, and Imagination.* Ed. Mark I. Wallace and trans. David Pellauer (Minneapolis, MN: Fortress Press, 1995).

Ross, Ellen. "The Use of Scripture and the Spiritual Journey in Walter Hilton's 'Scale of Perfection.'" *Augustiniana* 89: 119–131 (1989).

Ross, Ellen. *The Grief of God: Images of the Suffering Jesus in Late Medieval England* (New York: Oxford University Press, 1997).

Schwartz, Regina. *The Curse of Cain: The Violent Legacy of Monotheism* (Chicago: The University of Chicago Press, 1997).

Silvas, Anna. *Jutta and Hildegard: The Biographical Sources* (University Park, PA: The Pennsylvania State University Press, 1999).

Wallace, Mark. *Fragments of the Spirit: Nature, Violence, and the Renewal of Creation* (New York: Continuum, 1996).

Wiesel, Elie. *And the Sea Is Never Full. Memoirs, 1969–* (New York: Alfred A. Knopf, 1999).

Wyschogrod, Edith. *Saints and Postmodernism: Revisioning Moral Philosophy* (Chicago: The University of Chicago Press, 1990).

3

MEDIEVAL WOMANS' STORIES: STORIES FOR WOMEN TODAY

KIRSI STJERNA

After I gave birth to my daughter five years ago, I decided not to name her after Julian of Norwich, Birgitta of Sweden, or even the popular Catherine of Siena. But I did want Kaleigh Kirsikka to grow up appreciating and identifying with medieval women mystics as her spiritual foremothers, as inspiring, creative, charismatic figures in the Christian story. At the same time, I struggle to shield my daughter from these ladies' sometimes extreme devotional and ascetic practices and—it seems to us—anorectic behavior. Most likely one day Kaleigh Kirsikka will struggle with her own issues of identity, embodiment, and empowerment as did these women. She will test her identity and boundaries as a woman in relation to others. She will wonder about God and her self-image as a child of God. She will face suffering and look for redemption and grace. What could medieval women teach her in all this? Could she embrace them as her mothers of faith with an empathetic heart and a critical eye? Drawing from the examples of Julian of Norwich and Birgitta of Sweden, in particular, we can explore some of the problems, and promises, for women and faith communities today. I want to acknowledge the challenges the devotional lives of medieval women present to us: in their experience-based faith, passion, and intentional spiritual living, they can be seen as sources of inspiration for us today.

The Gap and the Continuum
between Medieval and Modern Worlds

At first thought it might seem irrelevant to look for spiritual inspiration from the Medieval Ages. After all, the gap between the medieval times and our times is huge—or is it? Yes, we'd like to understand the world less dualistically and with less superstition, yet we are by no means free of all dualism or superstition. In our rational, scientific approach to life, we have come close to losing our appreciation of the mysterious and unexplainable, the "beyond." If medievals saw this "earthly" life and the other "heavenly" life as enmeshed to the extreme, we grandchildren of the Enlightenment have built ideological barriers between the two. Yet, our existential, spiritual search leads us to wonder if "there is more to life" than what meets the eye. We also search for meaning, for God; we also struggle with good and evil (or whatever names we want to use). We tend to name our "demons" and "raptures" with less-religious terms, perhaps, but ultimately we connect with medieval people in our universal search for meaning, connectedness, purpose, and happiness. We battle our own demons—and experience an occasional rapture, too!

Compared to medieval people and their religious ways, we'd like to think we are different, yet we live in the centuries-old continuum where our faith *is* shaped by faith expressions of the past. We articulate our faith in relation to the traditions handed down from our fathers and mothers. Medieval women mystics sought an intimate knowledge of God, a personal experience, from which everything else would follow. We share their desire for repentance, redemption, and a new beginning. We, too, would like to be perfect, even though we differ in our understanding of "perfection" and how to reach it. As we develop a more holistic understanding of humanness and spirituality, fewer of us desire to renounce "the world." The comforts of sufficient nourishment, loving human relations, and possessions are no longer seen necessarily as obstacles to meaningful spiritual living. But we can be stretched to appreciate how the personal renouncement and discipline of medieval women mystics has been helpful for their growth and conversion. Through their stories we can also learn to appreciate the significance and uniqueness of religious experiences, even if our ability, willingness, and ways to "experience" faith might differ.

As a church, we have not always done justice to all our sources, especially those coming from medieval women. Now, as we learn more of the women of the past, we want to know more. What did they believe and experience? How did they appropriate their faith? What inspired their spirituality? During medieval times women were inspired to emerge as spiritual leaders with written testimonies of their faith journeys and emerging theologies. Knowing their stories and teachings complements our understanding of our own Christian heritage and may give us surprising points of connection. Knowing their stories will also show us where we do not connect.

In becoming familiar with the spirituality of medieval women, modern readers are easily alarmed by their sometimes extreme forms of asceticism and their mysterious revelatory experiences—the very two aspects that provide endless fascination for scholars and devotees alike. For example, by taking the discipline of fasting to an unhealthy extreme, both Catherine of Siena (1347–1380) and Catherine of Genoa (1447–1510) starved to death. They mortified their bodies with acts of extreme humiliation such as eating lice, kissing contagiously ill people, licking the floors, and not eating. (Their self-starvation is troubling as a not-so-healthy model for contemporary young women already prone to anorexia and rebellion by not eating.) These two women aimed to attain spiritual perfection by annihilating their body and human needs. Their practices were undergirded by dualistic teachings of the time that elevated spiritual life and perfection beyond ordinary humanness and bodily being. From our viewpoint, we could consider it their "loss," but acknowledge, at the same time, they "gained" something significant. Their ascetic purification often led to mysterious personal experiences of God, which then inspired a vision for reform and change.

In order to concretize and explore further the issues sketched above, we turn to the story of two well-known medieval women mystics: Julian of Norwich and Birgitta of Sweden.

Birgitta of Sweden (1303–1373)

Birgitta, a married woman with children, knew the struggles of a woman with a family and a vocation outside home. She was driven by her religious call and yearning for spiritual perfection. Different from some of her "role models"—those fellow ascetic heroines and saints whose lives she was familiar with—were her moderation and commonsense attitude in penitential practices (*Vita* 61; *R* VII:5). This saint ate (sometimes really well) and gave birth to children—eight in all. For her, the challenge in turning away from the "world" lay not so much in denying and punishing her body but in cutting loose from human commitments and relations. As one of the richest persons in Sweden, Birgitta had everything she wanted except the luxury to follow the ascetic impulse and her prophetic call full-time, unencumbered by human relations —and human love.

Only as a forty-one-year-old widow did Birgitta feel free to follow fully her spiritual call, leaving her then-grown children in Sweden and going on a thirty-year pilgrimage to Rome, where she would die of old age. She had experienced visitations of Christ and Mary since childhood but now, as a middle-aged widow, her entire life was transformed by her call from Christ to become his bride and bear spiritual children through her revelations and call for reform. Her new call allowed her to remain a mother in a spiritual sense, to mother the world with Mary, the Mother of God (*Vita* 25–26; *RE* 46–47). Leaving behind her life as a biological mother and a noble matron of a wealthy estate (and giving her possessions to her children), she lived in chosen, moderate poverty in Rome. During this time she labored to persuade the pope to return to Rome from Avignon, and to win an approval for her monastic order for women that was to the honor of Mary. She also worked endlessly for the unity of the Church, for peace in the world (the work her younger contemporary Catherine of Siena would continue), to care for the downtrodden, and to generally save souls with her penetrating, insightful visions and "preaching."

Birgitta was one of the first mother-saints in the medieval Church. As Clarissa Atkinson (1991, 144–193) has concluded, Birgitta stretched the category of holiness to include married women and brought "matristic" sensitivities into the realm of theology. She never stopped caring for her children, although she thought she should have; her maternal sensitivies (and her children) appear frequently in her revelations. As a mother, Birgitta felt pulled in opposite directions: between the responsibilities of "earthly" and "heavenly" life. Modern parents can relate to her struggle between parenthood and career, but with less-dualistic presuppositions: we would rather not see loving God and loving our families as mutually exclusive!

Birgitta, one of the more "moderate" saints in her ascetic practices, "mortified her body by living in toil and abstinence," says her *Vita Abbreviata Praedicate Sponsae Christi S. Birgittae*, written in 1492 for the canonization process by her confessors, both named Petrus Olavi. (References are from the English translation by Albert Kezel, 1990). As is the case with Birgitta, quite a few of medieval women did not write themselves but others—male advocates and confessors typically—wrote *about* and *for* them. The predominant source on women are their *vitae*: life stories more concerned with highlighting extraordinary characteristics of their lives rather than giving an authentic portrayal of the woman, her beliefs and experiences behind the "saintly image." This problem is often present with texts attributed to women themselves, texts they either wrote or dictated to a scribe.

It is troubling to us that we will never know how much women's texts were manipulated in the process of editing the language in order to make them fit into the acceptable expectations of the times. As an example, in Birgitta's case, her editor-confessors' role was essential in promoting the official approval of her visions, which they also compiled and prepared for publication. The extent of their "refinement work" remains unknown. But the fact that these men voluntarily worked for Birgitta for the publication of her visions suggests that they respected her visions as well as their divine origin and dared not to change in any essential way Birgitta's original ideas.

Although moderate, Birgitta's practices seem harsh today. On Fridays, for instance, she dripped candle wax on her flesh and plowed the wounds with her nails so that "her body would not be without the suffering of wounds, and this she did for the sake of memory of the passion of Christ." These practices were important to her search for an experience of God and holiness. Birgitta was rewarded with experiences that empowered her and made her appear particularly holy in the eyes of others who witnessed to her life and promoted her canonization in 1391—and who made sure her revelations were published and circulated.

Birgitta's revelations to the world—addressed to royalty as well as servants, popes as well as lay people—remain her major legacy. Through them she has spoken to generation after generation. Her *Vita* tells how, during prayer, she frequently became "absorbed" in ecstatic contemplation. While fully awake, she saw and heard divine revelations and entered into discussion with Christ, Mary, and the saints. In all, seven hundred of these revelations of different length have been recorded. Her confessors wrote down her visions and edited them for publication (since 1492) in eight books: *Reuelaciones* (=*R*); her monastic rule in *Regula Sanctissimi Saluatoris*; lessons for the order in *Sermo Angelicus* (=*sA*); various things in *Reuelaciones*

Extrauagantes (=*RE*), and four prayer books titled *Oraciones* (=*O*). These texts include reflections and instructions on biblical and theological subjects and spiritual life; didactic, ethical, and religious proclamations; and prayers, meditations, curses, praises, autobiographical data, and information about monastic life. (See Emilia Fogelklou, 1973, 196, 200, 86–92.)

Regardless of what can be speculated about the "supernatural" origins of the visions or the role of editors in molding her visions into publishable and orthodox form, we can consider Birgitta's visions testimony of her experience of God, that is of her insights into life, divine and human. Birgitta considered her revelatory experiences as the special "channel" of God into human life given not for her own glory but for the salvation of humankind. We can see them also as a vital means of authority that gave Birgitta a unique voice as "Christ's bride and channel" (*R* VII:7, 10, 19, 4).

Birgitta's collection of revelations displays a wide range of interests (personal, political, theological, and spiritual) and a strong desire to make sense of the world. As a mother and a matron, she wanted to maintain order in spiritual and earthly life. For her, that order came from keeping the right priorities, the first of which is loving God. Probably drawing from her parental experience, Birgitta envisioned right relationship with God as being similar to that of a parent/child relationship, a relationship grounded in an innate love and bond that mirrors some of the same dynamics. At the same time, she experienced her relationship with God as a heavenly marriage with Christ, the purpose of which was to produce spiritual children for God. Birgitta would see herself as "mothering spiritual children" for God by converting people back to God. Her thirty years of marriage to Ulf naturally shaped her grasp of mystical marriage as well and, paradoxically, provided her with less-erotic undertones when describing the mystical relationship, compared to the language her unmarried sister mystics used!

As a mother who had lost a child and a spouse, and as a mystic who had "revisited" Christ's death and his mother's sorrow in visions, Birgitta was deeply aware of suffering and evil in life. She drew consolation from her unshakable belief in her beloved Creator's eternal justice and endless mercy, as well as human beings' potential to make things right by willing right. Her motto could be: "You can do it if you really want it!" Her faith in human potential was as strong as her acknowledgment of the nuisance of ever-tempting devils around us. Birgitta found peace of mind from her conviction that nothing happens without a reason. The death of an unborn child, the creation of a beast, or the mischievousness of demons: she understood them all in the context of God's mysterious justice.

As a model of faith, Birgitta promoted Mary—the Queen of Heaven, who excels in her love for God, right use of will, and other human gifts—as a fully human and virtuous woman with divine powers over devils and evils. Mary dominated Birgitta's spirituality as the perfect mother, as a heavenly mother of mercy whose comfort she claimed to have experienced at the time of losing her own mother and at a difficult childbirth. To Birgitta, Mary presented a much-needed feminine model of how to follow and love Christ. Typical of medieval spirituality, the cornerstone of Birgitta's faith and the object of her most fervent love was Christ, who wishes to be known and loved by people as their bridegroom. Birgitta's God was Christ who wants intense love-relationships and spiritual children.

Birgitta's colorful theology, often touching upon practical concerns, was based on her experiences as a wife and a mother, as well as her mystical experiences of Christ's and Mary's presence in her life. Cardinal J. Ratzinger sees Birgitta among the high/late medieval saints who introduced a "female theology" and thus marked a turning point in spirituality with new emphasis on devotional life (1993, 71–92, 86–87, 89–90). In Birgitta's theology, praxis and theory connect. She complements patriarchal theologies with her "woman's perspectives" and parental interests, such as her curiosity about the theological and physical realities of childbirth as well as her insights on women's essential role in salvation history and special intimacy with God. As Auke Jelsma (1986, 169, 171) has pointed out, the prominence of women and Mary in Birgitta's theology and order is conspicuous.

In spiritual life, Mother Birgitta presents a model for extroverted, apostolic, and prophetic mysticism, exemplifying how to live "holy" *in* the "world." Holy living to her meant loving God and being active in one's calling. Her contemplative life was complemented by action, and both were elements of her intentional spiritual living, for which she had no particular model but embracing the basic virtues—faith, hope, and love (*RV*:8, rev. 1). As was true for most medieval women mystics, Birgitta saw love as the center upon which all depends and aims for: God is love and expects people to respond to that by loving God and neighbor. Loving oneself was not a positive concern for medievals. On this principle Birgitta built her message for "repentance" and "reformation"—two words central in Birgitta's theology, spirituality, and visions. Her remedy for the world's illnesses was reformation through right loving.

The ultimate goal of Birgitta's spiritual journey was not only to learn to love God better, but to change the world. In fulfilling this mission, she provided an example of how emancipation is possible even in the absence of freedom. As Auke Jelsma says, "Bridget [Birgitta] succeeded in using women's humble place in society as an advantage for her own position. Bridget did not revolt against the existing image of women, she used this image. By submitting herself to the authority of church, society, and God, she hoped to change the world." How? By making people will right and thus invoking God's mercy (*R* VII:8, 12, 27; Jelsma, 1986, 171).

Julian of Norwich (1343–1423)

Julian of Norwich, an anchoress from Norwich, England, presents another example of bodily suffering for spiritual goals. In order to be purified, Julian desired and prayed to God to have every kind of pain, both in her body and in her spirit. Her request was granted by God to the point where she nearly died of a mysterious "gift of bodily sickness." She described her three gifts of suffering as sickness itself, the experience of Christ's passion, and three wounds. As a result of this suffering, Julian received sixteen visions from God in May 1373, at the age of thirty. She subsequently compiled her visions and experiences in a book called *Showings*, first in a shorter volume (twenty-five chapters) that is the embryo for a longer text (eighty-six chapters) that she would contemplate over a period of twenty years. (For our puruposes here, references are from the longer book, unless otherwise indicated.) Julian's visionary theology is based on these revelations she received by words and images.

Julian is known more for her theology than her attempts to change the world, and yet that was also her ultimate goal. Her theology, which is her lasting, and by now widely recognized legacy in Christian history, grew from her mystical experiences of God. She wanted to know God and asked for the gift of suffering. Reflecting on that experience, she wrote *Showings,* a book that remains popular reading even today. "Her teaching is timeless," says Jean Leclercq, "meeting some of the urgent needs of those seeking

God in our age and answering many of the crucial problems of spiritual development and contemplative consciousness" (1978, 1).

We know very little of Julian. Our primary sources are her *Showings*, bequests made to her in fourteenth- and fifteenth-century wills, and the testimony of another English mystic, Marguerite Kempe (1373–1439). As far as we know, Julian was "living the solitary, enclosed life of an anchoress (but with a maidservant to tend her) in a cell adjoining the parish Church of St. Julia in Conisford at Norwich, opposite the house of the Augustinian Friars" (Edmunt Colledge and James Walsh, 1978, 18). Julian's *Showings* tell little of her personally, but they do portray a woman with great intelligence, eagerness to experience God, and ability to transform that experience into sophisticated theological insights on some of life's fundamental questions such as suffering, and (what she is most famous for) the maternal nature of God. She did not invent the idea of the motherhood of God, but she used it in an original fashion.

This understanding of a loving, maternal God shaped Julian's empathetic notion of suffering, another of her central concerns. Her notion of God combined with her personal experience of suffering, which nearly killed her (*S* ch. 1–5), supported her hope-filled conclusion that "all will be well"—because sin has no reality (*S* ch. 6, 27, 53), because God has no anger (*S* ch. 46, 49), and because Jesus is our mother (*S* ch. 58, 59, 60, 64) on whose love everything depends. For Julian, it was impossible for sin or evil to overwhelm us as long as Jesus is our creating and saving mother. "I saw that God does everything; I saw no sin, and I saw that everything was all right. But it was when God showed me sin that he said, 'Everything is going to be all right'" (*S* ch. 34).

Julian's suffering gave her a glimpse of her final goal; rest, and union "in nakedness" with her creator and heavenly mother. This experience is behind her empathetic encouragement to endure in the ambiguous spiritual journey of seeing and not seeing God during this life. Julian's "showing" for herself and others was that our basic source of hope in life is that God is our mother and foundation who has never left us but awaits us to fall back to God in prayer.

Like Birgitta, Julian focused on reconciling God and people, which both saw as the main problem and solution for human concerns. Both were bothered by the sin and brokenness they witnessed around them—a result of people falling from right love-relationship with God—and both saught answers on how to deal with the suffering caused by this broken-ness. They both knew suffering first-hand and were convinced of humankind's urgent need to repent and return to love God, the creator and source of mercy. Love is the way to correct our lives, it is the essence of God, the reason for our existence, the basic drive in life, human and divine. We all are by nature loving, passionate, desiring beings. While recognizing the sinfulness of human nature, the two women showed tremendous trust in, first of all God's loving goodness and mercy and powers over all things evil, and secondly in human potential to will and do good and love right. Everything, including a fulfilling spiritual journey, is possible in the bosom of the loving God that these women experienced. Transformation of the world is possible if people are willing to trust in God and one another. God is waiting. Birgitta's call for reform and Julian's assurance of hope seem to transcend time and place. There is even a sense of urgency in Birgitta's writings that may sound true for some people today that truly desire for a deep and profound change in their lives.

In addition to their similar basic theological conclusions, what unites Birgitta, Julian, and other medieval women teachers is their powerful mystical experiences, the yearning for them, their visions, and a sense of a call to serve as God's spokespersons. They also share their passion in fulfilling that call in ways appropriate to their situation in life. For medieval women this typically would have entailed transgression in the eyes of the "authorities" of the Church and bearers of the spiritual and theological "norms." In prayer and contemplation, in a focused search for the divine, they experienced God intimately enough to become transformed and "blessed" with a special kind of spiritual authority that placed prayer at the center of their lives.

Birgitta's and Julian's lives were transformed as a result of their prayer life and mystical experiences of God, and they relied on that experience in order to become God's transforming instruments in the world. They intentionally did not call themselves spiritual teachers or theologians—those were considered male realms. And yet, with their intimate knowledge of God and transforming visions, that is exactly what they became. Their spiritualities and theologies are visionary, existential, practical—and as such, timelessly inspiring.

Search for Suffering and Meaning

Visionary or "saintly" women from the Middle Ages typically suffered physically as part of their faith journey and "calling," some by choice, some more or less mysteriously. They tended to explain their afflictions in spiritual terms, as if bearing a pertinent divine meaning. Generally speaking, suffering and visions, accompanied by exemplary virtuous and chaste lives, provided spiritually active women with a measure of spiritual authority and notoriety. These also gave women a security blanket against "inquisition" by the Church, which did not officially allow women to exercise spiritual leadership. (The inclusion of women in ordained ministry and academia has happened only relatively recently, and even so is not universal.) Perhaps for a modern reader, it would be helpful to pay attention to the meaning these experiences had to the women themselves, instead of trying to appropriate their experiences and stories as direct examples for us.

For instance, one way to reconcile some of the difficult (and perpetually fascinating) elements in their devotional lives is to look at these as means of rebellion, transgression, and empowerment. As Elizabeth Petroff (1994, 176–177) suggests, "[I]n actuality there is only one real transgression for a [medieval] woman: to go public, to be a visible, speaking, informed moral leader." For medieval women to become visible and establish a public voice automatically meant transgression, a violation of the code of women's proper behavior, which could happen through contemplative and ascetic practices. Also, "[t]he conditions of women's lives [their devotional, ascetic, and contemplative practices and communities] led to visions, and visions gave an individual woman a voice, a belief in herself as chosen to speak. They also gave her the experience of inner transformation, which she felt compelled to communicate to others" (Petroff, 1994, 8).

> What Caroline Walker Bynum says about women's extreme fasting applies here as well: I argue that women's radical asceticism was not only a rejection of a world in which they had little control over their bodies and their destinies but also a rejection of a church which, as it touched more and more of life and provided ordinary folk with appropriate ways to be religious, seemed a threat as well as an opportunity to those pious women who wanted, without compromise or moderation, to imitate Christ (*Holy Feast*, 1987, 218).

In other words, what may seem alarming to us can be a surprisingly creative means of spiritual transformation and spiritual liberation for others. Birgitta and Julian are just two examples of women who embraced the traditional virtues of chastity, humility, obedience, poverty, and ascetic heroism. Renouncing their earthly lives and adapting disciplined spiritual lifestyles became the means of emancipation that allowed these women's spirits to rise rather than wither with their disciplined and frail bodies. Empowered simultaneously by their ecstatic and visionary experiences, they creatively transformed their otherwise limited lives and left a legacy of spiritual transformation and liberation for others.

The strivings of these women may reach across the centuries to stir our own inner longings for deeper self-understanding as well as a desire to understand God more deeply. Their striving may also aid us to be aware of opportunities to repent and start afresh, of methods to bring new energy into our lives, and to find our place, purpose, and direction in life. We may also relate to medieval mystics' existential questions on how to deal with suffering and evil in the world, how to find and name our God, or how to love, or live lovingly—a central concern for mystics aiming for the perfection of virtuous love.

However we name it, there is something universal and timeless in our spiritual search. We could call this a search for spiritual, meaningful living, or a search for the meaning, moment by moment, of the Divine mystery alive in our lives. The question, "What does your life mean?" is timelessly applicable—to the medieval mystics as well as to us today. Interpreting, or looking for the meaning below the surface of our lives, is foundational to a happy and productive life—and medieval women can give us witness to this kind of "life-long journey of growth." They spoke forcefully to the central concerns of the human condition that are easily recognized whether or not you are a believer, whether or not you go to church or belong to a faith community.

Reading the testimonies of the mystics who have gone before us, and learning from their intentional spiritual search, we may even find a mystic in ourselves. We can, in Carol Lee Flinders's words (1993, 9), make the "experiential discovery that the source of all meaning—the God of truth, beauty, and love, if you will—is a living presence within" us also. It is this realization that will connect us with women like Birgitta and Julian. Carol Flinders (1993, 10–11) suggests these women can speak to us of models of friendship, of the importance of institutions supporting spiritual growth, of the tranquillity resulting from finding one's calling, of the struggle women have with different claims put on them (such as "claims of family . . . and claims of their own emerging selves"). As subjects of powerful religious experiences and practices, these medieval women mystics emerged from institutional invisibility to become active players in the history of Christian spirituality.

We might even see them as religious "performers" who would induce reactions and transformation in their "audience," as Joanna Ziegler (1999, xx) proposes:

> By entering mystical behavior as theater, artistry . . . we begin to understand the most incredible acts of public pain and self-affliction. As in theater, that audience is moved to believe, to heal the pain and suffering, and to witness the effects of love. The freakish, outlandish, bizarre acts of personal piety that accompany mysticism, if interpreted as performance, may then be seen as dramatic vessels from which pour forth the entire and glorious range of ecstatic revelation.

Ironically, in order to sustain this visible and powerful role as visionary prophet or God's performers, women, at times, had to surrender themselves to the obedience of ecclesiastical authority and deny their own voice. Birgitta particularly exemplifies the ambiguity of power and powerlessness in the lives of medieval women. She had the courage to embrace a public teaching role within her obedience to the authorities and customs of the Church. "Paradoxically," says Claire Sahlin (1999, 84, see 69–99), "Birgitta's authority as an authentic spokesperson for God was never greater than when she relinquished her public speaking voice." For her survival, this was more critical than what she actually said. This is interesting because her theology contains some quite radical elements. For instance, her understanding of Mary's central, continuous role in salvation history pushes the limits of the traditional notion of God as a distant male Trinity. Birgitta played the rules, so to speak, yet managed to leave her unique footprint in the history of the Christian Church. A remarkable witness to her continuing influence is her status today as a globally celebrated saint, the new patron saint of Europe. In 1991, two widely attended international conferences were held, one in Vadstena, Sweden ("St. Birgitta, Her Proclamation and Example") and one in Rome, Italy ("Saint Bridget, Prophetess of New

Age") in order to explore Birgitta's significance for the modern world. As well, great festivities are to be expected in 2003 on the occasion of the 700th anniversary of her birth.

Birgitta's and Julian's stories demonstrate how medieval women have left us an ambiguous but rich legacy, sometimes quite complex and simple at the same time.

Conclusion

In evaluating medieval women's legacies and their appropriateness to us today, we can distinguish between two dimensions: 1) medieval women's lives, which entail religious practices; and 2) their visions and teachings. I would argue that medieval women's most significant legacy for later generations lies not in their devotional practices, at times extreme and brutal, but in the more universal aspects of their testimonies: they can inspire us with their zeal and passion in their spiritual journey and with their intense transforming religious experiences and resulting distinctive (sometimes more, sometimes less so) "matristic" (as complementing the "patristic") theologies.

Although the focus and treatment of issues by medieval women writers may often have been more practical than theoretical, their theological interests were emancipatory and brought along changes in devotional life. They exemplify spirituality in which mystical/religious experiences are intertwined with a call to reform and heal the world. We could call it apostolic and practical spirituality. Or prophetic spirituality. They evidence the interrelatedness of mystical experiences and reformative impetus, emphasize the relation between contemplation and action, and underline how being spiritually alive does make a difference in the world.

Past stereotyping and categorization may present a barrier in appropriating medieval women as theological and spiritual sources. Much of their writing has been characterized as predominantly devotional, didactic, and visionary and, as such, nonanalytical, subjective, romantic, emotional, repetitive, proverbial, and concrete—thus less weighty theologically and spiritually. Obviously these elements can be found in some, but not in all, women's sources, as Elizabeth Petroff (1987, 23–29, 48) and Katharina Wilson (1984, xx–xxi) have demonstrated. Indeed, instead of crafting academic treatises in a scholarly fashion, women often wrote (or dictated) in the vernacular (e.g., Julian wrote in English and Birgitta in Swedish as well as in Latin), following the form of a revelation or a prophecy, didactic or devotional proclamation. But that does not make their writings any less theological; just different. Experience complemented speculation in their theologies, which were inseparable from their lives and thus utterly existential. This, combined with their use of the vernacular and "different-from-academic" phrasing, enabled them to speak to a wide audience. As Jean LecLercq (1978, 3) has concluded, "To be sure, they did not teach in the same manner as the majority of the Schoolmen. Although most of the latter are forgotten and their sophisticated 'questions' remain buried in a few manuscripts, the existential message of the women who encountered God never ceases to be transcribed, translated and published."

As visionaries, seers, mystics, prophets, and theologians, Julian and Birgitta complement the traditional theological summae and mediate importantly between the academic speculative theology and lived theology of the people of the Church. With their very act of assuming the role of a spiritual teacher, they question the rightness of monopolizing theology and spiritual teaching by the academically learned and institutionally authorized, and claim that right for all people of faith. As teachers, they ponder faith issues and the teachings of their Church; in that, drawing from their personal experiences, they remind their readers of the mystery essential in all religiosity, of the experience without which faith fades, and of the spiritual and practical dimension of theology without which it remains an exercise of the mind. In their lives and writing, we see theology, spirituality, and living intertwined, thus forming a bridge between theology and life, and ideas and praxis. They show what living theologically and seeking God's meanings in one's life could be. They also suggest that faith and theology that are open to mystery and experience can, in surprising ways, promote emancipation, liberation, and spiritual transformation.

Learning from the spiritual lives and teachings of medieval women begins by appreciating them as "subjects," as real persons struggling with the real questions of the society and Church of their times. We need to take them as subjects of their religious experiences, of their spiritual lives, and of their theology. Learning of their struggles and their search for reform may give us a new sense of meaning in our lives today.

Resources

Auke Jelsma, "The Appreciation of Bridget of Sweden (1303–1373) in the 15th Century," *Women and Men in Spiritual Culture, XIV–XVII Centuries: A Meeting of South and North*, 163–175. Ed. E. Schulte van Kessel (The Hague: Netherlands Govt. Pub. Office, 1986).

Birgitta of Sweden. Life and Selected Revelations. Trans. Albert Kezel. The Classics of Western Spirituality (New York: Paulist Press, 1990).

Carol Lee Flinders, *Enduring Grace: Living Portraits of Seven Women Mystics* (New York: HarperSanFrancisco, 1993).

Caroline Walker Bynum, "Religious Women in the Later Middle Ages." Christian Spirituality. High Middle Ages and Reformation, 121–139. Ed. J. Raitt in collaboration with B. McGinn and J. Meyendorff. *World Spirituality: An Encyclopedic History of the Religious Quest.* Volume 17 (London, New York: Crossroad, 1987).

_____, *Holy Feast and Holy Fast: The Religious Significance of Food to Medieval Woman.* New Historicism: Studies in Cultural Poetics (Berkeley: University of California Press, 1987).

Claire L. Sahlin, "Preaching and Prophesying: The Public Proclamation of Birgitta of Sweden's Revelation," in *Performance and Transformation: New Approaches to Late Medieval Spirituality*, 69–96. Ed. Mary A. Suydam and Joanna E. Ziegler (New York: St. Martin's Press, 1999).

Elizabeth Petroff, ed. *Medieval Women's Visionary Literature* (New York: Oxford University Press, 1986).

Elizabeth Petroff, *Body and Soul: Essays on Medieval Women and Mysticism* (New York/Oxford: Oxford University Press, 1994).

Emilia Fogelklou, *St. Birgitta* (Stockholm: Albert Bonniers Förlag, repr. 1973).

Joseph Ratzinger, Cardinal, "L'attualità di santa Brigida de Svezia," *Santa Brigida profeta dei tempi nuovi/Prophetess of New Age* (1993), cit. op. 71–92.

Julian of Norwich, *Showings*. Translated from the critical text with an Introduction by Edmund Colledge and James Walsh; Preface by Jean Leclercq, The Classics of Western Spirituality (New York: Paulist Press, 1978).

Kari E. Börresen, "Birgitta of Sweden: A Model of Theological Inculturation," *Santa Brigida profeta dei tempi nuovi/Saint Bridget, Prophetess of New Age*, 190–198. Ed. Tekla Famiglietti, Proceedings of the International Study Meetings, Rome, October 3–7, Roma, 1993.

Katharina Wilson, ed. *Medieval Women Writers* (Athens, GA: The University of Georgia Press, 1984).

Vita Abbreviata S. Birgittae, in Reuelaciones S. Birgitte, 1492.

PART II

Setting the Stories of Women Christian Mystics into the Twenty-First Century

4

CATHERINE OF SIENA: CONTEMPLATING THE FRUITFULNESS OF CHRISTIAN SUFFERING

JANE MCAVOY

*I*s the willingness of medieval women mystics to suffer for their faith a model for our lives or a perversion of Christian faith? Is it ever a good thing to sacrifice oneself for the good of the Church, the stability of one's family, or the sins of the world?

A colleague struggles with his daughter's anorexia. He tells me that no matter how much I want to explain the eating disorders of medieval women mystics, it is a destructive practice that he can never condone. The pain and anguish in his voice leave me speechless. I realize that I will have to do more than explain away medieval women's self-inflicted suffering; I must respond to the reality of my colleague's pain.

Yet, I remain convinced that the answer is not a simple dismissal of the Christian ideal of suffering and all those who have suffered for their faith. In the novel, *Saint Maybe,* Anne Tyler presents an intriguing picture of a contemporary saint. The saint is a young man who decides to sacrifice his future career in order to raise his brother's children, because he believes that his actions will atone for his brother's death. As I read the book I am appalled by this idea of sacrificial atonement, and yet I am drawn to the possibility that this young man is (maybe) a modern-day saint. It is with the problems and possibilities of contemporary suffering in mind that I contemplate the meaning of Catherine of Siena's life.

Catherine is the ultimate test case for a study on the relevance of women mystics for contemporary spirituality. When Caroline Bynum wrote that medieval women mystics present us with the possibility that suffering can be fruitful (Bynum, 1987, 301), it is Catherine that she had in mind.

Catherine is one of the most famous Christians of all times, declared both a saint and a Doctor of Theology by the Roman Catholic Church, meaning that both her life and her teaching are considered outstanding models of Christian faith. When Pope Paul VI declared her a Doctor of the Church in 1970, he cited her emphasis on Jesus crucified and her obedience to the Church.

Catherine lived in the fourteenth century (1347–1380), a time of great suffering and turmoil in her city and in the Church. She is famous for her unswerving devotion to the pope during his exile to and return from Avignon. She also cared for plague victims, adjudicated family rivalries, and wrote numerous letters of counsel to civic and church leaders, all the while living a life of prayer and mystical devotion. Her holiness attracted numerous followers, and she wrote a book of spiritual instruction entitled *The Dialogue* (1378).

In her book Catherine talks about the ability to glory in suffering. She herself suffered from the inability to eat and considered this practice a way to pay for her sins. Her eating problems began during her youth, when she battled with her family over her desire to lead a religious life versus their desire for her to marry. The combination of refusing to eat and suffering a disfiguring illness finally convinced her family to let her join a Dominican lay order.

After a few years of private prayer and severe ascetical practice, Catherine had a death-like experience, when she heard Mary call her back to life so that she could free other people's souls through her pain. As a result, she turned to a life of willing suffering for the world. In her prayers, she asked that her life be sacrificed for the good of the Church. By 1380 the support for the papacy was crumbling in Rome and Catherine made one last effort to atone for the sins of the Church by undertaking a hunger strike. She died on April 29 at the age of thirty-three.

Catherine's life always has been controversial, her fasting being only one area that received a lot of criticism. During her day, in fact, critics wondered if she faked her visions. Members of her own order criticized her for wanting to lead a life of public ministry rather than private prayer. Others charged her with trying to be more pious than Jesus. To still the criticism, Dominican authorities appointed Raymond of Capua as her confessor. A noted Dominican leader and trained theologian, Raymond gave Catherine the approved status she needed as well as a dialogue partner to deepen her teaching and faith. It was Raymond who wrote her biography, *The Life of Catherine of Siena* (1395), and began her movement for sainthood.

With Raymond's efforts to spread the news of her work, Catherine's fame grew. Even before her death she was the most famous holy woman in Italy. Her own book, *The Dialogue*, and Raymond's book, *The Life of Catherine of Siena*, became popular works after her death. When translated into English, *The Dialogue* was depicted as instruction for the life of enclosure, while Catherine's active political role was ignored. When she was declared a saint and later patroness of Rome and Italy, the focus shifted to her work to bring the pope back to Rome, not on the influence of her spirituality. Later, as her fame grew, the fullness of Catherine's life, with its power and its suffering, fell into obscurity. Ironically, this most famous of medieval women is the hardest to recover from the legends of history.

Raymond himself understood the difficulty of the task. He states at the beginning of his work that to understand Catherine we must understand the outer and the inner nature of her life. "One would almost say there were two Catherines there: the outer one, in the body, worn to a thread by suffering; and the inner one, in the spirit, strong to keep that body on its feet, and filling it with energy" (Raymond, 1980, 61). If we are to recover Catherine's life from the obscurity of history and struggle with the meaning of her life for contemporary spirituality, we must follow Raymond's advice. While one could argue that Raymond, like all confessors, provides us with a biased view of Catherine, it is still the case that no one knew more intimately the details of Catherine's life. It is from Raymond that we glimpse an image of Catherine as a paradox of outer suffering and inner strength.

The Outer Suffering of the Spiritual Life

The greatest challenge that Catherine presents to us is her willingness to take on suffering to pay for sin. Raymond notes that the purpose of her lay order was to make satisfaction for their sins by the practice of penance, and he frames the story of Catherine's early life as the perfection of this calling. She exposed herself to the scalding waters of the sulphur baths (in the hopes of making herself undesirable for marriage), believing that she could exchange the pain she deserved in purgatory for the physical pain she

willingly endured on earth. Even as an adult, she willingly underwent tor-
turous practices of purging food as a means of penance. When Raymond
urged her to stop eating altogether to save herself from pain, she replied
that she saw this as an opportunity to satisfy her Creator by paying God a
finite debt for her sins (Raymond, 1980, 171). Later she imagined that
Christ asked her to choose between a crown of thorns and a crown of gold,
saying that she could wear one now and would wear the other after death.
She grabbed the crown of thorns, declaring that in this life she would take
suffering to herself for the refreshment of her soul. In these and many
other examples, Catherine seemed to accept and even seek out suffering to
satisfy God.

As her public ministry increased, Catherine began to take on suffering
to pay for other people's sins as well as her own. When the warring factions
of the Church spiraled out of control, she saw her role as not only mediat-
ing peace but also paying for the consequences of their sins. Catherine
urged a church official to ask for mercy for his sins, declaring that she
knew God forgave him because she had assumed the debts of his sins herself. While she counseled political leaders, military leaders, church leaders,
and anyone else whose sins she saw as threatening the stability of the Church,
her greatest concern was for the welfare of the pope, and her greatest suffering was on his behalf. "Let my bones be split apart for those for whom I
am praying, if such is your will," she prayed. "Let my bones and marrow
be ground up for your vicar on earth" (Noffke, 1983, 20). When all of her
efforts seemed in vain, her petitions increased, asking God to use her body
as an anvil on which the sins of the pope's adversaries could be hammered
out. That day she began a thirty-day fast that would lead to her death.

In *The Dialogue,* Catherine sets the meaning of suffering within the
context of the sinfulness of humanity and the justice of God. Infected by
the sin of Adam's disobedience, which Catherine describes as "stinking
pus" that has infected the whole human race, humanity declared war on
God's mercy and became the enemy of God. While Catherine describes
sin at various times as pride, selfish love, disordered will, nonbeing, and
sensuality, it is at base a perversion of our humanness and a denial of our
relationship with God. Sin is a poison that pollutes our nature and poisons
the world. Just as the plague had overcome Europe, so sin had overtaken
human life.

Having seen the devastation of war, Catherine knew that the war between humanity and God could not be reconciled without the restoration of justice, so Christ came to earth as mediator, taking on himself the punishment for humanity's injustice. While she does not clearly articulate why, Catherine states that divine justice demands suffering in atonement for sin, and by suffering in the body on the cross, Christ placates God's anger. Thus she prays, "You turned our great war with God into a great peace" (Noffke, 1983, 17). It is this belief in the centrality of God's justice that undergirded Catherine's own acts of suffering. Justice demands payment for sin, and the ongoing sins of humanity demand the continued suffering of sinners. It was faith in the uncompromising justice of God that compelled her to suffer for others. In her last prayer, just weeks before her death, Catherine prays, "My Lord, since it is impossible that your justice should be set aside . . . whatever punishment is due to this people, let it be worked out upon this body of mine" (Raymond, 1980, 321).

Catherine believed that she could suffer for others because Christ had served as not only the mediator but also the model for our salvation. She describes Christ as a bridge to salvation, reconciling the world to God and providing a straight path for our own life of faith. "I made of him a bridge for you," God declares, "because the road to heaven had been destroyed. If you travel along this delightful straight way, which is a lightsome truth, holding the key of obedience, you will pass through the world's darknesses without stumbling. And in the end you will unlock heaven with the Word's key" (Catherine, 1980, 166). Christ's body is stretched out from earth to heaven giving Christians a way through the perils of life. Outside his path is the way of disobedience that poisons the soul. The key to heaven is walking along the way of Christ's obedience even unto death.

Obedience is the theme of the last section of *The Dialogue* and the main theme of Raymond's record of Catherine's life. It is obedience that satisfies God's justice and reconciles humanity to God. Obedience to God modeled on the bridge of Christ compelled Catherine to defy her family, work tirelessly for the good of others, and suffer for the sins of the world. One of the best-known examples of Catherine's obedience was her caring for a sick woman named Andrea. Sickened by her cancerous sore, Catherine forced herself to suck from the woman's wound to overcome her revulsion. Whether true story or legend, the account serves as an example of the lengths to which Catherine was willing to go to live an obedient life. It also parallels the three stages of obedience, which Catherine describes as the three steps of the bridge of Christ. At his feet, one is stripped of the sin of disobedience; at the heart of Christ, one is dressed in love; and at the mouth of Christ, one finds the peace of perfect obedience. In service to Andrea, Catherine tasted the mouth of her bridge.

The symbol of this obedience is the blood of Christ, which became a central metaphor for Catherine of the sacrificial love of obedience. As one commentator notes, "At whatever point we enter her mind we encounter Christ crucified, and in particular the thought of his blood" (Foster, 1980, 29). It is the blood of Christ that nourished her soul as the model of suffering and as the food of communion. While many medieval mystics focused on the passion of Christ, Catherine took this imagery to new heights. In one of her most graphic visions, Christ rewards her suffering on behalf of the sick by allowing her to drink from his side. "Drawn close in this way to the outlet of the Fountain of Life, she fastened her lips upon that sacred wound, and still more eagerly the mouth of her soul, and there she slaked her mystic thirst for long and long" (Raymond, 1980, 156). Thus strengthened by the blood of Christ, Catherine was encouraged to continue her work.

This emphasis on blood was Catherine's way of responding to the bloody suffering of her day. Having cared for the sick during the plague, Catherine was surrounded by the blood of the ill and dying. Witnessing the warfare of the Church, Catherine had seen the blood of its victims. In a letter to Raymond, she recounts her presence at the execution of a young man caught in the civil wars of Siena. She held his head in her lap as he was decapitated. Then she writes to Raymond that she saw Jesus open his side and receive the blood of the man into his own blood, thus sanctifying his blood in Christ. She remained on the platform bathed in the fragrance of blood. When she opened this and many of her letters with greetings "in the precious blood of God's Son," she wrote with an awareness of the smell and feel of real blood.

Catherine was, indeed, worn to a thread by her suffering, and she accepted suffering in obedience to the justice of God and the example of Christ in order to eradicate sin. It was a suffering that appears to have been based on a theology of satisfying a wrathful and bloodthirsty God. Raymond presents her life as a perfection of Christian faith, which reinforces the idea that self-sacrifice is the means toward reconciliation with God. It is obvious that her later designation as a saint and Doctor of the Church is a result of the fact that her actions reinforced the dominant ideology of satisfactory atonement. But did she herself find strength in this understanding of satisfaction or did she understand the satisfaction of suffering within a framework of God's satisfying love? Answering this question will allow us to see how Catherine challenges rather than merely contradicts a contemporary spirituality. For this question we must turn to a study of the inner strength of Catherine of Siena.

The Inner Strength of the Spiritual Life

While a review of the life of Catherine suggests that suffering is the way to satisfaction, a study of *The Dialogue* reveals that it is not suffering that is the key, but the inner desire for God that lies behind it. Thus she notes that suffering makes one sad and happy. One is sad at the physical pain caused by suffering, but happy at the desire for charity that underlies the work. She calls suffering "fattening sadness" because it can increase the inner spirit and make love grow. It is not suffering but the desire behind it that has value. Behind suffering is love for God, born of the knowledge of God's goodness and the desire to eradicate the sin in oneself and others that denies that goodness. Thus Catherine is able to make the startling claim that she longs for suffering, not because she desires pain but because she desires God. Suffering is endured for the glory and praise of God (Catherine, 1980, 144).

Catherine's willingness to suffer is based on the pragmatic realization that in this life one cannot avoid pain. No one passes through life without suffering, she writes. The difference is that the servants of God suffer physically but not in their spirit, while the wicked suffer physically and spiritually (Catherine, 1980, 91). This difference is a matter of one's will being in conflict with God or in union with God. For the latter, suffering rests in the confidence that the soul is at one with the will of God. Since her suffering is understood within the framework of desiring God, Catherine concludes that suffering does not make her weary because her will is "in tune" with God's will. The servants of God feel no grief in suffering but, rather, feel God in the soul and are satisfied. God promises her that "in any situation or at any time whatever . . . I know how to and can and will satisfy (you) in wonderful ways" (Catherine, 1980, 296). Filled with this reassurance, Catherine"s spirit cannot suffer and she remains strong.

In her advice to others, Catherine is careful not to emphasize her suffering, but rather her desire for God as exemplary. In a letter to one of her followers, she writes that perfection does not consist in mortifying and killing one's body, but in killing perverse self-will. The goal is not to seek suffering, but to devote one's infinite desire to the honor of God and the salvation of souls. We nourish ourselves, Catherine concludes, at the table of holy desire. In another letter Catherine is more explicit, advising against fasting if the body is weak. Whether she wants others to avoid the dangers of fasting that have befallen her or merely wants to remind others that her own life is not a model for others is not clear. What is clear is that she wants to emphasize the proper understanding of her follower's desire. "Discretion," she writes, "proposes that penance be done as a means and not as a principal desire" (Petroff, 1986, 268). The principal desire is to enact God's will.

While desire for God makes suffering satisfying, it was Catherine's knowledge of herself as created in the image of a loving God that made desire possible. "In the gentle mirror of God she sees her own dignity: that through no merit of hers but by his creation she is the image of God" (Catherine, 1980, 48). This "cell of self-knowledge," as Catherine called it, served as the foundation of her strength. It was her sense of dignity that carried her through her struggle with her family, that gave her the confidence to follow a unique form of religious calling, and that empowered her to counsel popes and kings. Like many medieval mystics, she describes the image of God as the image of the Trinity in her soul. It is the ability to remember, understand, and will the goodness of God that is the mirror of God. As one turns inside oneself to the truth of one's being, there one finds God. In one of her prayers, Catherine proclaims, "You gave us our will so that we might be able to love what our understanding has seen and what our memory has held" (Noffke, 1980, 188). The truth of self-knowledge allowed Catherine to see the God in her as her true nature and all that countered this will as sin. Thus she notes that we have to strip ourselves of our own will to take on the gentle will of God as one "turns one's garment inside out when one undresses" (Noffke, 1980, 87). Inside the rebelliousness of will that is the poison of sin is the goodness of will to love God.

The foundation of this will is the memory of God's love. While both Raymond and Catherine talk about appeasing God's justice, the deeper reality for Catherine was that God is not a wrathful judge but a Gentle

First Truth, a truth of love. Catherine realized that her desire for God came from God's desire for her. In fact, she suggests that God is mad with love for creation. In *The Dialogue,* she writes, "O mad lover! And you have need of your creature? It seems so to me, for you act as if you could not live without her . . . You are pleased and delighted over her within yourself, as if you were drunk with desire for her salvation" (Catherine, 1980, 325). As Linda Woolsey notes, the powerful God that Catherine imagines as just becomes vulnerable through love (Woolsey, 1995, 29). It is this vulnerability that gave Catherine confidence in God even in suffering. God tells her, "Daughter think of me; if you do, instantly I will think of you" (Raymond, 1980, 90). She remained confident that if she would but remember God's love, she would remember that she rested in God's watchful care.

The nature of this divine care becomes clear in understanding the passion of Christ. Christ is more than the mediator of salvation; he stands as the vehicle of the love that accomplishes our salvation. Christ tends the wound of sin like a wet nurse who drinks the bitter medicine of the passion in order to pass on to humanity the wholeness of life. Like medicine that is too strong to be digested except through the nurse's milk, the cure for the disease of sin must come to us through the body of Christ. It is a painful cure, but one that heals the human race from the disease of sin. Only the scar and weakness from sin remain, which can be healed in baptism and strengthened in the ongoing nourishment of the Church.

Thus the love of God comes to us in the nourishment of the body of Christ in Communion. Christ is the food of souls strengthening the image of God in the soul and teaching the soul to understand the nature of God's love. God is the table that lays out the food; the Holy Spirit is the waiter that serves the food. In the understanding of the passion as the vehicle of salvation and nourishment of divine love, Catherine was strengthened and energized. Her letters end with the refrain, "Gentle Jesus! Jesus love!" In this greeting is the realization that in Jesus one understands the first truth of divine love.

It is the memory of the goodness of God as our essential humanity and the understanding that we are healed in the passion of Christ that gave Catherine the will to love. As she notes in one of her letters, those who eat at the table of God become like the food they eat, working for God's honor and the salvation of others. The response to salvation is not just perfect obedience, but perfect love. This fourth stage of faith is a perfect union with God in which the love of God is engrafted onto the heart of humanity. Catherine describes this union as like a fish in the sea in which water and fish intermingle. Or at other times she talks about the elements in a loaf of bread kneaded together until the individual ingredients are indistinguishable and a new reality emerges. More often Catherine speaks of Christ as engrafted onto the dead tree of humanity, thus enabling humanity to bear new fruit.

For Catherine, this union was so complete that she imagined herself engrafted with the heart of Christ. In response to her petition to have a clean heart created within, she imagined her side opened and her heart carried away by God. A few days later, she experienced another vision in which she saw her side opened again and the heart of Christ placed inside. At another point, she saw her heart entering Christ's side and becoming one with his heart. This mingling of hearts led her to greater and greater acts of love for others. Filled with the heart of Christ, she walked into all situations confident of the will of God.

One of the effects of this union of hearts was a powerful ability to demand mercy from God. Raymond records numerous accounts in which Catherine was able to pray for healing. During the plague, he was revived by her prayer on his behalf. At her sister's death, Catherine's prayers released her from purgatory. At her father's death, her petition was more pronounced and Catherine would not relent until God allowed her to take on her father's sins so that he could be released from purgatory. Raymond notes that Catherine wrestled with God, who held out for the demands of justice while she pleaded for the work of grace. At her mother's impending death, Catherine's prayer was bolder still. "Lord this is not what you promised me," she declared, and her mother was revived. Truly God is vulnerable in love, and Catherine was able to tap into the resources of that love, despite the demands of justice. "Nature bowed to God's command," Raymond notes, "issued through the mouth of Catherine" (Raymond, 1980, 234). And in the end, the ways of love always triumphed.

But that does not mean that Catherine could save the world. As the state of the Church declined in the months following the schism over papal leadership, Catherine became increasingly aware of the limits of her ability to love. When the pope ordered her to Rome, she complied and delivered a stirring speech to the cardinals that impressed even the pope with her courageous spirit. But when her health failed and there was nothing else to do, she prayed for her heart to be crushed and its blood squeezed out upon the Church. Yet even in this desperate act, Catherine remained confident of the saving work of God. Evil will be defeated, she writes, "not by what our bodies suffer, but by virtue of the glowing measureless Charity of God" (Foster, 1980, 276–277). With these hopeful words, she ended her last letter to Raymond.

With this image of the bleeding heart, we return to the centrality of the idea of blood. More than a symbol of sacrifice, blood is a symbol of the deep connection between humanity and divinity, oneself and one's neighbors. Blood is the sign of love. It is Christ's blood that waters the tree of humanity so that we might bear fruit. We are baptized into his blood and receive the nourishment of his blood in Communion. It is blood that is above all the sign of the union of humanity and divinity which "calls every believer to enter into the mystery not only as redeemed but as co-redeemer" (Noffke, 1983, 184). It is the flow of blood that empowers the soul to act in love for God.

Blood also represents the healing power of love in life. Given the context of her day, in which bloodletting was the primary form of medical treatment, it is not surprising that Catherine associated blood with healing. Just as the letting of blood was believed to draw off corrupt matter from the body, so the blood of Christ is able to draw off the corruption of sin. It is "in his blood" that Catherine acted in the world to mediate family rivalries, reconcile civil discord, and work for the healing of the corruption of the Church. As Elizabeth Petroff notes, "the healing power of blood was constantly revealed to her in ordinary brutal life" (Petroff, 1986, 240). Blood is a symbol of hope that no matter how broken the world, the blood of God works to nourish life.

Beneath the outer suffering of Catherine there was a spirit of connectedness that united her to the world and to God in the confidence of the love of God manifest in the midst of the pain of life. It was a love that she could depend on, be united with, and desire for the good of the world. Certainly it was an inner spirit that endured much for the sake of love, but it was in desire and hope that her spirit rested. Therefore, she could write that seeing God, she could love; "[L]oving, she is satisfied; being satisfied, she knows the truth; knowing the truth, her will is grounded firmly in [God]—so firmly and solidly that nothing can cause her to suffer, for she is in possession of what she had longed for, to see [God] and to see [God's] name praised and glorified" (Catherine, 1980, 151). In possession of such satisfying truth she was energized.

Contemporary Reflections

How are we to put together this picture of the outer suffering and the inner strength of Catherine? The uncommon nature of her life has perplexed interpreters and continues to elude most scholars today. The vast amount of literature on Catherine tends to polarize around a condemnation of her outer asceticism or a veneration of her inner spirit. To her critics, she is merely a medieval victim of anorexia. They condemn not only her practice but also the entire base of religious belief that undergirds her faith. To her most uncritical admirers, she was a free, loving, joyous figure of self-determination and a precursor of the feminist spirit. In the middle are a few scholars who try to see the active nature of her suffering in the context of a spiritual vision that was fully engaged in the world.

The question is how Catherine's life of outer suffering and inner satisfaction might broaden our understanding of the spiritual life. Is there any truth to Bynum's thesis that medieval mystics like Catherine challenge us with the possibility that suffering is fruitful?

In her 1995 article entitled "For Women in Pain: A Feminist Theology of Suffering," Patricia Wismer argues that feminist theology understands both the destructive practices of women's suffering and the reality of suffering as part of the web of life. We need to integrate the two so that we proclaim, "that suffering can never be redeemed and that meaning can be found in suffering" (Wismer, 1995, 148). This integration can be accomplished by analyzing the particularities of each experience of suffering. Wismer suggests looking at how suffering is caused and how it can be eliminated, looking for the meaning or growth that is possible in suffering, and looking at who suffers with us. Only then can we decide if or when we should take on suffering.

As we look at the particularities of Catherine's suffering, we see how Catherine's suffering is caused by external as well as internal factors, and how it is a means of growth toward realizing the satisfying love of God. Catherine's theology, as it has been handed down to us by her recorders, does emphasize the idea that suffering can placate God's anger. Justice requires payment for sin, and the crucifixion of Christ along with the ongoing suffering of human beings are part of the justice of God. There is no doubt that this ideology caused her to willingly suffer for sin. But in her prayers on behalf of those who suffer, she presents a different understanding of God as vulnerable in mercy. Remember that her prayers wrestled with the reality of justice and mercy. While God called for justice, she called for mercy and argued until the mercy of God relented. Only then did she take on the suffering of others. Catherine believed that suffering is both caused by and eliminated by God, and in this she rested her hope.

Catherine's hope was based in the idea of the cell of self-knowledge that underlay her suffering. It was the knowledge that we are created in the image of God with the memory of God's goodness, the understanding of the passion as the lengths to which love will go, and the will to realize fully the depths of our desire to live in unity with that love that motivated Catherine's life. Underlying her actions was a relationship of identity with the love of God. Catherine called it the mad love of God. She took on suffering for the sake of this love and found meaning in not only the growth that resulted from her suffering but also in the knowledge that she suffered with Christ for the sake of the world. Because she believed that Christ suffered with her, suffering became for her a means of growth.

This leads us back to some interesting insights about suffering as a possible mode of contemporary spirituality. First and foremost, we must not glorify Catherine's self-inflicted suffering, and we must seek ways to eliminate any theology that celebrates her example as a model of faith. Catherine herself prayed to God to overcome her weakness and advised her admirers not to follow her example, because she realized that this form of suffering was not a means toward growth. Given the epidemic of eating disorders in our day, the outer suffering of Catherine's life must be recognized and mourned. Catherine was mistaken when she said that she sought to satisfy her Creator in her purging, and we should do all we can to eradicate the theological justification that leads to such actions of self-inflicted sacrifice today.

Given the theological climate of her day, it is not surprising that Catherine believed she had to satisfy the justice of God. What is surprising is that she dared to argue with this theology, even to argue with God. She wrestled with the idea of God's justice and demanded that God act with mercy. She was confident that God's love seeks us out and desires our salvation. She was sure that her own will, working in concert with God, could free souls. This confidence led her to suffer on behalf of others as a work of protest against the sin of the world. Today, it raises for us the possibility that suffering is meaningful when it connects us with the work of God in the world.

Catherine stands as a reminder that the spiritual life is not an easy life of feeling good—not a life of indifference or escape—but rather a life that realizes salvation in the midst of brokenness. It is a life of full engagement with the world. In her book on suffering, Dorothee Soelle writes that the acceptance of suffering is a "part of the great yes to life" (Soelle, 1975, 108). Soelle argues that we either carry out the act of suffering or we are passive recipients of suffering, indifferent as stones. More recently, Soelle has described meaningful suffering as like labor pain in that it is oriented toward joy and undertaken in an effort to work for resistance and change (Soelle, 1995, 74). Catherine's suffering for the transformation of her world was truly a labor of love.

What Catherine has to teach us is that suffering is not an option in life. What is an option is whether we have the courage to be fully engaged in the suffering of our day in solidarity with others and with God. She refused to be indifferent to plague victims, casualties of the civil war of Siena, the corruption of the Church, or the political infighting of her day. From her unwavering care of Andrea to her support of a criminal at the guillotine, Catherine showed suffering as a life wholly engaged in the world.

Catherine also challenges us to realize fully the depths of what it means to understand ourselves as wholly connected to God and to the world. For Catherine, the image is one of the flow of blood that connects us to God and to one another. The blood of Christ was a reminder for her of the saving work of God in the suffering of the world—a suffering that results from the depth of God's connection to creation, of God's vulnerability of love. Likewise, Catherine suffered for others because she realized that the sins of one affect the whole. Here Catherine gives us the possibility of rethinking the meaning of the blood of Christ, especially in Communion, as an image of connectedness. Like the power that flows in and through the world, the blood of Christ reminds us of the power of God in and through the pain of life. The Crucifixion is the power of connectedness at work in the world. For Catherine the blood of Christ provides a power in suffering, a power of the image of God in her life working for the reconciliation of the world.

One of Catherine's most fruitful ideas is the nature of Christ's saving work. While the idea of Christ as our bridge, and therefore role model, is more prevalent in her writing, the theme of Christ as wet nurse is more thought provoking. As wet nurse, Christ provides the medicine for our salvation in a manner that puts his own body in service for humanity. The flow of blood, like the flow of milk, contains the life-giving elements of wholeness. The wet nurse mediates salvation in a bodily form. Catherine saw the work of Christ leading toward a healing of the world. In Communion, that healing continues and gives us the food to be reconciled and become reconcilers for God in the world.

And so in the end, we consider the possibility that suffering can be fruitful. My colleague cannot escape the brokenness of his daughter's illness. Day by day he stands beside her, suffering with her in love. Only time will tell if his daughter's struggle will lead to self-knowledge or self-destruction. It is not a pain that is oriented toward joy, but a suffering that is caused by insecurity and doubt, and we should condemn it as such. On the other hand, the young man who sacrifices for the sake of his brother's children finds joy and meaning in his life, sees his sacrifice as a means to a greater good, and finds spiritual growth in his new identity. He, like Catherine, may, indeed, be a saint. They both challenge our ideas about the spiritual life and remind us that our hope rests in the fact that nothing, not even suffering, can separate us from the fruits of the Spirit.

RESOURCES

Bynum, Caroline Walker. *Holy Feast and Holy Fast: The Religious Significance of Food to Medieval Women* (Berkeley: University of California Press, 1987).

Catherine of Siena. *The Dialogue.* Trans. Suzanne Noffke (New York: Paulist Press, 1980).

Foster, Kenelm. Introduction to *I Catherine: Selected Writings of St Catherine of Siena* (London: Collins and Co., 1980).

McAvoy, Jane. *The Satisfied Life: Medieval Women Mystics on Atonement* (Cleveland: Pilgrim Press, 2000).

Noffke, Suzanne, ed. *The Prayers of Catherine of Siena* (New York: Paulist Press, 1983).

Petroff, Elizabeth Alvilda, ed. *Medieval Women's Visionary Literature* (New York: Oxford University Press, 1986).

Raymond of Capua. *The Life of Catherine of Siena.* Trans. Conleth Kearns (Wilmington, DE: Michael Glazier, 1980).

Soelle, Dorothee. *Suffering.* Trans. Everett Kalin (Philadelphia: Fortress Press, 1975).

Soelle, Dorothee. *Theology for Skeptics: Reflections on God.* Trans. Joyce L. Irwin (Minneapolis: Fortress Press, 1995).

Tyler, Anne. *Saint Maybe* (New York: Alfred Knopf, 1991).

Wismer, Patricia. "For Women in Pain: A Feminist Theology of Suffering." In *In the Embrace of God: Feminist Approaches to Theological Anthropology.* Ed. Ann O'Hara Graff (Maryknoll: Orbis Press, 1995).

Woolsey, Linda Mills. "Feather, Spark, and Mustard Seed: Hildegard of Bingen and Catherine of Siena." *Daughters of Sarah* 21: 28-31 (1995).

5

MARIE D'OIGNIES: FEMALE VISIONS OF STRENGTH

ANNETTE ESSER

*I*n his *Vita Mariae Oigniacensis,* Jacques de Vitry (1160/70–1240) presented his spiritual teacher and friend, Marie d'Oignies (1177–1213), as the modern saint whose example and virtues might "strengthen the faith of the weak, instruct the unlearned, incite the sluggish, stir up the devout to imitation, and confute the rebellious and unfaithful" (*Vita,* Prologue; King, 1). Jacques de Vitry was himself a high-ranking and well-known Catholic of his time: he was a canon, crusade preacher, later bishop and cardinal, so his enthusiasm about Marie d'Oignies and the other Flemish women, whom today we call Beguines, carried weight.

Once, while Marie was in a state of "ecstasy of mind," she used a knife to cut out a large piece of her flesh, thus giving herself wounds like Christ had received in his passion. Jacques de Vitry applauds this self-infliction of wounds; he even calls it *virtus,* a male virtue, and places Marie in the tradition of the great athletes of faith, the desert fathers St. Simeon the Stylite and St. Anthony. As a Catholic woman today, rather than willing or able to share in Jacques's fascination with Marie's "fortitude," I felt disgusted by this act of self-mutilation. And, as a feminist theologian, I tried to look at her life and her visions with a critical feminist perspective; thereby revisioning her visions in the light of current historical and psychological knowledge.

Reading again the chapter on mysticism in Simone de Beauvoir's book *The Second Sex,* I was reminded of the distinction she has made between two kinds of women mystics. Although both may fully experience divine love in their body, de Beauvoir looks critically at those who remain in the socially constructed emotional realm of their womanhood, while she appreciates others who transcend this realm in their mystical experience and develop a clear concept of action. In my own religious search as a German Catholic theologian, it was that latter type of women mystics to which I was drawn first. My growing awareness of my personal journey as well as knowledge of Eastern forms of meditation had started my search for a specific Christian way of prayer and meditation, which I then found in studying the great women mystics, especially Teresa of Jesus (1515–1582) and Hildegard von Bingen (1098–1179). However, I was later amazed to find in a history class at Columbia University, New York, in 1997, young secularized American students interested in the rather unusual women mystics whom I had rejected, and whose mystical phenomena (visions, stigmata, and elevations) I had learned to regard as secondary and at times irrelevant. It was by this detour that I came to deal with Marie d'Oignies, a mystic of the second kind, whose fame as a holy woman remained somewhat unknown until she was re-discovered in the twentieth century and subsequently has been characterized as the first Beguine.

As a feminist theologian, I still have not overcome my disgust of Marie's excesses of extreme physical self-denial. As I studied the life of Marie d'Oignies, I started to realize that her story reveals something about the darker and probably more neurotic roots of Catholic spirituality that many women, including myself, have deeply internalized. So, I found that dealing with her *vita* has led me to deal with some remnants of my own deeply internalized dispositions. I have been led to deal with sources of guilt and a longing for passion rather than action; to deal with a romantic or psychopathic desire for self-sacrifice in the light of a divine realm that could also be demonic; to deal with a suppressed and guilt-loaded sexual life; and to take notice of a strong missionary impulse that could turn out to be disturbingly naive.

In order to understand some of these darker roots of women's spirituality, my journey led me to search for Marie d'Oignies expressions of self-hood in her visions. I will look critically at Jacques de Vitry, the author who presented these visions, as well as at the political and historical context of Marie's life. However, my interest goes beyond a mere historical and critical presentation. Asking about the impact of Marie d'Oignies visions for the spirituality of Catholic women today, I am also searching for a connection through history that is not one of mere written tradition but rather handed on indirectly through practices and traditions. Being sensitive to current psychological theory, I am assuming that the medieval and modern psyche, our consciousness and unconsciousness, are not principally different from each other. As will become clear, a number of theological questions arise that require our attention: questions about a spirituality of passion versus a spirituality of action and creation; about the recognition of mystical versus pathological elements in the identification with the passion of Christ; about a destructive body-denial versus a holistic affirmation of the body, including sexuality; about a so-called holy fasting that covers a neurotic anorexia versus a healthy asceticism that spiritually transcends the fixation to one's body; and about the demonization of enemies versus an experience of the divine realm as the root of our mission.

An Interpretation of the Life of Marie d'Oignies in the Context of Her Time

The simple fact that Marie d'Oignies did not write about her life and her mystical experiences poses a significant difficulty. It means that we can only reach out to her through the eyes of her medieval biographer, and that we cannot be sure that any of our interpretations do justice to her spiritual life. Jacques de Vitry wrote his *Vita Mariae Oignacensis* in Latin, the language of the Church for centuries. Consequentially this *vita* was not written for unlearned women but, rather, exclusively for educated men who were to use her life as *exempla* in their teaching. The most recent translation into English, by Margot King in 1989, is very helpful; yet we have to remember that this is not the Flemish language of the holy woman herself (nor my own German language); thus, trying to read, write about, and listen to the voice of Marie is always open for new errors of interpretation. Another difficulty for today's reader is that the *Vita Mariae Oignacensis* is not written in the style of a modern biography. At first glance it is rather pious and hardly concrete, giving only a few biographical data of Marie's life. So, it seems right to name it a "mystical" *vita*.

The few chronological data of Marie's life can be summarized as follows. Born in 1177 in Nivelles, Brabant-Flanders, to wealthy bourgeois parents, Marie was extremely attracted to voluntary personal poverty from an early age; for example, she rejected the pretty clothes her parents wanted her to wear. In 1191, her parents married her at age fourteen, but she, having not chosen this form of life herself, was able to persuade her husband, John, that they should not permit sexual intimacy in their relationship. Instead, they would live a life of chastity and poverty, distribute their wealth to the poor, and serve at the leper colony in Willambrouk, outside Nivelles. Doing this, they were not praised but criticized by their relatives.

In 1207, Marie moved to a cell at the Augustinian priory of St. Nicholas of Oignies, which was founded by Giles (Guido), the brother of her husband. There she lived a life of prayer and complete poverty, save for what she earned with her spindle. More and more followers were attracted to her, and she supported many of her friends with her visionary gifts and healing power. In 1209, sharing in the contemporary enthusiasm for the crusades, Marie prophesied the Albinguensian crusade after a vision in which she saw a great number of crosses descending from heaven.

In 1211, Jacques de Vitry became a canon in the Augustinian convent in Oignies, possibly drawn there by Marie's fame as a visionary. Marie must have exercised a considerable influence over him and he was personally very close to her, identifying himself as a crusade-preacher with her work. At her instigation, he was ordained in 1210 and remained in the community as her confessor. Marie died June 23, 1213, only thirty-six years old.

Greatly saddened by Marie's death, Jacques de Vitry was anxious to secure relics of Marie's body, as was the practice of the time, especially when an individual was considered to have possessed a special holiness. Evidently, Jacques carried with him a reliquary containing one of Marie's fingers, which was attributed to have had healing power.

To enhance Marie's memory and to counter heresy in the south of France, Jacques wrote her *vita* two years after her death (1215). This *vita* not only included the inspirational story of her life, but was also a propaganda effort to gain official ecclesiastical recognition for these holy women, the Flemish Beguines, which he achieved at least orally from the pope (Innocent III). Jacques was one of the best and most famous preachers of his time and later became a bishop (1216) and a cardinal (1229). In his time, Jacques was regarded as an accomplished and effective preacher. Through his personal report, the spirituality of Marie and the other Flemish holy women may have also influenced the Franciscan movement and gained wider recognition. Upon his death on May 1, 1240, Jacques was buried in Oignies as requested in his will.

The political and historical context in which Jacques de Vitry wrote the *Vita* of Marie d'Oignies was that of the crusades and the battle against the heretical Cathars in Southern France. Marie's and Jacques' lifetime was full of a general enthusiasm for the crusades in which, in 1212 and in 1214, even women and children participated. The pope had officially called for the fourth crusade in 1202 that lasted until 1209, and for the fifth in 1213, shortly before Marie's death. Marie, who had had a vision about a crusade, was probably herself eager to join, but Jacques convinced her not to go. One may argue, however, that Jacques saw her whole life as a spiritual crusade against the heretics. This specific intention becomes clear in the prologue, where Jacques mentions that the *Vita* was written upon the request of Bishop Fulk of Toulouse, who had been "exiled from his city by the heretics." To him Jacques describes these holy Flemish women as "soldiers of God" in the struggle against the "enemies of faith." The heresy of these "enemies of faith," the Cathars, is rooted in their denial of all but one sacrament, their dualistic teaching of God and Satan as equally strong, as well as their belief that Christ was not truly human.

As a preacher, Jacques de Vitry was famous for his widespread use of *exempla*, examples of holiness. Thereby, he stressed not only one of Marie's virtues—one spiritual gift of a holy woman—but rather her many virtues. Thus, Marie's *vita* is written as a sequence of *exempla* in which many of her virtues are demonstrated. In the *Vita* of Marie, men and women of the time of the crusades were to be challenged in their own faith journeys. But how do we feel about these virtues today?

To get a better feel for her virtue, let us look at Marie through the eyes of her contemporary biographer. Jacques describes her as a "humble female soldier" and a "column of strength" in the struggle against the heretics. Are Jacques' words about the "fortitude in the frail sex of a woman" merely his construct, or do they indeed mirror Marie's strength? Considering how Jacques was influenced by Marie, I find it improbable that he made up these from his own imagination. It is by examining her visions that we may come closest to Marie's original voice, even given the religious climate of the day that had an inclination toward the extraordinary and at times bizarre.

Toward an Understanding of the Visions of Marie d'Oignies

Jacques de Vitry's *Vita* of Marie d'Oignies is full of visions. This fact alone is remarkable, as it opposed the belief-system of the heretical Cathars who did not have or believe in visions. It was also important for Jacques to stress Marie's visions because, otherwise, Marie's religious life resembled very much that of the Cathars. For, like the Beguines, they also practiced handwork, poverty, chastity, continuous prayer, genuflections, extreme fasting, and active charity. So in order to prove her orthodoxy, it was important for Jacques to show the charismatic-prophetic element in Marie's religious life, especially in her visions. Just because Marie and the other holy women venerated relics, honored the saints, and participated in the sacraments of the Church, their ascetic life was not politically conspicuous.

But what is a vision? Peter Dinzelbacher gives a definition in his work published in 1981 titled *Visions and Visionary Literature in the Middle Ages* (1981, p.29).

> We talk about a vision when a human being experiences to be transformed in a supernatural way from his/her environment into another space/realm; he/she sees this space/realm or its contents as an image that he/she can describe; the transference happens in ecstasy (or in sleep), and through it; secrets that were so far hidden for him/her get revealed to him/her.

This definition appears technical and sometimes hard to evaluate. For instance, in many of Marie's "visionary experiences," an ecstasy is not mentioned, yet the text refers to her experiences as visions. Or sometimes, the word *vision* is not named explicitly but the described experience can possibly be labeled as such. Also, Dinzelbacher's use of the medieval scholastic distinction between "natural" and "supernatural" is problematic. A more modern theological definition would transcend this dualism and argue for the unity but not the sameness of these realms. I would rather follow, therefore, Caroline Bynum's (1987, p. 8) appreciation of these phenomena.

> I am not concerned with whether medieval accounts of phenomena such as stigmata, levitation, miraculous bodily changes, extended inedia, visions and food-multiplication are "true." As a phenomenologist would say, I "bracket" the question of cause, either natural or supernatural, for such events. I am interested in what medieval people experienced; and

while I have a historian's skepticism about all evidence, I, also as a historian, prefer to start my study of the past with what people in the past said themselves.

As a theologian, I also need to listen to what people in the past said about what they experienced, yet I intend to go beyond historical questioning. That means that I am still interested in whether these accounted phenomena are true, be it in a real-physical, in a personal-psychic, or in a transpersonal-spiritual way. I am also interested in the theological and symbolic contents of these visionary experiences and the effect they had for the spirituality of later generations of Catholic women. A review of four of Marie d'Oignies's visions as presented in the firt book of her *vita* can help us pursue these reflections further.

1. VISION OF FIERY EXCESS

The context of Marie's first vision in Jacques de Vitry's *Vita* took place shortly after Marie's marriage to John. Jacques writes:

> Then removed from her parents, she was set on fire with such an excess of ardor and punished her body with such warfare and brought it into servitude that frequently when she had toiled for a large part of the night with her own hands, she would pray for a long time after her labor. As often as was licit for her, she passed a very little part of the night in sleep on concealed planks which she had hidden at the foot of her bed. And because she obviously did not have power over her own body, she secretly wore a very rough cord under her clothing which she bound with great force. I do not say this to comment the excess but so that I might show her fervor. In these and in many other things wherein the privilege of grace operated, let the discreet reader pay attention that what is a few does not make a common law. Let us imitate her virtues, but we cannot imitate the works of her virtues without individual privilege. Let us rather admire than imitate (*Vita,* Ch. 12; King, p. 14–15).

Marie was a young woman of fourteen. At that age, after her first menstruation, a young woman in the twelfth century was regarded as grown-up for marriage. It was in this new situation of marriage, "removed from her parents," that "she was set on fire with such an excess." According to medieval reading, this fire shall surely indicate the experience of divine love. With the insights of modern psychoanalysis, one may look at this "fire" as a symbol of Marie's sexuality and be aware of the very physicality of Marie's religious experience. Yet, Jacques' description intends to indicate the opposite, for it connects the experience of fire with the "warfare against the body," and we may assume that it also includes Marie's warfare against the physical encounter with her husband. In a Freudian understanding, this "warfare" could be interpreted as sublimation or suppression of the awakening sexual Eros-drive in this age of adolescence. However, such an interpretation reflects modern thinking, which directly opposes medieval values. While modern thinking embraces the body and regards physical-bodily experience as real and superior to spiritual constructs, this twelfth-century text has an opposite intention: the soul is regarded as superior to the body, even though spiritual experience also has a physical effect. Marie's own desire is to escape her body, and thus her warfare against a body that has to be "punished" and brought "into servitude."

This language may also indicate a connection to the warfare against the heretics. When Jacques describes Marie as a "female soldier," I also see Marie's battle against her body in the same line as the harsh regimen of soldiers: sleeping on planks and wearing a rough cord instead of women's underwear. The fact that Marie deliberately treated herself in this way indicates that she really saw herself as a soldier of God in the warfare against the heretics. Jacques de Vitry's commentary shows that he admires Marie's struggle and does not find her behavior insane, as it was already seen in the eyes of some contemporary critics. Jacques does not recommend to imitate but rather to admire Marie. For it is admiration, that may lead to inspiration, that is owed to a holy woman or a heroine whose virtues are a divine gift; through imitation we cannot gain those gifts of grace since they are a free gift from God. Jacques recommendes that admiration alone can give strength to others who have to fight in the same battle against the heretics, the "enemies of the faith."

2. ECSTASY ABOUT THE PASSION OF CHRIST

Jacques described the "cross and the passion of Christ" as the first content of Marie's devotion (*Vita*, Ch. 16; King, p.17–18):

> The beginning of her conversation to You, the first fruits of love, was your cross and your passion. She "heard you hearing and was afraid" (Hab.3:2); and she "considered your works" (Eccl. 7:14) and feared.

One day she was anticipated and visited by You, and she considered the benefits which You have shown forth—mercifully created—in the human flesh, and found so much grace of compunction, and such an abundance of tears was pressed out by the wine-press of your cross in the passion, that her tears flowed so copiously on the floor that the ground in the Church became muddy with her footprints. Wherefore for along time after this visitation she could neither gaze at an image of the Cross nor speak nor hear other people speaking about the passion of Christ without falling into ecstasy through a defect of her heart. Therefore she sometimes moderated her pain and restrained the flood of her tears and would raise up her soul to the divinity and majesty of Christ and, by thus leaving behind a consideration of his humanity, tried to find consolation in impassability. But when she tried to restrain the intensity of the flowing river, then a greater intensity wondrously sprang forth. When she directed her attention to how great He was who endured such degradation for us, her pain was renewed and new tears were revived in her soul through her sweet compunction.

Jacques comments on Marie's devotion:

You have lost the love of your relatives but you have found the favour of Christ! With how many miracles have you decorated her who is degraded and mocked by worldly men.

Marie's *vita* is possibly a central piece of witness for the new (female!?) kind of devotion to the passion and humanity of Christ developing in the twelfth century in opposition to older forms of devotion to Christ's divinity and his kingdom.

To understand this kind of female spirituality more deeply, we need to ask about the effect of this form of devotion. Is identifying oneself with the suffering of Christ (as *Imitatio Christi*) only a path of self-destruction? What does it mean to suffer Christ's wounds at the cross in the body of a woman? Looking at Marie's example, I found a wild mixture of effects, feelings, and beliefs that I either liked or disliked as a Christian woman today: physical effects of painful joy and bodily nourishment; feelings of satisfaction and love; beliefs of being elevated through grace while experiencing contempt for worldly things; faith in a coherent concept of rightness and wrongness; support for the faithful and an aggression against the enemies of faith; and real insight or conviction about a clear path to pursue or a battle to be fought. These diverse ways of viewing the Christian journey have been influential in women's beliefs and spirituality up until today.

3. ECSTATIC VISION AND SELF-STIGMATIZATION

Jacques described Marie's act of self-mutilation as follows (*Vita*, Ch. 22; King, p. 22):

> As if inebriated and from the fervor of her spirit, she began to loathe her flesh in comparison to the Paschal Lamb and in her mistaken fervor, she cut out a large piece of her flesh with a knife which, because of her modesty, she buried in the earth. So inflamed had she been by an exceeding fire of love that she had risen above the pain of her wound and, in this ecstasy of mind, she had seen one of the seraphim standing close to her.

This form of *imitatio Christi* has to be seen within the context of Marie's desire for a mendicant life that was denied to her. In not being able to follow Christ in the outside male world, she at least tried to identify with his life and death within the limitations of a female life.

In the initial words of this chapter, Jacques had described a spiritual process in which spirit and flesh are dualistically juxtaposed, and in which the increasing "taste of the spirit" means loosing any interest in the "delights of the flesh." Thus, he describes Marie's extreme fasting as an experience in which the "the fervor of her spirit" opens her up for the desired vision of the Divine. Looking more critically upon this experience, a psychological view might assume that here a state of advanced anorexia took place in which the withdrawal of food has already become an addiction and where even thinking of food makes one feel sick. But where we may talk of "holy anorexia," Jacques de Vitry was convinced that in extreme fasting, Marie proved her "holiness."

In describing this vision that occurred during her fasting, Jacques talked about the "fervor of her spirit" that had "inflamed" her by "an exceeding fire of love" before she had the vision of a "seraphim standing close to her." Surely, Marie herself was spiritually supported and elevated by this ecstatic vision of an angel. And her physical and spiritual experience is directly connected to the image of the angels as the angels represent the symbol of fire. In the ancient and scholastic tradition, the seraphim belong to the first hierarchy of angels, whose wings cover their faces as they are closest to God; they are the pure fire of God's love. Marie's vision of a seraphim thus means truly an experience of the divine fire. This position seems to justify her deed of self-mutilation that overcomes or transcends the loathsome flesh. In other words, the contempt and violation of one's flesh is justified by divine power.

In this state of mind, the paschal lamb is perceived as "sweet" and one's own flesh is found to be disgusting. "Mistaken fervor," as Jacques evaluates it, led Marie to cut off her own flesh, but he explains this as an act of recompense for her eating some meat before. He uses her "modesty" to explain the fact that she buried her flesh in the earth. In the historical context of twelfth-century relic-cults, this kind of modesty may indicate that the cut-off flesh of her body was seen as a relic that could be venerated already in Marie's lifetime (as Jacques himself was most eager to do with her finger after her death).

In his interpretation, Jacques de Vitry compared Marie's wound to the ones of Simeon and Anthony, the two desert fathers and columns of faith, and praised "such fortitude in the frail sex of a woman." Thus, in Jacques' view, this female act of self-mutilation did not indicate self-hate but the opposite; it demonstrated a form of love and strength. I find this same kind of understanding in the testimonies of (female) psychiatric patients today who practice acts of cutting their flesh. And even though I perceive this as a form of masochism, it may be useful to listen more carefully to the emotional superstructure of these women themselves, in order also to understand a long history of women's (neurotic?) spirituality.

4. VISION OF HANDS FROM PURGATORY

Marie's prayerful visions of the souls in purgatory occurred repeatedly when she had debilitated her body by fasting and while she was working hard with her hands at the spindle (*Vita*, 27; King, p.26–27).

> She prayed without interruption by crying to the Lord with a silent heart or by expressing her affectivity through the office of the mouth of the heart. Aromatic smoke continually ascended to the sight of the Lord from the altar of her heart, for while she worked with her hands and put her hand to the test and her fingers clasped the spindle, she had her Psalter placed before her from which she would sweetly belch forth psalms to the Lord.

On three occasions, probably always in her cell where she lived like an anchoress close to the Church of Oignies, Marie experienced the "eternal fires" or the "purgatory," whose hands she "sees."

Once when she was offering prayers to the Lord for the soul of a certain dead man, it was said to her, "Do not pour out your prayers for him because he had been condemned by God. He has been transfixed by a mortal wound and has miserably died in a tournament and has been sold into the eternal fires." One day she was in her cell close to the Church of Oignies and she saw a multitude of hands before her as if in supplication. Amazed and not knowing what this vision was she was struck by some little fear and fled into the church. On another occasion when she was in her cell, she once again saw these same and was terrified, but when she again fled into the church, she was held back and detained by the hands. Then she ran back to the Church as if it was a tabernacle so that she might have counsel from the Lord. She begged the Lord that he certify what those hands wanted of her. The Lord's response to her was that the souls of the dead who were being tortured in purgatory were asking for the prayers of her intercession which would soothe their sufferings as if with a precious ointment.

Marie's prayers seem to have had that sweet effect. They were a "precious ointment" for the souls in purgatory. But from time to time, Marie interrupted these "useful" prayers to flee to the nearby church.

Looking more closely at the text, the language in which Jacques describes Marie's prayer life is enlightening. By using metaphors such as "crying to the Lord with a silent heart" or "expressing her affectivity through the office of the mouth of the heart," Jacques expresses a new form of (female) spirituality that transcends traditional forms of prayer and whose core is the "action of the heart." The heart is described as a sacred place where the office (Psalter) takes place like in a church building. The real church building, then, is seen as "a tabernacle" of the body of Christ! Marie's prayer is also described in very sensual terms: from the "altar of that heart" now "aromatic smoke continually ascended to the sight of the Lord." This sensual component of sweet aroma seems to be important throughout the text: clasping the spindle, Marie would sweetly belch forth psalms. After her "spirit was fastened to the Lord with the fat of devotion," Marie would "sweetly grow sleek in prayer" and thus Marie reached the state of "sweetness of contemplation."

The request of "the dead who were being tortured in purgatory" has to be seen in this context. They ask "for the prayers of intercession which would soothe their sufferings as if with a precious ointment." It seems here that the souls were asking for something that Marie truly had to offer. Their requests underlined that which was happening spiritually. We might call this experience *office of the heart* and see it as equally valid as the official Church Psalter when it comes to reaching toward, and praying for, the faithful departed. Jacques makes it clear that the dead souls do not reach out to just anybody here but to a holy woman whose spiritual aroma and bodily suffering can soothe their sufferings. Marie must haven been aware of this holiness herself when she enjoyed the sweetness of contemplation afterwards. And the only point where she is criticized by Jacques is when she is not willing to give enough of that precious ointment, which Jacques perceived as her central vocation in life.

The reaction of Marie to the visions related in these pages show her fear of, and compliance to, this vocation. In the description of the visions, we can see an intensification of the degree of terror that preoccupies her. Marie understood that these visions were the means by which she was able to pray for the dead souls in purgatory. But did Marie really see the "hands from purgatory" that pursued her? It is difficult to define what the physical, psychic, and spiritual reality of a vision is and whether visions have a material and physical reality that goes beyond the individual person into the transpersonal realm—in other words whether the "souls of the dead" are "real" or not. But without answering this question, we can observe that the experience of these visions had a strong psychic and spiritual effect on Marie. She would not have been terrified for nothing; something important happened to her and that is a "real" experience.

Marie was very conscious of the situation of the "souls of the dead" in the "eternal fires" who were "being tortured in purgatory," as the Catholic Church was officially teaching it. Yet, in the experience of the visions, it was not the image of purgatory itself that became more forceful upon her, but the relationship between her and these souls, or in other words, her own specific calling to do something for them. Whereas she first distanced herself from a dead soul at the order of a voice, she began to grasp the intention of the hands reaching out to her, and finally, in the third vision, the supplication addressed to her became outspoken. Marie was terrified. This "vision" touched her most deeply, so much so that when she tried to escape, "she was held back and detained by hands."

This reminds me of those familiar dreams in which we have the experience of wanting to run away but are held back. One psychological interpretation of this is that one has to stand still and look back upon whatever it is one runs away from; there is an important psychic energy that needs to be dealt with by envisioning it. This modern depth-psychological insight is exactly what Marie did, when she "begged the Lord that he certify what those hands wanted of her." In truly having asked this question, she also received an answer, and in this answer also lies Marie's calling, to use her power of helping others with prayers and active love.

The suffering of the "poor souls in purgatory" was visualized in the time of the twelfth century in the most dramatic pictures. Therefore, the question of salvation or liberation of this pain was of the most existential relevance. After the Reformation deconstructed the system of indulgence (buying graces to lessen one's time in purgatory) in the Roman Catholic Church, what remains of these beliefs today? It is not my intention to defend the belief in the dead souls in purgatory that are helped by intercessional prayers, even if this is still the teaching of the Roman Catholic Church. Rather, I prefer to look at the image of Marie's holiness and consider what it means today, that is, what can we retain from her visions for today? Talking of holiness as a precious ointment lets me understand that holiness is not just a necessary moral or prayerful act, but that holiness has a dimension of sensual beauty and existential power as well. And it was Marie's female power that was not afraid to overcome her own fear of dead souls that impresses me. In later visions, she demonstrated this power even in acts of exorcism. But can and should we still learn from this kind of holiness today?

Conclusion

Having presented some of Marie d'Oignies visions, I now ask about the theological impact of her visionary life for the spirituality of Catholic women today. Does Marie set an example that we should follow, or should saints like her be admired rather than imitated, as Jacques de Vitry says: "Let us imitate her virtues, but we cannot imitate the works of her virtues without individual privilege. Let us rather admire than imitate."

For this, we have to ask, What are these values that we should admire rather than imitate? Had we asked Jacques de Vitry, he might have said that this was about the veneration of the sacraments, and about the love for Christ and the battle against his enemies. But having looked at Marie's visionary life more deeply, surely there are some other virtues at play here.

Marie d'Oignies, the Beguines, and other pious women of their time presented a new form of female devotion and prayer. The core of this was the emotional and spiritual "action of the heart" versus a mere, superficial or passive belief in the teachings of the Church. Acknowledging this in itself has been very influential for the spiritual life of many women over the centuries and still touches me (positively) today. We must look deeper, and beyond, Marie's act of apparent self-mutilation as a "raw" participation in the passion of Christ. There was far more going on than mere physical degradation: through Marie's suffering she was connected to God's community of saints and sinners. The problem is not the passion of Christ that we may identify in the passion of a suffering people; rather, the problem lies in the passion that we would deliberately and "rawly" want to follow as some spiritualities dictate. There are even what I would call "secular imitations," that is, the self-mutilating acts of psychiatric patients today.

Another problem I see is the idea that saints have the power to pray for us or for the "poor souls in purgatory." This thought may be comforting, but it also raises a question about the effects of our own prayer and the power and truths of visions that we ourselves might have (or might be afraid of having). Marie did not hand over her prayerful responsibilities to others. She actively participated, according to the norms of her times, in the salvation and peace of all souls. By handing spiritual responsibility over to the saints, we risk distancing ourselves from a deeper understanding of what prayer and visions really mean or could mean in our lives. And thus we not only accept an image of saintly power that could be questioned, we also, implicitly, affirm our traditional status as women who need to connect to God via exterior means. Often this means through male priests and their presiding over the official "prayers of the Church," sacramental and nonsacramental alike. Marie's *office of the heart* moved beyond institution to true charism. And while our status as married women might be socially superior to what it was before, we also have internalized for ages that the status of unmarried women who reject a sexual life is something more powerful, something that brings them closer to God. But could not the opposite be true?

Having looked more deeply at the devotional prayer life of the "holy woman," Marie d'Oignies, I must confess that I did become suspicious whether all her struggles were not a dangerous exaggeration of devotion that was truly self-destructive. And I wondered whether and how this kind of struggle could be distinguished from that of psychotic people who also envision all kinds of "demons," and get lost in the world in which we daily live. Here it was helpful again to remind myself of the work of Anton Boisen (1936, p. ix), who found that:

> [C]ertain types of mental disorder and certain types of religious experience are alike attempts at reorganization. The difference lies in the outcome. Where the attempt is successful and some degree of victory is won, it is commonly recognized as religious experience. Where it is unsuccessful or indeterminate, it is commonly spoken of as "insanity."

I believe that Marie d'Oignies has won her victory against the "hands" and the "demons" that pursued her and that, in the end, we cannot classify her or her brutal act of self-mutilation as insane. Jacques de Vitry's described Marie d'Oignies in the image of the "humble female soldier" by describing her life as a battle and often using military language to do so. This battle is fought in the name of Jesus and the battlefield is her own body; and her weapons are extreme fasting, self-flagellation, and self-mutilation. Do we still want to applaud a victory that is seen as control over the female body—no more hunger, no sexual desire, or the conscious blocking of natural functions like menstruation? It seems to be important to emphasize that this image of Marie, and women like her, was surely not only Jacques'. The spirit of her time longed for this kind of "modern saint" that lived outside the strict boundaries of the Church and society of her day and thus was fascinated by her.

But how can I, as a feminist theologian, evaluate Marie's voice in today's world? I question whether Marie did transcend the realm of her womanhood, as Jacques indicates when he described the strength with which the "handmaid of Christ" treated herself like a "female soldier." I don't think that Marie's battle was a role-reversal. What was and is important was the way she "fought" *as a woman* with her whole body. I would also suggest that Marie was aware of her own strength and that this awareness was more important to her than the physical effects of her struggle. Historically, Marie really fought a battle for the Church and contributed to a Catholicism that, whether we like it or not, is still present today: Marie struggled with a dualistic worldview, body-denying attitudes, belief in demons and exorcism, prayer for the "poor souls in purgatory," all of which were very influential in popular Catholic belief and are still present today. Even though I was personally disgusted by many aspects of Marie's *vita* in the beginning, I saw that looking more closely at it brought me to a deeper understanding of my own tradition. It showed me the turning points where the Catholic Church made important decisions in its history, and has won "victories" that women continue to regret today. For what kind of victory was truly won against a woman (representing women in general) who was forced to self-mutilation in order hold up her side of the battle?

As a Catholic theologian, I have raised questions about this belief-system. I have asked about the distinction between a spirituality of action and creation versus a spirituality of passion; about the recognition of mystical versus pathological elements in the identification with the passion of Christ; about a holistic affirmation of the body (including sexuality) versus a destructive body-denying attitude, specifically about a healthy asceticism that may constructively transcend a splitting fixation to the body versus "holy" or "neurotic" anorexia; and about the experience of the divine realm as the root of our mission versus the demonization of our enemies. By asking these questions, I have already expressed the kind of holistic spirituality I am searching for. I believe that, in order to nurture this kind of holistic spirituality, we have to carefully work through our own (self-) destructive images. That means that we have to look at our own love for passion; our destructive attitudes toward our physical body; our unconscious images and beliefs about God; our hidden and perhaps destructive missionary intentions; and our negative images of the other.

In short, we need to "re-vision our visions," that is, search for a spirituality of creation and life, a spirituality of the body and of the divine realm, and a spirituality that neither denies passion nor long for it for its own sake. Formulating this in more depth is a task of feminist spirituality and theology today.

As a final thought, I suggest that the self-induced wounds in Marie's body symbolize wounds within the souls of Catholic woman today who continue to take their stand in a world-denying tradition. She has wounded herself and her wound continues to bleed for us. What she denied to herself, we have denied to ourselves or at least felt guilty about. What she longed for, her passion, is our passion as well, and we must learn to allow that passion to turn us toward, and not away from, the creative and forward-looking possibilities of our lives. Marie's "fortitude" for us is to acknowledge the wounds and strength that empower us in the "frail sex of a woman."

RESOURCES

Boisen, Anton. *The Exploration of the Inner World: A Study of Mental Disorder and Religious Experience* (New York: Harper & Brothers 1936).

Bolton, Brenda M. "Mulieres Sanctae," in: *Women in Medieval Society*. Ed., Susan Stuard (1976), 144–145.

_____. "Vitae Matrum: A further Aspect of the Frauenfrage," in: *Medieval Women*. Ed., Baker, Derek, (1978), 253–273.

Bynum, Caroline. *Holy Feast and Holy Fast: The Religious Significance of Food to Medieval Women* (Berkeley: University of California Press, 1987).

Dinzelbacher, Peter. *Vision und Visionsliteratur im Mittelalter*, Stuttgart 1981.

Geyer, Iris. *Maria von Oignies: Eine hochmittelalterliche Mystikerin zwischen Ketzerei und Rechtsgläubigkeit* (Frankfurt/M, 1992).

Jacques de Vitry. *Vita Mariae Oigniacensis*, ed. D. Paperbroek, in *Acta Sanctorum* 4 (June 23,v), pp. 636–666; Margot King, trans. "*The Life of Marie d'Oignies by Jacques de Vitry.*" Second revised edition (Toronto: Peregrina, 1989).

6

The Contribution of Julian of Norwich's Revelations to Finding Religious and Spiritual Meaning in AIDS-Related Multiple Loss

JANE F. MAYNARD

*M*y pastoral interest in HIV/AIDS began nearly eleven years ago when I worked for a year as a chaplain intern on Ward 5A, the special-focus AIDS unit at San Francisco General Hospital. In this setting, I encountered the devastation wrought by AIDS, the stigmatization that persons living with AIDS and HIV experience, and the hope and healing that can come through acceptance of and care for persons with AIDS. My work with AIDS provided me with the greatest theological challenge I have ever experienced, as AIDS seemed to oppose all that was creative and life-giving. My work with AIDS also brought to center stage questions about the nature of God and God's response to suffering, and a need to reconcile the goodness of creation with the destructiveness of AIDS.

After three years of pastoral involvement with persons living with AIDS and AIDS loss, my quest for understanding received a new impetus when I encountered these words in Julian of Norwich's *Revelation of Love*:

> But of all the pains that lead to salvation, this pain is the most: to see your love suffer. How might any pain be more to me than to see him who is my whole life, my bliss and all my joy suffer? Here I truly felt that I loved Christ so much more above myself that there was no worse pain I might suffer than to see him in pain (1996, Chap. 17, 34).[1]

Julian, a fourteenth-century recluse who lived from 1342 to at least 1414, uttered these words while viewing a vision of Christ's suffering and death on the cross. Two written accounts of Julian's vision exist, a short and a long version. Most scholars believe that Julian composed both versions herself, one shortly after the vision in 1373, and a longer one some twenty years later. Julian's remarks above reflected her experience of Christ's passion described at some length in both texts.

When I read these words, I was greatly stirred. They reminded me instantly of the sentiments of the partners, friends, and family members of those who had died of AIDS with whom I had worked as a chaplain. Further, they reminded me of my own pain in witnessing the deaths of friends and family members. In short, Julian's words articulated the perspective of a survivor. I knew upon reading them that Julian was well acquainted with death, and in that moment, I became curious about her. Who was she and how had she come to express her compassion for suffering so clearly?

Addressing these questions yielded two results. First, I developed the understanding of Julian's theology and spirituality within her own situation of loss due to the plague. Second, I have used this knowledge to create a context within which we can reflect on her experience in relationship to the experience of a twentieth-century San Francisco Episcopal congregation whose life and ministry have been marked by significant AIDS loss. Elucidating Julian's theology in the context of the plague offers significant promise for interpreting the contemporary experience of AIDS loss.[2]

The Effects of the Plague on Julian

Three theses summarize my approach to Julian and her experiences of suffering and healing. First, Julian may be understood as a survivor of plague-related loss. She experienced multiple loss in the plague pandemic of the fourteenth and fifteenth centuries, and it shaped both the form and effects of her religious experience. Further, surviving this loss may also have motivated her to articulate and disseminate her vision and theological reflections upon it at some personal risk. Second, Julian's traumatic loss affected her significantly. Understanding the effects of loss on her life and vision is enhanced when they are viewed through the lens of survivor psychology. Third, Julian's vision, a creative act of the religious imagination, enabled her to heal from traumatic loss. Her vision and reflection upon it gave inner form and significance to the death immersion she had experienced and to the rest of her life in relationship to it. Let us explore each of these theses, in turn, as we consider the implications of Julian's theology for AIDS loss.

Julian in Her Own Context

We know few things for certain about Julian and her life. She tells us in her writing (Chap. 2, 3) that she experienced a life-changing vision on the eighth day of May in 1373, when she was thirty years old. From this we can infer that Julian was born close to the end of 1342. A bequest by Roger Reed, rector of St. Michael's Church at Coslany, in 1393 to "Julian anakorite" suggests that Julian had adopted the distinctive lifestyle of an anchoress by that time. That she continued in this ministry into the next century is supported by the prologue to the short text identifying her as "a recluse at Norwich living yet in 1413." The flamboyant Margery Kempe, a contemporary of Julian's from nearby King's Lynn, describes her visit to Julian, lending supports to the view that Julian was known in her day as a respected spiritual counselor.[3]

The fourteenth century in which Julian lived and wrote may be thought of as a time characterized by the best and worst of human achievement. On the one hand, the age was distinguished by religious and artistic genius. A flowering of mysticism marked the fourteenth century, both on the continent and in the British Isles, and literary giants such as Dante and Petrarch and Chaucer and Langland produced their masterworks in this period. On the other hand, the fourteenth century was marked by a great discrepancy between its moral and philosophical ideals and the behavior they were intended to guide. In her engrossing history of the fourteenth century, *A Distant Mirror*, Barbara Tuchman (1978, xiv) quotes the Swiss historian de Sisimondi, who describes the fourteenth century as "a bad time for humanity." Evil and misfortune abounded, including famine, ecological disaster, papal schism, the Hundred Years War, taxes, and brigandage.

Perhaps the most significant fact about Julian's times for our purposes, however, was that they were marked by a series of outbreaks of the plague (Jantzen,1987, 7–8). The first and most serious one occurred when she was just seven years old. Besides this initial outbreak in 1348–1349, Julian survived other plague epidemics in 1361 and 1369. While we cannot be certain that Julian was living in Norwich at this time, we do know that wherever she was living in England, she would have experienced the plague. This factor, along with the suffering sustained by the people of Norwich, would surely have influenced the ministry of spiritual care Julian exercised later in her life.

The arrival of the "pestilence" or "Great Mortality" in the fourteenth century heralded one of the greatest disasters ever known. The plague, arriving in Europe from the East, was spread primarily through well-established trade routes from parts of Eurasia where it was endemic. While nineteenth- and twentieth-century historians have disagreed about the mortality rates associated with the plague, most recent estimates suggest that it resulted in an average mortality of forty-seven to forty-eight percent (Horrox, 1994, 229). Entering Europe through Messina in Sicily, the plague progressed rapidly throughout continental Europe. It traveled from Italy to the Holy Roman Empire within a year and entered France through coastal towns, infecting Avignon in the spring of 1348 and Paris in June of 1348. Death rates were stunning: between February and May up to four hundred people a day died in Avignon. At the time, Paris was the largest city of Northern Europe, with a population of between 80,000 and 200,000. It experienced eight hundred deaths per day in November and December 1348 (Gottfried, 1983, 50–55). The plague moved to the West as well as to the North and entered England by ship in the summer of 1348 where, scholars estimate, nearly half the population died within eighteen months. While the rate of infection and death varied from region to region, nearly all agree that East Anglia, the region of England containing the city of Norwich, was the most severely afflicted. At the time of the first epidemic, Norwich's population was roughly 10,000 to 12,000. The plague arrived in Norwich in January of 1349 and remained until the spring of 1350. Surviving records suggest that half of the beneficed clergy and forty to forty-five percent of the general population died in the first epidemic.

Undoubtedly, the most horrifying aspect of the plague was the massive amount of death it caused. Death on this scale had two main consequences, each described repeatedly in eyewitness accounts. First, observers were overcome with the sheer number of dead and decaying bodies they encountered.[4] Towns resorted to mass graves and the stench of death was omnipresent. Second, over time, survivors simply became insensitive to the horror in order to survive. Boccaccio captures this growth of apathy.

[I]n fact, no more respect was accorded to dead people than would nowadays be shown towards dead goats. For it was quite apparent that the one thing which, in normal times, no wise man had ever learned to accept with patient resignation had been brought home to the feeble-minded as well, but the scale of the calamity caused them to regard it with indifference (Horrox, 1994, 32–33).

Because of the sheer volume of deaths accompanying the plague, many locales experienced the collapse of normal customs for death and burial (Horrox, 1994, 331). In some cases, such customs as the ringing of "passing bells" were outlawed for the sake of public morale. Certainly in most places, the magnitude of death simply made it impossible for clergy, physicians, and society in general to respond with sensitivity to individual cases.

The plague was terrifying, dehumanizing, and devastating. These facts lead to a third effect the chroniclers repeatedly described: the dead and dying were abandoned through fear of contagion. Flight was a preferred mode of escape for the rich, in keeping with advice in a German manuscript: "Clever doctors have three golden rules to keep us safe from pestilence: get out quickly, go a long way and don't be in a hurry to come back" (Horrox, 1994, 108). Clearly, those who were not sick harbored ambivalence and guilt about abandoning the sick, factors that may only have contributed to their burden of grief. Other troubling effects of the plague experienced by the well included concern about how best to avoid infection and suspicion toward outsiders who may have been carrying the infection (Horrox, 1994, 29). The tendency to blame foreigners and strangers for inexplicable misfortune appears to be a nearly universal psychological phenomenon, as the continued existence of scapegoating in times of tragedy attests (Horrox, 1994, 34–35 and 224–226).

Contemporary accounts of the plague suggest that it induced a full range of difficult and conflicting emotions in those afflicted with its presence, and this was undoubtedly most unsettling. Perhaps the most difficult experience of all, however, was attempting to understand why: *Why* had this suffering come to afflict the population?

Perhaps the most common and troubling explanation for the plague was theological: the plague was understood as a form of divine vengeance for human sinfulness (Horrox, 1994, 14–26). In a time when scientific and medical knowledge seemed grossly inadequate in the face of human pain, it is perhaps understandable that religious explanations would be invoked. The starkest theological accounts conceived of the plague as a reversal of creation, as the "undoing" of the goodness of the world because of human sin. Several categories of sin were understood as occasions for the unleashing of divine wrath, among them the seven deadly sins, a lack of good faith and equity among judges, the pettifogging of lawyers, the hypocrisy of religion, and the vanity of ladies. Perhaps the most commonly cited causes for God's disfavor, however, included divine disapproval of tournaments and the scandalous fashions of the day (Horrox, 1994, 130–134).

Alongside the view that the plague was a form of divine punishment was the notion, promoted by some, that it was a spiritual blessing, since it prompted people to repent and be spared of the pains of hell (Horrox, 1994, 98). Others believed that the plague heralded the end of the world. Religiously speaking, regardless of the particular theological explanation one adopted, the remedy was the same: the faithful must repent and be saved. A variety of pastoral and penitential resources were exploited to this end, including processions, recitation of psalms, pilgrimage, attendance at Mass, confession of sins, and meditation on the passion of Christ. Intercession was also considered a potent remedy, and favored saints included St. Sebastian and St. Roche as well as the Blessed Virgin Mary.[5]

Unfortunately, some people adopted extreme religious responses. These included the Flagellants, bands of men and women who roamed continental Europe, particularly Germany and the Low Countries. They marched from town to town, flagellating themselves publicly for their sins. Over time, they became more and more extreme in their practices and threatened the authority of the Church and the public order. They were condemned and ultimately dissolved through Clement VI's papal bull in 1349. The University of Paris also opposed their activities. Unfortunately, their practices and the emotional public reaction to them led mobs to persecute and execute thousands of Jews. The Flagellants blamed Jews for the origin and spread of the plague. Their efforts, along with general public intolerance in the wake of the plague, led to the destruction of 60 large and 150 smaller Jewish communities and 350 massacres of Jews by 1351 (Ziegler, 1969, 109).

We can assume several things about the effects of the plague on Julian through drawing on existing facts about the plague and the experience of twentieth-century survivors of multiple loss.[6] Articulating these assumptions supports the thesis that Julian may be understood as a survivor of plague-related loss. These assumptions are as follows:

- Julian would have been exposed to the physical horror of death on a large scale at a young age. She would have been seven years old when the plague arrived in England, and she would have experienced the death of half the people she knew.

- Julian would have experienced a diminished capacity to absorb these deaths and to feel their effects. In addition, she would likely have experienced impaired mourning because the plague disrupted normal customs associated with death and burial.

- There is every reason to expect that Julian would have experienced cumulative effects of multiple loss, since she would have lived through repeated outbreaks of the plague.

- There is also every reason to expect that Julian's memories of these events would have been vivid and lasting, since this phenomenon characterizes trauma survivors.

- As all survivors do, Julian would have asked herself, "Why am I alive, whereas others have died?" Her contemporaries raised this question, but as a survivor of repeated outbreaks, Julian may have experienced this question as especially urgent.

- It is likely that Julian would have dreaded potential recurrences of the plague and would have asked, in living through repeated outbreaks, whether God and the world were reliable.

- It also seems reasonable that Julian would have experienced ruptures in the fabric of her community as a result of the plague.

- Julian may have experienced severe psychological effects of the plague, including a sense of foreshortened future, a death-dominated life, unresolved or incomplete mourning, a restricted emotional range and temptations to despair.

Finally, plague experiences may have heightened Julian's concerns with sin and salvation, as she would have been exposed to the dominant theological explanation for the plague in her day. Feelings of shame and guilt that often accompany the experience of surviving multiple loss may also have heightened these concerns. The central role that sin plays in Julian's second, longer text makes this assumption seem quite reasonable.

Let us now explore Robert Jay Lifton's psychology of the survivor in an attempt to understand the significance of these assumptions for the development of Julian's theology and spirituality.

Robert Jay Lifton's Psychology of the Survivor

Robert Jay Lifton's work on the psychology of survivors (Lifton, 1968) greatly assists the attempt to understand the plague's effects on Julian. Lifton defines a survivor as "one who has encountered, been exposed to, or witnessed death and has himself or herself remained alive" (Lifton, 1987, 235). According to Lifton, survivors normally pursue one of two options: either they confront the death immersion they have experienced and seek insight and healing, or they confront the death immersion and respond with cessation of feeling or psychic numbing. Lifton has identified five distinctive psychological themes that characterize the psyche of the survivor. With a better understanding of these themes, we can further comprehend and appreciate Julian's experience.

The first psychological theme characterizing survivors of massive death is the presence of the death imprint and associated death anxiety. The death imprint consists of "indelible images not just of death but of grotesque and absurd (that is, totally unacceptable) forms of death" (Lifton, 1987, 235). The death imprint is recalled with great clarity and immediacy many years after the original event in which it was created, and the survivor has a sense of being bound by it. Associated with the death imprint is an element of frustrated enactment, for frequently in situations of overwhelming death, survivors feel guilt or self-blame because of what they did *not* do or feel (Lifton, 1979, 171).

A second feature of survivor psychology is death guilt. Death guilt is epitomized by the survivor's question, "Why did I survive whereas others died?" Survivors feel a responsibility and debt toward the dead because of their inability either to act in a way they would ordinarily have thought of as appropriate in a death situation or to feel the feelings they ought to have felt for the dead and dying (Lifton, 1987, 236–237).

The third psychological theme characterizing survivors is psychic numbing, the diminished capacity to feel that emerges in situations of trauma. Psychic numbing is a necessary psychological defense against overwhelming images and stimuli. It results from a disconnection between cognitive images and the emotions that normally accompany them. Recovery from psychic numbing involves recovering the capacity to feel again (Lifton, 1987, 239–240).

Lifton labels a fourth psychological feature of survivors as counterfeit nurturance. This feature has two aspects. The first aspect, related to relationships, has two characteristics. On the one hand, survivors struggle with issues of autonomy in interpersonal relationships. They feel the effects of their ordeal, but are often reluctant to receive support, for to do so is to acknowledge the effects of the trauma they have experienced. On the other hand, survivors struggle with issues of contagion. They feel marked by their experiences and perceive themselves, and know that others perceive them, as tainted. These feelings may lead survivors to mistrust in relationships and to mutual antagonism and even avoidance of others.

The second aspect of counterfeit nurturance describes how trauma affects the survivors' perceptions of daily life. Survivors encountering massive death, particularly death from persecution, may feel that they have come from a world in which living and dying are divested of moral structure and have lost their logic. Living in such a world, survivors must decide either to reject it as counterfeit or to adapt to its inverted logic and survive. These conflictual dynamics may paralyze survivors. At other times, however, survivors may also be more sensitive to falseness of any kind and appreciate more the authenticity of life (Lifton, 1987, 240–241).

Lifton labels the final psychological dynamic characteristic of survivors as formulation. This term describes survivors' struggles for meaning and sense of inner form in the face of the trauma they have experienced. Again, this dynamic may have several aspects. Some survivors become "collectors of justice," seeking some acknowledgment of the crimes committed against them and attempting to reestablish the sense of a moral universe that was lost in the atrocities they experienced. Others feel compelled to bear witness, to develop a survivor mission related to the injustices they have experienced. The essential task of the survivor is to find meaning in the trauma, to recover the capacity for creating symbols that was lost in the process of surviving. Survivors must find ways to assert the continuity of life and the integrity of the self that are true to the experiences of death they have known (Lifton, 1968, 525–539).

This summary of Lifton's theory captures the essential aspects of his psychology of the survivor. We are now better equipped to understand Julian's life and vision as they may have been affected by the Black Death.

Julian as a Survivor of Traumatic Loss

Applying Lifton's theory enables us to understand how Julian healed from the traumatic effects of plague loss, for the theory describes how Julian may have experienced relief from the debilitating effects of the plague.

Julian's vision of the crucified Christ was the most important resource for healing she possessed, for Julian's vision of Jesus' suffering and death may be understood as a death imprint. Julian's *effective interaction* with the death imprint of her vision allowed her to heal from the destructive impact of her original, plague-related death imprint. Using Lifton's language, the vision constituted a death imprint, because it was an "image of death" that was both grotesque and absurd (Lifton, 1968, 480). On the one hand, the image was grotesque because it captured the painful effects of the inhumane suffering that Christ experienced. Julian described this aspect of the crucifixion in excruciating detail. On the other hand, the image was absurd because Julian would have understood Christ's passion and death as unnatural and indecent. These qualities, in Julian's view, would arise from the fact that Christ experienced no human comfort in the midst of this painful death, that he who was reduced to nothing was God and, therefore, that he who was highest and most worthy was completely humiliated and despised in this shameful death. Further, it is clear from the text that Julian experienced death anxiety as she witnessed the vision, for she states that she regrets praying the prayer that resulted in it:

> Little did I realize what pain I asked for and like a wretch I regretted it, thinking to myself, if only I had known what it were like, I would never have prayed for it. For I thought these pains of mine surpassed even bodily death (Chap. 17, 34).

Julian was able to heal from the damaging effects of her earlier plague-related death imprint because, in staying with the vision of crucifixion despite her pain, she was able to move through death to new life.

While observing the vision, Julian crossed over the threshold of death with Christ into new life (Chap. 21, 39). This movement through death to life occurred in the context of a near-death experience. Thus, Julian's healing was strengthened because her vision occurred when she herself was suspended between death and life. The fact that she literally returned to life following her encounter with death in her vision *and* her illness undoubtedly helped to provide her with healing from death anxiety.

Second, in remaining with the dying Christ despite her pain in witnessing Christ's suffering, Julian may have healed from the death guilt she experienced in her earlier encounter with death. The experience of death guilt arises when survivors are immobilized by painful feelings amid overwhelming death. In Chapter 19 of the longer text, Julian describes how she decided consciously during her vision, despite the temptation to look away, to remain with Christ and to witness his suffering. Her ability to withstand this temptation and to remain with Christ constitutes a significant turning point—it becomes a successful enactment in the face of a painful death experience. Julian's effective choice undoubtedly healed her from the sense of inactivation she may have experienced in her earlier encounters with death.

Further, in the course of her vision, Christ communicated to Julian his willingness to suffer and die for her because of his love for her:

> This is my joy, my bliss, my endless liking that I was ever able to suffer for you. For truly, if I could have suffered more, I would have suffered more (Chap. 22, 40).

Experiencing Christ's willingness to die for her relieved Julian from the burden many survivors bear of living halfheartedly because of guilt. Julian learned that Christ's atonement for her sin freed her from the need to atone.

Psychic numbing represents the survivor's diminished capacity to feel. It arises in situations of trauma that impair the survivor's capacity to form mental symbols of the death experience. Survivors seem to retain the capacity to form cognitive images of the horror they are experiencing, yet they disconnect these images from the feelings that accompany them. Lifton believes that, in psychic numbing, the self becomes severed from such psychic forms as compassion for others, communal involvement, and other ultimate values. Psychic numbing results in a sluggish despair characterized by chronic depression and a constricted life space that is often covered over by rage and mistrust (Lifton, 1968, 500–510).

Julian's vision provided her with an opportunity to heal from psychic numbing. She experienced healing because she allowed herself to feel fully the compassion and empathy she held for the dying Christ. As already noted, Julian experienced these feelings at some personal cost because they were much more intense than she anticipated. Nevertheless, the fact that she remained with the vision despite her pain demonstrates that she did not dissociate from her feelings of compassion.

The text does not support the notion that Julian suffered from the degree of anger and mistrust in interpersonal relationships that sometimes characterizes survivors of multiple loss. In fact, the text reveals little about Julian's relationships, and thus we cannot know if she experienced counterfeit nurturance. The evidence does suggest, however, that Julian was a woman of deep compassion who felt great empathy for others. Nevertheless, it is interesting to speculate about Julian's decision to live as an anchoress. In making this choice, she effectively removed herself from the social sphere. Was she at all motivated by a sense of contagion, or did this lifestyle provide her with the time and means to engage in her "survivor mission," sharing the fruits of her vision with others? Unfortunately, the text does not allow us to decide between these alternatives.

The text does suggest, however, that Julian may have experienced life prior to her vision as counterfeit, as lacking in authenticity. Julian tells us, for example, that before her vision, she

> . . . had a great longing and desire, by God's gift, to be delivered from this world and this life. Frequently [she said] I witnessed the woe that is here and knew the well-being and bliss that is there. And even if there were no other pain in this life apart from the absence of the Lord, sometimes this alone seemed more than I could bear. And this made me mourn and long more eagerly, and also my own wretchedness, sloth and very weakness made me reluctant to live and labor on as I knew I should (Chap. 64, 129).

Prior to her vision, therefore, Julian appeared to experience life as tiresome and drab. Her vision relieved her somewhat from her sense of this present life as counterfeit, however, for she saw more possibility for joy in daily life through God's sustaining love. Nevertheless, she was very much a child of her age in one respect: she awaits the final hope of bliss in the life to come. That is, her otherworldly desires causes her to de-emphasize the joys of the present life in favor of bliss in heaven.

Finally, let us consider Lifton's notion of formulation. According to Lifton, recovery from the trauma of multiple loss occurs as survivors are able to find meaning in their experience of death and dying and to make sense of the trauma they have experienced. He notes that survivors frequently undertake a mission, and Julian's efforts to write down and disseminate the contents of her vision may be understood in this way. Her efforts take on particular significance because first, Julian's text was the first written in English by a woman and second, she was at some risk of being condemned as a heretic for writing it. These facts testify to her courage in producing this work.

Julian's vision represents a creative attempt to give form and meaning to the experience of painful and absurd death. As a result of her vision, Julian achieves the symbolic immortality that survivors seek in Lifton's view, for Julian emerged from her vision with Christ's assurance that she would not be overcome by sin and death (Chap.68, 137). Freed from anxiety about her death and salvation, Julian was able to devote herself as an evangelist to sharing the good news of God's love. Her vision, therefore, represented a confrontation with death, a reordering of her emotions and imagery, and a renewal of a sense of life's meaning and vitality. Further, Julian's attempts to find meaning through her vision provide evidence for three traits Lifton notes as crucial in survivors' attempts to make meaning. First, Julian experienced a heightened sense of connection to both God and her fellow Christians as a result of her vision. Second, Julian emerged with a greater sense of symbolic integrity, and she continued to develop this through her long-term reflection and writing on her vision. Finally, she was able to move forward through life. No longer paralyzed or robbed of vitality through mourning, she was able to embrace the life of a theologian and counselor.

In summary, therefore, Lifton's psychology of the survivor enables us to understand first, the psychological effects of traumatic loss upon Julian and second, the means through which she healed from it as a result of her vision. Let us now explore some parallels between Julian's experience and theology and that of All Saints' Episcopal Church in San Francisco. These parallels will illustrate how Julian's theology, arising in the context of the plague, compares with a contemporary theological and spiritual response to AIDS loss.

Towards a Constructive Theology of
AIDS-Related Communal Bereavement

As noted above, my attempts to understand Julian as a survivor of plague loss arose from echoes I heard between her words and the words of loved ones surviving persons with AIDS. My attempts to describe and to understand the relationship between these two experiences is a larger project than can be neatly summarized here. Clearly, however, there are some points of contact between Julian's experience of plague loss and the contemporary experience of AIDS loss.

All Saints is an Anglo-Catholic community in the Haight Ashbury district of San Francisco. An average of ninety members attends worship each Sunday, and altogether, the parish boasts about two hundred active members. Between March 23, 1987 and the end of 1997, the parish participated in the funeral and/or burial of thirty-four men who died of AIDS. These figures do not tell the whole story of loss, however, because they do not reflect other parishioners and men associated with the parish who were living with AIDS and who left the parish to return to their families to die or to have their funerals elsewhere. As part of the research, interviews were conducted with fourteen lay and clergy members of the parish. Preliminary data suggest that these individuals lost an average of 61.5 acquaintances and 8.8 close friends and partners to AIDS, including those within and outside the church. Acquaintance loss ranged from 5 to 200, while close friend and partner loss ranged from 0 to 30. Clearly, individual members of the parish *and* the community as a whole suffered a devastating amount of loss.

Some key similarities and differences emerged in my comparison of Julian's theology and spirituality with that of All Saints. Turning first to similarities, the church community is central both to Julian and to the All Saints community. Despite the flaws of the fourteenth-century Church, Julian refers repeatedly and in positive terms to Holy Church. Underlying her positive sense of church is a self-acceptance and acceptance of others that result from healing from traumatic loss. Julian repeatedly mentions the importance of unity with her fellow Christians and the necessity of looking beyond others' sins.[7] This attitude exemplifies the perspective of a healed survivor: Julian came to view herself as no more or less guilty or worthy than others and thus opened herself up to the possibility of full communion with others. Further, the text suggests that Julian was also open to communion with non-Christians and lapsed Christians as well, a position that was rather extraordinary for her day.

In this regard, an All Saints parishioner, Lucinda Grey, voiced sentiments particularly consistent with Julian's views on this issue. When asked to describe the effect of AIDS loss on her relationship with God, she responded:

> I think it's gotten me away from thinking of God as being very judgmental and gotten me away from thinking that there are standards for behavior and belief that people need to follow to get God's approval and go to heaven . . . It's gotten me more to a conviction that whatever the life of the world-to-be may be, that we'll probably all be there and that I don't think that God sweats the small stuff.[8]

In her response to follow-up questions, Lucinda described how she also has come to believe that *she* is among those who will be with God. When asked how she had come to this acceptance of self and others, she responded:

> I've seen so many very good people that the vast majority of people would consider undesirable die in the church and have been to the funeral services with those hymns, those readings . . . I cannot imagine that God would not accept Stephen (naming a young gay man who died of AIDS), that he would not be pleased with Mike or Hank or any of those people.

Clearly, through participating in the liturgy and prayers for her friends, Lucinda reached the conclusion that God is indeed merciful and that God's mercy extends to her, to her friends, and to others who may or may not be Christians, a point she mentions explicitly. Surviving traumatic loss appears to allow people to see themselves as friends of each other and as friends of God. This notion of friendship embraces both saints who are alive and saints who have died but live on in the hearts and minds of others.

A second key parallel between the experience of Julian and that of All Saints relates to the process of healing from traumatic loss. Applying Lifton's psychology to Julian's religious experience suggests that healing from trauma is facilitated when the survivor is able to reexperience painful feelings associated with trauma in the context of symbolic meaning and community support. Julian imaginatively "reworked" the imagery of the crucifixion, and she had the aid of others in integrating her visionary experience (Chap. 66, 133–134). In a similar fashion, the people of All Saints developed a devotion to St. Michael the Archangel, defender of the defenseless, and constructed a beautiful shrine in his honor in the AIDS memorial garden. This shrine and the devotion to Michael have become a focal point for the annual AIDS memorial liturgies in which the names of the beloved dead are read and their lives remembered and celebrated. Participating in this ritual together strengthens, heals, and empowers the parish—it provides parishioners with a place where they may come together around their loss as well with a patron who strengthens their resolve to seek justice for those living and dying with AIDS.

The importance of mystery and transcendence in healing exemplifies a third parallel between Julian's theology and spirituality and that of All Saints. Julian emphasizes mystery and transcendence most clearly in her eschatology, in her invocation of that great deed through which Christ will make all things well. Rather than seeing this as a "pat solution" that allows her neatly to tie up conceptual loose ends, Julian's writing on this subject communicates a profound trust, the fruit of her encounter with a loving God. Julian believes in God's goodness and love and in the effectiveness of God's actions on our behalf. As she notes:

> [W]hen the doom and judgment is given and we have all been brought up above, then we will see clearly in God those secret things that are hidden from us now. Then will none of us be stirred to say: "Lord, if only it had been thus, then it had been full well"; but we shall say all with one voice: "Lord, blessed may you be! For it is thus, it is well . . ." (Chap. 85, 162).

Julian's eschatology is a dynamic solution worked out in trust and love. She grounds this solution in the profound awareness of human limitations that clearly is a legacy of surviving traumatic loss.

At All Saints, mystery and transcendence are expressed most clearly in the parish's rich Anglo-Catholic liturgy. This beautiful liturgy fully engages the senses, draws effectively on the Church's sophisticated musical heritage, and is replete with verbal and nonverbal cues to the presence of the Holy. I soon became aware in my observation of the parish's liturgy of its power to serve as a "container" for the complex and confusing emotions associated with loss. That is, the nonverbal richness of the liturgy and its sheer beauty facilitated experiencing and expressing the heightened joy and sadness that were part of life with AIDS. The parishioners themselves described how central the liturgy was to their healing process. Over time, their perception and appreciation of the liturgy deepened—not because *it* changed, but because they brought to it so many feelings and memories of love, loss, and longing. Further, the eucharistic liturgy at All Saints integrates two theological themes central to the life of the community: remembrance and resurrection. The Eucharist, with its twin anemnetic and proleptic aspects, allows the congregation to cherish past memories and express future hopes in a dynamic and sacredly constituted present moment.

Besides these rich parallels informing our understanding of multiple loss, one key difference has emerged between Julian's theology and that of All Saints. In keeping with the emphasis on sin in her day, Julian devotes a great deal of attention to working out a theology of sin and redemption. She reaches the very hopeful conclusion that sin is inevitable, but that God does not blame us for it. This stance on sin allows Julian to attribute to its existence the manifold suffering that humans experience. She is careful, however, not to view suffering as a punishment for sin. Instead, she uses the concept of sin to account for the presence of misfortune and pain in the world.

In contrast, the people of All Saints devote very little attention to the notion of sin *per se*. They attend much more, however, to the notion of injustice, particularly the injustice associated with sexism, heterosexism, and racism. The members of the parish are painfully aware that the dominant American culture and the wider Church do not fully share the vision of inclusiveness that guides their life. It seems likely that the notion of injustice at All Saints functions similarly to Julian's notion of sin, for it provides a way of accounting for the suffering associated with massive loss. The notion of injustice, however, exemplifies a corporate and systemic understanding of sin, rather than the more individual understanding Julian develops. Perhaps the emphasis on the corporate understanding of sin and evil at All Saints may be viewed as a natural outgrowth of the corporate culpability associated with the Holocaust and other experiences of massive death in the twentieth century.

Conclusion

In ten years, my exploration of AIDS loss has come full circle. It began when I was a chaplain with pastoral experiences of loss and empathy and the ensuing struggle for meaning these created. My search for answers serendipitously resulted in an encounter with a fourteenth-century solitary. In coming to understand and to appreciate Julian's awareness of God's courteous love, I have been brought face to face yet again with the painful reality of AIDS loss, this time in a small urban congregation. In the course of this journey through grief, I have learned to face pain honestly, to give myself fully to the doubts and questions it engenders, and to persist in the quest for meaning. In this regard, I have been inspired by Julian's courage and twenty-year devotion to articulating the truth of her visions. In teaching me how central faithfulness, love, and community are to healing, Julian and the people of All Saints have been visionaries and cotravelers in my own quest for meaning. I have been both humbled and privileged by their companionship.

NOTES

1. The references to Julian's text are all drawn from John Skinner's 1996 translation of Julian's Long Text, *A Revelation of Love,* published by Arthur James. Hereafter, parenthetical references to the text will show the chapter number and page.

2. This research is the basis for my doctoral dissertation entitled *Finding Religious and Spiritual Meaning in AIDS-Related Multiple Loss: A Comparative and Constructive Theological Analysis of Communal Bereavement,* Claremont School of Theology, forthcoming. I am grateful to Robert Rennicks for his comments on this chapter, and to Mary Elizabeth Moore, Kathleen Grieder, and William Clements for their assistance with the dissertation.

3. These and other facts about Julian's life may be found in Grace M. Jantzen, *Julian of Norwich: Mystic and Theologian* (London: SPCK, 1987).

4. Rosemary Horrox, translator and editor of *The Black Death,* Manchester Medieval Sources Series (Manchester, England: Manchester University Press, 1994), provides a number of sources testifying to this effect. See especially Section I: The plague in continental Europe, 32, 59 and II: The plague in the British Isles, 70.

5. On processions, see Barbara Tuchman, *A Distant Mirror: The Calamitous Fourteenth Century* (New York: Knopf, 1978), 99–100. For various forms of prayer, see Horrox, 147–148.

6. Some readers may question the advisability of applying twentieth-century research on survivors to Julian's experience of plague in the fourteenth century. I would argue that this comparison is appropriate based on the striking similarities I have observed between twentieth-century accounts of multiple death experiences and accounts of plague loss. Even within the twentieth century, survivors of widely varying disastrous situations, such as the Holocaust, Hiroshima, the Vietnam War, AIDS loss, and natural disasters like the Buffalo Creek flood, appear to experience very similar effects. It would appear that post-traumatic stress and its symptoms are fairly constant across time. However, we must be careful to note as Lifton does that *"to observe common psychological responses of survivors . . . in no way suggests that the historical events themselves can be equated"* (emphasis his). See Robert Jay Lifton, "The Concept of the Survivor" in *The Future of Immortality and Other Essays for a Nuclear Age* (New York: Basic Books, 1987), 235.

7. See, for example, Chapter 8 in the Long Text.

8. These and subsequent quotations are from the author's interview with Lucinda Grey [pseud.], 29 August 1999. Tape recording, San Francisco, CA. The names of the men have been changed for the sake of confidentiality.

RESOURCES

Robert S. Gottfried. *The Black Death: Natural and Human Disaster in Medieval Europe* (New York: The Free Press, 1983).

Rosemary Horrox, trans. and ed. *The Black Death.* Manchester Medieval Sources Series (Manchester, England: Manchester University Press, 1994).

Grace Jantzen. *Julian of Norwich: Mystic and Theologian* (London: SPCK, 1987).

Julian of Norwich. *A Revelation of Love.* Trans., John Skinner (Evesham: Arthur James, 1996).

Robert Jay Lifton. *Death in Life: Survivors of Hiroshima* (New York: Random House, 1968).

_____. *The Future of Immortality and Other Essays for a Nuclear Age* (New York: Basic Books, 1987).

Barbara W. Tuchman. *A Distant Mirror: The Calamitous Fourteenth Century* (New York: Knopf, 1978).

Philip Ziegler. *The Black Death* (New York: Harper & Row, 1969).

7

NEAR-DEATH EXPERIENCE AND JULIAN OF NORWICH'S DOCTRINE OF PRAYER

ANN W. ASTELL

O n the afternoon of August 26, 1987, while I was working at home on my preparations for a course I was teaching at the University of Wisconsin-Madison, there was a knock at my door. Sister M. Terese stood there, her face pale, and said, "Come quick. I cannot awaken Christine." We found Sr. M. Christine Pauly (b. 1928), a longtime muscular sclerosis patient, sitting in her chair in a coma. Rushed to the hospital by ambulance, she was immediately placed on life-support—and I can still remember how corpse-like she looked. The doctors, judging by the barely perceptible vital signs, said that Sr. Christine had probably had a massive stroke. After repeated tests over the next couple of days, she was declared brain-dead. The decision was made to remove her from life-support and to entrust her into God's hands. "She will not be able to breathe on her own," the doctors speculated, "without the aid of the respirator." When the fateful hour arrived, people all over the city of Madison, Wisconsin, were surrounding Sr. Christine with their prayers, for she was and is greatly loved.

To everyone's amazement, Sr. Christine drew breath when the machine was turned off. In the early morning hours of the next day, she opened her eyes and, several hours later, she began to speak. Ater two more days of convalescing, Sr. Christine walked out of the hospital, perfectly coherent and radiant in her disposition.

When we asked her, "What happened to you? Do you remember anything?" Sr. Christine hesitated, but then confided that the Blessed Mother had come to her in her room. "While I was asleep in my chair at home, I

• 109

saw the Blessed Mother coming toward me down a cliff. I was in darkness below. She was dressed in blue and white and had a crown of stars around her head. Then she reached out her right hand, and I took hold of it with mine. She said, 'Child, do not be afraid.'" Mary then told Sr. Christine that she was ready for heaven, but that her time was not yet; that she was still needed for a while on earth. Hearing this word from Mary consoled Sr. Christine greatly and gave new meaning to her suffering. The first word Sr. Christine uttered when she regained consciousness was "Mary."

In the thirteen years following her near-death experience, Sr. Christine never lost the peacefulness, the transfiguration of her personality that she received then, despite a steady, crippling decline in her health due to the ravages of multiple sclerosis. She was a source of courage and consolation to many people who came to her seeking counsel in the face of their own suffering. She lived compassionately in the hope of Mary's promise to her, which echoes Simeon's prophecy in Luke 2:34–35: "This child is destined for the falling and the rising of many in Israel, and to be a sign that will be opposed so that the inner thoughts of many will be revealed—and a sword will pierce your own soul too." During the Thanksgiving holiday this past month, I was able to spend some precious time alone with Sr. Christine and spoke with her again about her near-death experience. Less than a week later, on the night of November 27, 2000, Sr. Christine died suddenly and unexpectedly of a severe stroke. Seen in retrospect, our Thanksgiving conversations together, during which we recalled all the details of her near-death experience, were an immediate preparation for her actual dying, her second death, and her entrance into eternal life.

Sister Christine's miraculous recovery in 1987 was, for some time, the talk of the town, especially in St. Mary's Hospital, where the doctors remained baffled by it. Her experience seems no less wonderful, but less unusual, in the light of recent studies of near-death experience (henceforth abbreviated NDE). Since psychiatrist Raymond A. Moody's best-selling 1975 book, *Life After Life*, which examined 150 case studies of NDE, and his 1977 sequel, *Reflections on Life after Life*, academic researchers from a variety of disciplines—physicians, sociologists, and psychologists—have conducted similar research involving thousands of cases. Psychologists Karlis Osis and Erlendur Haraldsson summarize as follows: "Some [deathbed patients] see apparitions of deceased relatives and friends. They see religious and mythological figures. They see nonearthly environments

characterized by light, beauty, and intense color. These experiences are transformative. They bring with them serenity, peace, elation, and religious
emotions" (*At The Hour of Death*, 2).

In their 1997 book titled *The Eternal Journey*, medical sociologists Craig
R. Lundahl and Harold A. Widdison assert:

> We now know that demographic variables . . . do not significantly influ-
> ence the incidence or contents of NDEs. . . . However, prolonged
> unconsciousness does affect NDE incidence and depth. Research also
> shows NDE incidence as well as depth is greatest for illness victims,
> moderate for accident victims, and weakest for those who attempt sui-
> cide (*The Eternal Journey*, 6).

Thanatologist Elisabeth Kübler-Ross concurs: "At the portal of death
human experiences . . . are alike and do not much vary depending on
religious and cultural backgrounds. They are more influenced by the depth
and authenticity of a belief system" (cited in *At The Hour of Death*, ix).

Julian of Norwich's Near-Death Experience

The medieval mystic Julian of Norwich recorded sixteen revelations that
she received during her NDE, in 1373, in a book called *Showings* or *Revelations of Divine Love*. About twenty years later, she wrote a longer version
of these same revelations. To my knowledge, the *Revelations* of Julian of
Norwich have never been examined systematically from the point of view
of contemporary NDE research.[1] At least some of the reasons for this
neglect are obvious. Strong disciplinary boundaries separate the method-
ologies employed by psychologists and sociologists on the one hand, from
those used by theologians, church historians, and historical linguists on
the other. There is also the difficulty, as Lundahl and Widdison admit, of
"separating out the core dying experience from cultural expectations of
what should be happening at death" (*The Eternal Journey*, xxv). And yet
enough crosscultural research has been done to suggest "that the NDE is a
pervasive phenomenon occurring across time, culture, and ages" (*The Eternal
Journey*, 5).

Obvious similarities exist between Julian's experience, recorded in the
Revelations, and that of contemporary NDE reporters. A severe illness
brought Julian close to death in May 1373. The revelations she received
convinced her of God's unconditional love for her and for humanity, and

of her mission to proclaim to others what she had learned. What differentiates Julian's revelations from that of most people nowadays who experience near-death is their theological depth, and the degree to which Julian was spiritually prepared to receive them by a life of prayer and virtuous striving. Julian emphasizes that she experienced near-death as *a fulfillment of her own desire expressed in petition to God.* Her sense of her own prayer as inspired and answered by God contributes substantially to her general doctrine of prayer and extends into her crucial, theological understanding of God's will, whereby everything, even sin and death, works to the good. She draws an analogy between her own experience of near-death and recovery, on the one hand, and Christ's death and resurrection on the other. Indeed, her experiential sharing in the passion and resurrection of Christ through her rescue from pain, the devil, and death informs her theology of universal salvation. Hers is, quite simply, a theology based on a near-death, mystical experience.

Julian is careful to present her near-death experiences as God's answer to her urgent prayer:

> I quite sincerely wanted to be ill to the point of dying, so that I might receive the last rites of Holy Church, in the belief—shared by my friends—that I was in fact dying. . . . In this illness I wanted to undergo all those spiritual and physical sufferings I should have were I really dying, and to know, moreover, the terror and assaults of the demons—everything, except death itself! (*Revelations*, 63)[2]

Julian desired to have this illness at a young age as a powerful means of altering her life, detaching herself from earthly desires, and cleansing her soul. "Because of that illness," she hoped to live afterwards in a manner more worthy of God and to die a "better death" (*Revelations*, 64) in the end. She did not, however, cling to this desire for a near-death experience. She prayed for it earnestly, but in a conditional manner, and she even "forgot all about [it]" (*Revelations*, 64), until her petition came to be fulfilled. Julian's forgetting of the petition rules out the possibility that her illness onto death was self-induced.

Revelations begins with a listing of Julian of Norwich's three-fold petition to God: (i) to understand his passion; (ii) to suffer physically while still a young woman of thirty; and (iii) to have as God's gift the "three wounds" of contrition, compassion, and longing for God. In retrospect, these petitions, especially the request for a near-death experience, are now seen to have been prophetic and inspired, for her prayers are answered perfectly. Part of Julian's wonderment and theological reflection concerns the source and nature of her own prayers. The first revelation causes Julian to ask in Chapter Six "how we should pray." The fourteenth and longest of Julian's revelations begins with three important chapters on prayer (Chapters 41-43), which are followed by a discussion of the divine and human will, sin, and salvation; into the parable of the Lord and the servant; and finally, into the discussion of Mother Jesus. The final chapter of *Revelations* returns to the theme of prayer with which the book began, and names God once again as "the foundation of [our] praying" (*Revelations*, 211). Julian's doctrine of prayer is thus inseparable from her mystical theology, her image of God, her understanding of human nature, and her salvific experience of near-death.

At the beginning of the *Revelations*, Julian, like the respondents in contemporary NDE studies, witnesses with clinical precision to her own process of dying: "On the third night I was quite convinced that I was passing away—as indeed were those about me" (*Revelations*, 64). She describes a progressive paralysis: "By then my body was dead from the waist downwards. . . . My eyes were fixed, and I could no longer speak. . . . Then my sight began to fail. . . . Then the rest of my body began to die, and I could hardly feel a thing. As my breathing became shorter and shorter I knew for certain that I was passing away" (*Revelations*, 65).

Propped up on her sickbed in what appeared to be her final hour, Julian fixed her eyes on the face of the crucifix that the parish priest had placed before her. Thus the two sufferers, Jesus and Julian, faced each other as mirror images. Julian's three petitions—to be physically present at Christ's last agony, to be granted a life-threatening illness, and to be pierced with the wound of compassion—simultaneously found fulfillment, as Julian's suffering was incorporated into Christ's, and his into hers. Even as she was awaiting her own death, Julian "looked with all [her] might for the moment of [Jesus'] dying . . . And just when I was thinking that his life was about to finish, and that I must be shown his end, suddenly, while I gazed on the cross, his expression changed to cheerful joy! The change in his blessed countenance changed mine too, and I was glad and happy as could be" (*Revelations*, 95). Julian interprets this unexpected change in Christ's face as a prophecy of the soul's abrupt translation at the moment of death from an earthly share in Christ's passion to an eternal share in his resurrection: "Between the one thing and the other no time shall intervene: all shall be brought to joy" (*Revelations*, 95).

Julian similarly reports an instantaneous change in her own condition at the start of her revelations: "Suddenly all my pain was taken away, and I was as fit and well as I had ever been; and this was especially true of the lower part of my body. I was amazed at this sudden change, for I thought that it must have been a special miracle of God, and not something natural" (*Revelations*, 65). This description of an instant loss of pain is typical of NDE case studies. Lundahl and Widdison quote numerous examples of people separated from pain through an out-of-the-body experience. One person, an accident victim, reports: "One minute I was racked with tremendous pain, the next I was out of my body and free of all pain" (*The Eternal Journey*, 89). Julian does not actually describe being out of her own body, but she reports a promise of the Lord to her that presents death as a sudden release from pain: "Suddenly you will be taken from all your pain, all your sickness, all your discomfort, all your woe. . . . Suddenly you will be taken" (*Revelations*, 177). She goes on to describe an out-of-the-body experience that may be an image of her own:

> At this time I saw a body lying on the ground, heavy and ugly, without shape or form, a swollen mass of stinking filth. And suddenly out of this body sprang a most beautiful creature, a little child, perfectly shaped and formed, active and lively, whiter than a lily: and he quickly glided up to heaven. The swollen body stood for the great misery of our mortal flesh, and the little child for the clean and pure soul. I thought, "With this body this child's beauty cannot live, and on this child no physical filth can stay" (*Revelations*, 178).

The soul was frequently depicted in medieval art in the form of a small child. Similarly, contemporary accounts of deep, near-death experiences frequently include encounters with children, often the souls of children yet unborn, who are destined to be the children or siblings of the one who is near death (*The Eternal Journey*, 29–46). The child in Julian's vision appears to be her own soul, as a representative of all souls who are destined to be born into eternal life. As Julian writes: "All this living and waiting here is but a moment: when we are taken suddenly out of suffering into bliss, the suffering will be nothing" (*Revelations*, 178).

Julian describes her sudden freedom from physical pain as a "special miracle of God" (*Revelations,* 65). Not surprisingly, her revelations include "special insight and instruction about miracles" (*Revelations,* 117), past and present. They are all characterized, Julian understands, by two elements: first, the "sorrow, distress, [and] trouble" that inspire people in their weakness to cry to God "for his grace and help;" then the miraculous intervention of God's "supreme power, wisdom, and goodness" (*Revelations,* 117). Human distress is for Julian the prelude to, and sure promise of, a miracle: "It is always like this before miracles" (*Revelations,* 117). This law holds true also in the case of moral weakness and sin. Cast down by our failures, we acquire humility, expressed in contrition, and then "suddenly we are delivered from sin and pain, and raised to blessedness, and even made great saints!" (*Revelations,* 120). Here and elsewhere Julian stresses the sudden, instantaneous quality of a miracle, which always involves a shift along a vertical line. Even as the soul leaves the mortal body behind and is thus delivered from physical pain, so, too, God's grace is an infused lightness that allows the soul to be lifted up into a seat in its higher part, away from its lower inclinations.

Freed from the physical pain of the body, Julian describes a feeling of "heartfelt joy" in the presence of the Trinity: "And I knew that all eternity was like this for those who attain heaven" (*Revelations,* 66). Later, in the seventh revelation, this bliss of hers was intensified: "This experience was so happy spiritually that I felt completely at peace and relaxed: nothing on earth could have disturbed me" (*Revelations,* 86). Such feelings of peace and joy are the hallmark of contemporary near-death experiences, even in the cases where, as in Julian's, heavenly visions are combined with infernal ones, and emotions of elation and pleasure alternate with those of depression and pain.

People who confess to having had a near-death experience frequently report meetings with others, usually deceased relatives or religious figures, described as beings of light. Similarly, Julian encounters Jesus in his passion and sees his mother Mary: "In my spirit I saw her as though she were physically present, still in her youth, and little more than a child" (*Revelations,* 67). Three times she sees Mary, the only saint with whom she has a personal encounter. She sees the Lord in glory in her twelfth revelation. In the sixth revelation she sees Jesus in the company of all the saints: "Utterly at home, and with perfect courtesy, himself was the eternal happiness and comfort of his beloved friends, the marvelous music of his unending love showing in the beauty of his blessed face" (*Revelations*, 85).

This vision of the heavenly reward granted to God's servants seems to be part of a divine review of Julian's life. People typically see their lives pass before them in an examination of conscience or flow of memory during their NDE. Julian's sixth revelation includes the Lord's judgment of Julian. It begins with the Lord giving thanks to Julian: "Thank you for all your suffering, the suffering of your youth" (*Revelations*, 85). The Lord then teaches Julian that each person's "reward is governed by the willingness of his service and its duration. In particular those who willingly and freely offer their youth to God are rewarded and thanked, supremely and wonderfully" (*Revelations*, 86). Near death at age thirty, this word must have come as a great consolation to Julian, who declares: "The more the loving soul sees this courtesy of God, the more gladly will he serve him all the days of his life" (*Revelations*, 86).

Julian's NDE was of relatively long duration. After a week of serious illness, she received the last rites. Shortly thereafter, within the space of five hours, from 4:00 a.m. to 9:00 a.m., she had fifteen different revelations, the sixteenth coming as a confirmation during the following night. In keeping with the findings of Raymond Moody's 1977 research into prolonged and deep NDE, Julian's *Revelations* exhibit not only the usual NDE features but also four less common ones: the sight of unusual landscapes, an encounter with demons, the experience of a supernatural rescue for herself and others, and visions of knowledge.

Like many people who have had NDE, Julian reports seeing a heavenly city: "Then our Lord opened my spiritual eyes, and showed me the soul in the middle of my heart. The soul was as large as if it were an eternal world, and a blessed kingdom as well. Its condition showed it to be a most glorious city" (*Revelations*, 183). She also describes being led "down onto the sea-bed," where she saw "green hills and valleys looking as though they were moss-covered, with seaweed and sand" (*Revelations*, 77). The colors painted here by Julian are vivid, as are the colors in contemporary NDE reports of ethereal landscapes, especially light-filled cities and paradisiacal gardens.

Julian, however, mainly focuses on the changing coloration of Christ's body, which seems to reflect seasonal alteration in the weather. "Great drops of blood rolled down," Julian writes, from the crown of thorns, "and they came down a brownish red colour—for the blood was thick—and as they spread out they became bright red. . . . Their abundance was like the drops of water that fall from the eaves after a heavy shower" (*Revelations*, 72). There were "frequent changes of colour" in the face of the crucifix (*Revelations*, 76), Julian observes. "Dry, bloodless, and pallid with death," it became "more pale, deathly and lifeless. Then, dead, it turned a blue colour, gradually changing into a browny blue, as the flesh continued to die. . . . [H]is dear body became black and brown, as it dried up in death; it was no longer its fair, living colour" (*Revelations*, 87–88). Julian pictures Christ's body in a winter landscape, facing "a strong, dry, and piercingly cold wind" (*Revelations*, 88), which causes extreme dehydration. Mortally sick herself for a week, Julian characteristically identifies her own body with Christ's: "And it seemed to me, that with all this drawn-out pain, he had been a week in dying" (*Revelations*, 88).

Among the landscapes that are not described in Julian's *Revelations* are the places of torment and purification. Indeed, Julian's case challenges the oft-repeated scholarly claim that what distinguishes medieval NDE from contemporary ones is the frequency with which Christians of the Middle Ages see visions of hell. Julian relates that she had asked "to get a real sight of hell and purgatory" (*Revelations*, 111), but that that request of hers was not granted: "But for all my desire I saw absolutely nothing, except . . . in the fifth revelation where I saw the devil reproved by God and condemned eternally" (*Revelations*, 111). Julian interprets this as a sign not of hell's nonexistence, but of heaven's lack of involvement with "all creatures who are of the devil's sort and die as such" (*Revelations*, 111).

Julian does encounter the fiend, however. At the end of her fifteenth revelation, she falls asleep and sees the horrible, red face of a nightmarish demon, who attempts to strangle her (*Revelations*, 182). This trial is connected with Julian's temptation to doubt the revelations she has received. After the sixteenth and final revelation, the fiend comes to her a second time at night, in order to tempt her to despair. Whereas the first fiendish attack focused on the senses of sight and touch, the second involves smell and hearing. Julian is revolted by the demon's "foul and nauseating" stench and distracted by the sound of "a distinct chattering" (*Revelations*, 185). Her perseverance in prayer throughout these ordeals and the eventual departure of the enemy strengthen her belief in God's saving power.

Julian's vivid, visionary encounter with the devil parallels otherworldly meetings with demonic beings in contemporary NDE accounts. Although researchers emphasize the more common, positive, euphoric reports of light and consolation, a significant number of people confess that they have had frightening or hellish near-death experiences. Psychologists Lundahl and Widdison distinguish the heavenly City of Light from the hellish Realm of Bewildered Spirits as NDE places, and describe the latter as a location resembling Dante's Inferno, "filled with hate, despair, terror, hopelessness, darkness, and animal passions" (*The Eternal Journey*, 238). Such descriptions directly contradict Carol Zaleski's characterization of contemporary NDEs as radically unlike medieval ones: "Gone are the bad deaths, harsh judgment scenes, purgatorial torments, and infernal terrors of medieval visions; by comparison, the modern other world is a congenial place, a democracy, a school for continuing education, and a garden of unearthly delights" (*Otherworld Journey*, 7). Indeed, if, as cardiologist Maurice Rawlings claims in his 1978 book, *Beyond Death's Door*, the number of frightening NDEs equals that of consoling ones, then medieval near-death experiences may be much more similar to modern ones than some scholars are willing to admit.

Many reports of near-death experience include a prophecy of a final age, characterized by love and peace, which comes to humanity after a time of purifying suffering. Some include a prophetic sense that even the souls in the Realm of Bewildered Spirits will eventually be brought out of darkness into the City of Light (*The Eternal Journey*, 236). This sort of prediction resembles the word of the Lord oft-repeated by Julian: "All will be well." It especially recalls Julian's prophecy of a final "great deed," to be performed by the Trinity: "There still remains a deed which the blessed Trinity will do at the last day—at least so I see it—yet when and how it will be done is unknown to all God's creatures under Christ, and it will remain so until it takes place. . . . This great deed . . . is known only to [God] himself. By it he will make everything to turn out well" (*Revelations*, 110).

The hope and promise of a general deliverance of humanity from sin and suffering accords, first of all, with the dying Julian's experience of instantaneous freedom from physical pain during her revelations; second, with her vision of the sudden change in Christ's countenance from deathly pallor to living beauty; and, third, with the Lord's promise to her that she would be "suddenly taken" from pain into bliss at the end of her earthly life. At the same time, as Julian recognizes, the assurance that "everything is going to be all right" seems to be at odds with both our human sense of justice and the Christian doctrinal belief that "many creatures will be damned" (*Revelations*, 110): "We see deeds done that are so evil, and injuries inflicted that are so great, that it seems quite impossible that any good can come of them" (*Revelations*, 109). In the face of this apparent contradiction, she maintains her firm trust in God's providence: "For the great deed that our Lord is going to do is that by which he shall keep his word in every particular, and make all that is wrong turn out well" (*Revelations*, 111).

Julian's experience of God reveals God's nature to be unconditional love. Many people encounter such love and happiness during their near-death experience that they are unwilling to return to earthly life. Julian seems to fit this category. At the beginning of her fifteenth revelation she confesses, "I had had a great and longing desire that God should give me deliverance from this life. . . . Besides, because of my own wretchedness, slothfulness, and incapacity, I did not want to live and to toil as it fell to me to do" (*Revelations*, 177). God convinces her to fulfill her mission on earth with the promise of heaven, on the one hand, and the gentle indication that he wills her to endure awhile longer on the other: "Never again will there be any sort of suffering, or sickness, or unhappiness, or failure of will. It will be all joy and bliss eternally. Why should it grieve you to suffer awhile, seeing that it is my will and my glory?" (*Revelations*, 179)

Julian's return from a mystic state to a normal state of consciousness is accompanied by much pain. She writes:

> I had no pain to trouble or distress me all the while the fifteen revelations lasted. But at the end, everything closed up and I saw no more. At one moment I was feeling that I was going to survive, and at the next my sickness returned, first in my head which began to throb, and then suddenly my whole body felt as ill as it had ever been. . . . Wretch that I was, I moaned and cried as I became aware of my bodily pains and lack of comfort, both spiritual and physical (*Revelations*, 181).

This sort of desolation after a deep, rapturous, near-death experience is not uncommon, as NDE research shows.

Julian, however, quickly regains her composure after a time of temptation and takes firm possession of the faith, hope, and charity that her revelations had inspired in her. Already in the first of her revelations she had had a sense that she had a mission yet to fulfill on earth:

Throughout all this I was greatly moved with love for my fellow Christians, that they might know and see what I was seeing, for I wanted it to cheer them too. The vision was for all and sundry. . . . I was sure that I was dying, and this was a cause both of wonder and disquiet, for I thought the vision was meant for those who were going on living (*Revelations*, 74).

Entrusted with the task of recording her revelations, Julian insists: "It is God's will that you should receive it with great joy and pleasure, as if Jesus himself had showed it to you all" (*Revelations*, 74).

Julian's Doctrine of Prayer

Julian's visions of knowledge—her physical sights, such as that of the hazelnut; her insights into theological mysteries; and her prophetic foresights—are many, and it is the purpose of the *Revelations* as a whole to record them. Among Julian's teachings, her doctrine of prayer holds a special place. Because she received her revelations in prayer with God, her doctrine of prayer is inseparable from her theology. Julian received her near-death experience, including her visions of Christ, moreover, as an answer to her explicit petition. The precision with which her request was answered and the generosity of God's gift led her to the recognition that God had inspired her desires in order to make her receptive and cooperative: "Everything that our Lord makes us ask for he has ordained for us from before time. . . . He moves us to pray for what it is he wants to do" (*Revelations*, 124, 128).

This simple insight, based on her own near-death experience, has profound theological and practical consequences for Julian. The three chapters (41–43) specifically devoted to prayer are numerically at the center of the *Revelations*. There she reports the mysterious word of the Lord: "I am the foundation of your praying" (*Revelations*, 124). She anticipates this revelation in the second and third chapters, where she describes her petitions, and she returns to it in the final chapter, where she repeats the mystic sentence: "I am the foundation of your praying" (*Revelations*, 211). She concludes with the assertion that the whole of the *Revelations* is about the need for us to pray for charity: "Thus does our good Lord will that we should pray. This is what I understood his meaning to be throughout" (*Revelations*, 211).

The great mistake of people, according to Julian, is to suppose that prayer is self-generated, rather than coming from God. Whatever comes from God necessarily leads us back to God; whatever desire, whatever petition, God inspires in us must necessarily accord with his own will and is, therefore, certain of fulfillment. If we think that prayer originates in ourselves, then we are tempted to imagine that we can pray without communicating with God, without God's hearing and answering us. Our prayers, therefore, are lacking in trust, and "we do not fully honour our Lord in our prayer" (*Revelations*, 126). But if we recognize that God is "the foundation of [our] praying" (*Revelations*, 124)—that is, its root, its deepest source, and its support—then God is already speaking to us in our prayer. God speaks with the voice of our souls. No genuine prayer can occur, except as an expression of a union with God that already exists and as a means for a closer union with God.

Our "ability to pray is itself given to us by his loving grace" (*Revelations*, 126), Julian insists. Since prayer itself is God's gift to us, it stands as a guarantee of other gifts to be given: "No one genuinely asks for mercy and grace without mercy and grace having been given him first" (*Revelations*, 126). Thus every petition already entails thanksgiving for the gift that God has in store and for which human longing and willing prepare the way. "Thanksgiving," Julian writes, "is a real, interior knowledge" that recognizes God's gift precisely as a gift, even before it is actually received: "With prayer goes gratitude" (*Revelations*, 125). Remembering that the greatest deeds [e.g., the Creation, the Incarnation, the Resurrection, Pentecost] are already done," we should pray "for the deed now in process" (*Revelations*, 127) and cooperate as far as possible in the fulfillment of God's will.

Julian stresses the need to pray consciously and deliberately, but she also maintains that part of us prays without our knowing it in the form of an inarticulate, perhaps even unconscious, yearning for God, a spiritual thirst that orientates us to God as the one who alone can satisfy the immensity of our desire for love. Julian likens this most basic prayer to the body's hunger and thirst. For Julian, Christ's dehydrated body on the cross is an embodied prayer, a physical and spiritual thirst for souls and for the salvation that God intends for all creation. Similarly, the aridity of the saints who pray when they are "dry, empty, sick, or weak" (*Revelations*, 125) is a prayer that prophesies and enables the nourishing rain of grace.

The suffering of sinners on account of their distance from God is also a form of prayer, whether or not they are conscious of it. Indeed, every human being prays. For Julian, prayer is natural. Created in the image and likeness of God (Genesis 1:26–27) and through the Incarnate Word of God (John 1:1–3), a human being can and must pray, because our very being is always already found in relation to God. As Julian puts it, "By nature our will wants God, and the good will of God wants us" (*Revelations*, 71).

In keeping with the teaching of St. Bernard of Clairvaux (1090–1153), Julian maintains that this inescapable, natural prayer can, however, either be resisted or embraced and enhanced. People can resist the prayer that is natural to them because, through the fall, humanity has lost its moral likeness to God, while retaining God's image. People can also choose instead to affirm and to cooperate with the prayer of their nature through the conscious practice of prayer—a practice that brings them more and more into conformity with God's will for them, thus restoring the moral likeness to God that was lost. As Julian writes:

> By his grace [our Lord] aims to make us as like himself in heart as we are already in our human nature. This is his blessed will. So he says, "Pray inwardly even if you do not enjoy it, though you feel nothing, see nothing. Yes, even though you think you are doing nothing.". . . Because of the reward and everlasting gratitude he wants us to have, he is eager to see us pray always (*Revelations*, 125).

According to Julian, "the outcome and purpose of our prayers" is that "we should be united with our Lord and like him in everything. . . . Prayer unites the soul to God" (*Revelations*, 126, 128). The soul "by prayer conform[s] to God" when it prays "fervently, wisely, and earnestly," asking God "to do what [God] is going to do" (*Revelations*, 128). Since the ultimate purpose of all prayer is a deeper union with God, all prayer is really a petition for charity, for divine love; a crying out for God who is "uncreated charity" (*Revelations*, 210): "When by his special grace we see him clearly, there is need of nothing further. We have to follow him, drawn by his love into himself" (*Revelations*, 129). When Julian sees Christ in the first of her revelations, she declares, "To know the goodness of God is the highest prayer of all, and it is a prayer that accommodates itself to our most lowly needs" (*Revelations*, 70).

To be sure, on earth we recognize imperfectly the details of God's plan, especially in the beginning, when the soul is less conformed to God's will. As Julian observes, "The desire of the saints in heaven is only to know such things as our Lord wills to show them. Their love and their longing likewise are ruled by the Lord's will. And this ought to be *our* will too, like theirs" (*Revelations*, 107). The important thing is that we pray, trusting in God's goodness and expressing our needs and desires to him in the childlike faith that "[God] does not despise the work of his hands, nor does he disdain to serve us, however lowly our natural need may be. He loves the soul he has made in his own likeness" (*Revelations*, 70). Indeed, "the love of God Most High for our soul is so wonderful that it surpasses all knowledge" (*Revelations*, 70). If we contemplate "the supreme, single-minded, incalculable love that God, who is goodness, has for us," then we "can ask of our lover whatever we will" (*Revelations*, 71), knowing that God will do what is best for us, in the best way, and at the proper time.

Prayer, Medieval and Modern

We began with the story of Sr. Christine and her near-death experience. I conclude by drawing some parallels between Julian's doctrine of prayer and that of Sr. Christine. As a Schoenstatt Sister of Mary, Sr. Christine's way of praying was strongly influenced by the spirituality of the Schoenstatt Movement, which was founded in Germany on October 18, 1914, at the outbreak of World War I. Now a worldwide movement of moral and religious renewal with members on six continents, the Schoenstatt Movement aims to strengthen and secure the Christian baptismal covenant with God through a childlike Covenant of Love with Mary, the thrice admirable Mother of God, of the Redeemer, and of the redeemed. Sister Christine's baptismal name was Hedwig, but when she became a Schoenstatt Sister of Mary in 1954, she chose the name "Christine" as a sign of her calling to follow Christ as Mary did. For both Julian of Norwich and Sr. Christine, the motherly love and mercy of God were plainly visible in the person of Mary and in Mary's Son, Jesus. Mary is the only person, besides Christ, whom Julian meets in the course of her revelations. Even as Mary is venerated as "thrice admirable" in Schoenstatt, Julian sees Mary three times: "The first occasion was when she was with child, the second sorrowing under the cross, and the third as she is now, delightful, glorious, and rejoicing" (*Revelations*, 102). Similarly, Mary is the one who appeared to Sr. Christine in her near-death experience and who said to her, "Child, do not be afraid."

As an image of God's merciful, fatherly, and motherly love, Mary inspires childlike forms of prayer in both Julian's spirituality and in Schoenstatt. As Fr. Joseph Kentenich (1885–1968), the founder of Schoenstatt, observes: "Mary has accepted the task of being our mother. . . . Through sincere love for Mary, a child receives a nest in a warm, motherly heart" (*God My Father*, 68). As a creature and child of God, Mary also models for her spiritual children a trustful, obedient way of praying to God: "Here I am, the servant of the Lord; let it be with me according to your word" (Luke 1:38). For both Julian and Sr. Christine, these words of Mary, spoken at the hour of the Annunciation, "convey the infinitely simple, childlike surrender of the whole nature to the eternal God's will" (Kentenich, 1977, 58). Such a Marian surrender is lived in daily life through a practical faith in divine providence and an active, affectionate cooperation with God in every circumstance.

The Marian dimension of both Julian's and Schoenstatt's spirituality is very deep and deserves an extended comparative treatment. Here I would like to note only that the *Revelations* reveal Julian of Norwich to have been one of the many medieval Christians who believed in the doctrine of the Immaculate Conception, according to which Mary was preserved by the grace of Christ from original sin and its effects from the first moment of her existence in the womb of her mother.[3] Mary thus stands as a new Eve at the side of Christ, the new Adam. Her sinless being represents a perfect, paradisiacal human nature, as it was originally intended and created by God. Julian discovers "in the soul of our blessed Lady St. Mary" the constant working of God's will and the "action of truth and wisdom" (*Revelations*, 130). For both Julian and Sr. Christine, Mary was the Immaculate Conception, the realization of the unspoiled concept, the "essential nature," of humankind (*Revelations*, 131). As such, Mary is the radiant ideal to inspire our striving for holiness and our hope for a perfectly redeemed humanity. Thus Sr. Christine saw Mary crowned with stars, and Julian beheld her "delightful, glorious, and rejoicing" (*Revelations*, 102).

To Sr. Christine, Mary promised a share in the "sevenfold sword" of sorrow that had pierced her heart as Christ's compassionate mother, permanent companion, helpmate, and coredemptrix beneath the cross. Sister

Christine had prayed in her youth for this gift of suffering with Christ and for him, and she renewed that petition daily during the forty years of her illness. In Schoenstatt, such a prayer is called an *inscriptio* dedication.[4] Julian, too, prayed in her youth for the wound of "genuine compassion" with Christ (*Revelations*, 64). In the course of her revelations she renewed that petition, asking that she might "in [her] own body fully experience and understand his blessed passion" (*Revelations*, 66): "I wanted his pain to be my pain: a true compassion producing a longing for God" (*Revelations*, 66).

Why would anyone ask God for the gift of suffering? As Fr. Joseph Kentenich understood it, God uses suffering to form us into the likeness of his Son Jesus, who, "although he was a Son, . . . learned obedience through what he suffered" (Hebrews 5:8). Suffering is part of God's redemptive plan for each of us, but it is hard for our nature as sentient beings to say "yes" to what is painful. Even Jesus struggled on the eve of his passion, praying, "Father, for you all things are possible; remove this cup from me; yet, not what I want, but what you want" (Mark 14:36).

When we pray in the Lord's Prayer, "Thy will be done," we give God, as it were, a blank check. When we make an *inscriptio* dedication, we petition God to write on the blank check and to take from us whatever God wills, even our very lives. In this way, by begging God ahead of time to give us whatever God's plan of love holds in store for us, we prepare ourselves to accept with courage and love the crosses that come our way and to find a genuine, redemptive value in them. Such an attitude helps us to see both the sorrows and the joys of life as God's gift. In times of persecution, such as the Nazi persecution that brought Fr. Kentenich and other Schoenstatt members to the concentration camp at Dachau in 1941–1942, and in the face of other, similarly great hardships, the attitude of *inscriptio* is indispensable; one cannot hope to live a truly Christian life without embracing the cross.

Julian had a comparable understanding and experience. She asked to suffer with Christ, and God answered the prayer God had inspired in her. Given a choice whether or not to accept the cross, she chose "only Jesus for [her] heaven, come what may," despite "the natural demurring and reaction of the body" (*Revelations*, 93). Later she confessed, "Had I known the sort of suffering it would involve, I should have thought twice about praying for it" (*Revelations*, 93). But she never withdrew her petition for suffering, for her soul, unlike her body, "was not protesting"; on the contrary, it was "deliberately and eternally set on being united to our Lord Jesus" (*Revelations*, 93). According to Julian, the soul can never reach its full development if its lower, sensual part, which is joined to the body, does not come into conformity with the will of God through a share in the cross of Christ, who laid down his life for us. Suffering that is freely accepted opens the soul to its very depth, permits us to know "our own soul thoroughly" (*Revelations*, 161), and allows grace to penetrate the very ground of our being. Julian writes: "We can never be completely holy . . . until our sensuality has been raised to the level of our substance through the virtue of Christ's passion and enriched by all the trials laid upon us by our Lord in his mercy and grace" (*Revelations*, 161). Julian calls these trials the loving "touch" of God (*Revelations*, 161). Similarly, Fr. Kentenich speaks about the soft hand of God in the iron glove.

Julian emphasizes the contrary responses to suffering of the body and the soul, of the animal will and the godly will, of the sensuality and the substance, of the lower and the higher, essential nature. As Julian emphasizes, our prayer brings these contrary responses together and serves to harmonize them. Similarly, Fr. Kentenich, who was Sr. Christine's spiritual father, counseled his Schoenstatt children to pray to God with a divine smile and a human cry. The divine smile represents the prayer of Christ in us, the prayer that trusts in God's goodness and that wants to do and to suffer whatever God wills for us. This is the prayer of our higher nature, the desire of our godly will, the longing of the child of God in us. The human cry is the prayer of the fallen Adam within us and of the crucified Christ—weeping, helpless, hurt, hungry, and thirsty. Both belong together, the divine smile and the human cry. Despite her heavy cross and indeed because of it, Sr. Christine was known, as the homilist at her funeral remarked, as the "little Sister with the big smile."

For Julian, human beings are creatures who are not only mixed (because of the combination of body and soul, reason, and affect), but also mixed up, due to our sinfulness. The Son of God, however, accepted the whole of human nature as his own in order to redeem it. Indeed, Christ who died and who rose from the dead is so alive in human nature that even when we seem to be "spiritually dead," due to "the trouble and distress that we ourselves fall into, . . . in God's sight the soul to be saved *never was dead, and never will be* (*Revelations*, 139, emphasis added). Such an observation is all the more powerful, coming as it does from a mystic whose own near-death experience taught her the meaning of death and filled her with the hope of eternal life. Like Sr. Christine, who first "died" and then returned to life because she was "needed yet on earth," Julian was entrusted with the work of writing the *Revelations* and of teaching her doctrine of prayer: "We all need to pray to God for charity. God is working in us, helping us to thank and trust and enjoy him. Thus does our good Lord will that we should pray" (*Revelations*, 211).

NOTES

1. Carol Zaleski (1987) compares medieval and modern accounts of NDE, but she does not deal with Julian of Norwich. In dealing with the Middle Ages, she focuses on the sixth through the early thirteenth centuries.

2. I use Clifton Wolters' Penguin Classics translation throughout, *Revelations of Divine Love*, citing page numbers parenthetically. Julian's book is also referred to as the *Showings*, a title that captures the meaning of the Middle English word *shewings* better than does the word *revelations*.

3. The English Franciscan John Duns Scotus (d. 1308) formulated a theological basis for belief in the Immaculate Conception that was later to gain official ecclesiastical acceptance in 1854, but only after centuries of debate in which English theologians, notably Eadmer of Clare (d. 1124), Anselm of Edmunsbury (d. 1148), Osbert of Clare (d. 1170), Robert Grosseteste (d. 1253), and William of Ware (d. 1300), played a leading role as advocates of the dogma.

4. As Jonathan Niehaus explains, "The *Inscriptio* literally means to inscribe one's heart into the heart of another. . . . Like the Blank Check, this consecration developed during the difficult Nazi years. . . . Its importance lies in overcoming our natural aversion to sacrifice and the cross. To find its ways to the *Inscriptio*, the soul must face up to this inherent fear and strive to overcome it by doing the opposite—by *embracing* the cross. By freely asking God to send us whatever crosses he has foreseen for one's life, the soul can reach an attitude of greater inner freedom and covenant dedication" (19).

RESOURCES

Julian of Norwich. *Revelations of Divine Love*. Trans. Clifton Wolters (New York: Penguin, 1985).

Kentenich, Joseph. *God My Father* (Waukesha, WI: International Schoenstatt Center, 1977).

Lundahl, Craig R. and Widdison, Harold A. *The Eternal Journey: How Near-Death Experiences Illuminate our Earthly Lives* (New York: Warner Books, 1997).

Niehaus, Jonathan. "Introduction." In Joseph Kentenich, *Schoenstatt's Covenant Spirituality*, 8–26. Ed. and trans. Jonathan Niehaus (Waukesha, WI: Schoenstatt Fathers, 1992).

Osis, Karlis and Haraldsson, Erlendur. *At The Hour of Death* (New York: Avon Books, 1977).

Zaleski, Carol. *Otherworld Journeys: Accounts of Near-Death Experience in Medieval and Modern Times* (New York and Oxford: Oxford University Press, 1987).

8

From *The Cloud* (Unknown Author) to *The Castle* of Teresa of Avila: Teresian Metaphor as Transition from "Unknowing" to "Being Known"

Roseanne McDougall

*T*he *Cloud of Unknowing* and *The Interior Castle* are two medieval/ late medieval texts that are valuable for instruction in contemplative prayer. *The Cloud of Unknowing* is important because it presents a practical method whereby one might dispose oneself to receive the gift of contemplative prayer. A person drawn to begin contemplative prayer could turn to *The Cloud of Unknowing* for guidance. *The Interior Castle* goes a step further than *The Cloud of Unknowing* in that it presents metaphors that enable the contemplative to situate prayer within the Western contemplative tradition and to reflect more deeply upon her or his experience. The metaphors in *The Interior Castle* serve as lenses for interpreting one's prayer in such a way that having experienced "unknowing," one does not "know" or understand one's "unknowing;" rather, one experiences oneself as "being known" by God. When read in sequence, *The Cloud of Unknowing* and *The Interior Castle* provide both a practical method for disposing oneself to contemplative prayer and metaphors for reflection upon the experience of contemplative prayer. Reflection upon the metaphors can lead to a deepened realization that, while one may have had the experience of "unknowing" and one does not "know" much about it, one is nevertheless "known" by God. Even with this brief overview to a sequential reading of *The Cloud of Unknowing* and *The Interior Castle,* the reader is encouraged to explore for oneself *The Cloud of Unknowing* and *The Interior Castle* as valuable means of instruction and growth in contemplative prayer.

The Cloud of Unknowing, written in England in the fourteenth century by an anonymous Author, contains simple, clear instructions for anyone who experiences a desire for a deep encounter with God in prayer. Despite its simplicity, *The Cloud of Unknowing* is not easily comprehended.

The experience of "unknowing" is paradoxical and can leave the twenty-first century practitioner of prayer with desires both to deepen one's experience of God while in the state of "unknowing," and to "know," or to have one's experience affirmed. At its best, "unknowing" requires the willingness to proceed without such affirmation, while, on the other hand, confirmation of one's experience provides assurance that one is on a genuine path. Affirmation also brings encouragement, direction, impetus, and inspiration to continue one's commitment to the kind of prayer described in *The Cloud of Unknowing*.

The Interior Castle, written in Spain in 1577 by Teresa of Avila (1515–1582), draws upon metaphors derived from nature and from literature to elucidate, at least indirectly, her own experience in prayer. The contemplative who reflects upon the "unknowing" component in the metaphors suggested by Teresa of Avila in *The Interior Castle* can derive an intuitive sense that one's own experience is being, to some degree, described. Thus, the metaphors of the sixteenth-century *The Interior Castle* can serve to validate the contemplative experience of the twenty-first century. Further, reflection upon the metaphors of *The Interior Castle* can leave the contemplative with a sense of "being known" by God.

With close attention to the experience of contemplation in *The Cloud of Unknowing* and after a review of *The Interior Castle*, one can apply metaphors from *The Interior Castle* to the experience of "unknowing." Then, from that vantage point, one is better prepared to explore the paradox of both "unknowing" and "knowing" or "seeing through a glass darkly." While the authentic mystical journey requires the commitment to continue the practice of prayer while "unknowing," nevertheless, bits of intuitive "knowing," provided through reflection upon metaphors in *The Interior Castle*, give clarity, depth, insight, and affirmation to one's experience of the Divine active in one's day-to-day life.

Such affirmation is more necessary in the twenty-first century than it may have been in the fourteenth or the sixteenth centuries because the would-be contemplative of the twenty-first century is a post-Enlightenment, post-modern person. Many, although not all, present-day contemplatives have developed a worldview shaped by the Enlightenment and by the development of the modern world. They have acquired a critical consciousness through which they look to the application of their own reason to empirical data rather than to extrinsic "authority" for the validation of their experience. In order to live in the fullness of one's humanity as it has evolved during the past several centuries, one should seek interior validation of spiritual experience. In the seeking, one may find that one is deeply "known" by God. Without this search for validation of experience, one becomes less reflective, more robot-like, and less a fully human person. One might also fail to experience the satisfying joy of "being known" by God.

The Author of *The Cloud of Unknowing*, while offering concrete instructions, recommends blind obedience to method in contemplative prayer (Johnston, 1973, 92). Teresa of Avila in *The Interior Castle* presents metaphors through which one can reflect upon one's experience in contemplative prayer, critically discern God's presence and invitation in prayer, and experience oneself as "being known" by God.

The Cloud of Unknowing *and Contemplation*

The Author of *The Cloud of Unknowing* offers pithy observations regarding contemplation throughout the seventy-five brief chapters that comprise the short book. A careful reading suggests that, while there are few clearly delineated boundaries, the Author does, in fact, subtly address four questions: What is contemplation? How does one contemplate? What are the effects of contemplation? How does one discern the call to contemplation?

The Author's observations on contemplation are found throughout the book with little apparent order. The original synthesis of the Author's work offered below is intended to make *The Cloud of Unknowing* accessible to the reader by paraphrasing the Author's main ideas on contemplation in a systematic manner. The sequence has been imposed upon the content of *The Cloud of Unknowing* in order to assist in bringing about clarity in understanding the work.

First, the Author addresses the question, "What is contemplation?" According to the author of *The Cloud of Unknowing*, contemplation is a calling, a drawing, a desire for a deepening life rooted in the talents and abilities given by God from the beginning of the individual's existence and developed by the human person over the course of a lifetime. Contemplation both nurtures human goodness (of which God is the source) and brings about healing within the one who contemplates. The person who practices contemplation engages in an act of love, both toward God and toward other people.

Second, the Author addresses the question, "How does one contemplate?" One approaches the act of contemplation through the general practice of some good habits as well as through the specific practice of turning to God. Such general good habits include: "purifying one's conscience," regular reading and/or listening to the Word of God, reflecting upon the Word of God, and seeking the "all-merciful God" (Johnston, 1973, 85, 92–93). Habits of seeing, hearing, and reflecting upon the Word of God are, perhaps, self-evident.

Purifying one's conscience involves the desire to become more authentic, that is, to refine the quality of one's character. In the fourteenth century, purification of conscience was expressed in practices such as examining one's conscience, confessing one's sins to a priest, and performing acts of penance.

Seeking the all-merciful God recognizes that God has given unique talents and gifts of personality to the individual (Johnston, 1973, 129, 140). At the same time, one also acknowledges that one is the recipient of frail human nature, also given by God, but containing "the blind root of evil and tendency to sin," which is also described as "the root and ground from which evil springs," "the lump of sin," and "the root and pain of our original sin" (Johnston, 1973, 93, 85, 137–138). The individual shares in the ground of evil residing in frail human nature. With this recognition, one continues to seek the all-merciful God in all of the actions of one's life.

In addition to the general practice of cultivating good habits, the Author of *The Cloud of Unknowing* articulates four specific "guidelines" for the practice of turning to God. The first guideline: choose a simple meaningful word, and attend to it. This action is a "naked intent towards God," the "desire for God alone" (Johnston, 1973, 56).

The second guideline: the resulting experience will be a "darkness" of mind, a "cloud of unknowing," or "nothing except a naked intent towards God in the depths of one's being" (Johnston, 1973, 48–49). One will feel "frustrated." One should continue to turn to God with a "burning desire" for God alone; one should "rest in the blind awareness of God's naked being" (Johnston, 1973, 59). The patient practice of such intent toward

God, amidst the sense of distance from God, will become like a "keen shaft" of love (Johnston, 1973, 63–64).

The third guideline: while thoughts and desires will arise within consciousness, one should abandon them and thereby place them under "the cloud of forgetting" (Johnston, 1973, 57–58). One should return to the awareness of the simple word or to the intent toward God.

The fourth guideline: if unduly powerful thoughts and desires arise, one should humbly give oneself over to God with them, and then return to the awareness of the simple word or to the intent toward God. One should patiently and peacefully await the coming of God (Johnston, 1973, 88–89).

These four concrete "guidelines" constitute the core of the Author's practical instruction for disposing oneself to contemplation. The person who follows the Author's advice over an extended period of time may perhaps find that the lived experience of being immersed in "unknowing" leaves her or him with a readiness for the significance of Teresa's metaphors as introduced in *The Interior Castle*.

Third, the Author addresses the question, "What are the effects of contemplation?" The Author of *The Cloud of Unknowing* is less focused in discussing the effects of contemplation than in defining it and in explaining how to go about it; however, the Author's varied perspectives of the effects of contemplation are both understandable and advantageous. After all, the Author, is no doubt, very personally involved in the practice of contemplation. When one is deeply affected by an experience, it can be difficult to be, at the same time, analytical and descriptive about it. However, the reader can be assisted by the identification of some of the specific effects of contemplation, and can resonate with aspects of their description.

Fourth, the Author addresses the question, "How does one discern the call to contemplation?" The Author of *The Cloud of Unknowing* offers several criteria for discerning the call to contemplation. The first criterion is one of freedom, in which the Author states directly that *The Cloud of Unknowing* is not intended for everyone. The reader should feel free to put it aside. However, if *The Cloud* strikes a chord in the heart of the reader, then one should be thankful and pray for its Author (a personal touch). Further, one should examine oneself to ascertain if one is purifying one's conscience, if one is attracted to simple contemplative prayer, and if one is drawn to fix one's "secret little love" upon the "cloud of unknowing" as one's principal concern. These are "the signs" of discernment (Johnston, 1973, 143–145).

In conclusion, the Author of *The Cloud of Unknowing* leaves the practitioner of contemplative prayer with God in the state of "unknowing" or in "the cloud of forgetting;" both of these states are left mysteriously undefined. One "knows" them because one has experienced them, however vaguely.

For some, the silent mystery of "unknowing" or of "the cloud of forgetting" is more than enough. After all, it is of God. Others seek some small assurance that they are treading an authentic path as they seek God in contemplative prayer.

While Teresa of Avila reiterates many of the teachings of the Author of *The Cloud of Unknowing,* she also provides penetrating analysis of what may be taking place in contemplative prayer. In addition, she suggests metaphors or allegories enabling the reader to understand her analysis and to identify the reader's own experience within the contemplative tradition.

The Interior Castle and Its Metaphors

Teresa of Avila (1515–1582) wrote *The Interior Castle* in Spain in 1577. It is considered to be the fruit of her mature reflection on the spiritual life and the culmination of her teaching on prayer. Teresa wrote *The Interior Castle* as an act of obedience in response to the order of Fr. Jerome Gratian (1545–1614), her spiritual director, confessor, and religious superior.

While Teresa was writing in obedience to Gratian's directives, she was well aware that her work was subject to the meticulous scrutiny of the Spanish Inquisitors. In her day, Teresa endeavored to maintain a delicate balance in the midst of apparently conflicting expectations. Over four hundred years later, *The Interior Castle* serves as a lens through which to view aspects of the contemporary experience of "unknowing."

It was evident that Teresa had known deep interior experiences of God, she was articulate about them, and that, as a woman, she was uniquely suited to instruct and to guide other women in the ways of prayer. Furthermore, Gratian wanted to understand Teresa's experience in prayer. Since her earlier writing, *The Life* (1562), in which she had discussed prayer, was in the hands of the church authorities in the Spanish Inquisition, Gratian directed Teresa to convey her experiences in a new work (Kavanaugh and Rodriguez, 1980, 263, n. 1, 481).

In completing *The Interior Castle,* Teresa contributed that for which she had longed during her own spiritual formation, namely, guidance derived through seasoned experience in the ways of contemplative prayer.

The Interior Castle consists of a "Prologue," seven sets of "Dwelling Places" (each containing between one and eleven chapters) and an Epilogue. Teresa's first three sets of "dwelling places" can be interpreted as an allegory describing the remembrance of one's lost identity, the invitation to return to a higher life, and the obstacles experienced along the way. The last four sets of "dwelling places" can then be seen as a description of the journey toward heaven or a return to the ideal world, a world far more real than one's lost idyllic world.

In "The Prologue," Teresa expresses her desire to be obedient to her religious superior (Jerome Gratian) and to the teachings of the holy Roman Catholic Church. She relies upon God as her source of strength. She will address the questions raised by her sisters about the journey of prayer, the mystical life.

Teresa assumes that "the language used between women" will be readily understood by her sisters. This last comment is important because, in Teresa's day, ordinarily, the individual sister spoke primarily with the male priest/ confessor about the progress of her spiritual life. To his credit, Gratian seems to have understood that sometimes the gender difference, with its consequent difference in life experiences, contributed to a gap in understanding a matter so intimate as a sister's prayer life. Such understanding contributes greatly to a fruitful working relationship between the one seeking spiritual guidance and the one offering it (Kavanaugh and Rodriguez, 1980, 282, Prologue, no. 4).

"The First Dwelling Places" suggests that each individual soul can be compared to a diamond or clear, crystal castle containing many dwelling places, a paradise wherein God and the soul commune, one with the other. The castle of one's soul contains many rooms surrounding the center wherein the King (the Lord) dwells. Temptation, however, lurks in some of these rooms. While the first dwelling places are those furthest from the center, the soul is encouraged to enter the castle, to wander about within it, and to explore the rooms of self-knowledge and the rooms where the

King's glory radiates. The brilliance of God's goodness should be the measure with which to evaluate one's own frailties and consequent need for growth. "By gazing at His grandeur, we get in touch with our own lowliness"(Kavanaugh and Rodriguez, 1980, 292, I.2, no. 9).

"The Second Dwelling Places" shelter those who are "vulnerable" to the Lord; yet these souls still choose to place themselves in "occasions of sin." They should persevere in the knowledge of God and in self-knowledge; they should embrace the cross and try to live in conformity with God and the desires of God. They would be wise to discuss their experiences with those who reside in dwelling places closer to the center of the castle. As they continue to pray and to seek the Lord, the Lord will carry them from one dwelling place to another.

"The Third Dwelling Places" houses those who try to refrain from "venial sins;" these persons practice penance, recollect themselves, engage in good works, strive for balance in their lifestyle, and desire deep union with God. Their focus should be upon love of God, and they should persevere in "nakedness and detachment" for God will give inner peace. While one is invited to become more like Christ, it is important to let go of anxiety and to humbly seek God's mercy.

In the first three "Dwelling Places," the metaphor of the castle itself, made from a diamond or clear crystal, suggests the beauty of one's soul, made in the image of God. Through the metaphor of a "call," one is invited to return to one's true self by entering the castle through the door of prayer and reflection. Insects, snakes, and other poisonous animals depict the temptations preventing a generous response. The faithful, steadfast soul experiences these temptations as kinds of suffering which may take many forms, including pain, loneliness, and the need for patience.

While temptations and suffering, although in different forms, continue as companions through one's life, the individual is nevertheless now ready to enter the "Dwelling Places" closer to the center of the castle, where "His Majesty" dwells. The metaphors of these inner "dwelling places" are Teresa's way of offering spiritual direction to the practitioner of contemplative prayer (Kavanaugh and Rodriguez, 1980, 283–284, I.1, no. 1; 294, I.2, no. 14; 298–299, II.1, nos. 2–4).

After lengthy experience in earlier dwelling places, one is brought to "The Fourth Dwelling Places," which are closer to the King and very beautiful. As the soul lives in dependence upon God and continues to strive for a balanced life of prayer and good works, God bestows consolations; one's heart becomes opened.

One is carried beyond discursive meditation to the grace of an awakened will, given to God. "The important thing is not to think much but to love much; and so do that which best stirs you to love." The faculties of the soul may be taken up completely with God, while at the same time the mind is being buffeted with distracting thoughts. This experience may be one of deep union in which the faculties of the soul are "suspended" in God. At a subsequent time, the gift of "suspension" (being taken up in God) is not present. While continuing without the concrete experience of being taken up in God can be painful, doing so provides an occasion to remain both peaceful and patient (Kavanaugh and Rodriguez, 1980, 319, IV.1, no. 7).

God gives deep delight, peace, quiet, and sweetness. God may absorb the intellect and instruct it in ways that cannot be explained; on the other hand, the intellect may remain active, while the will finds rest in God. One should surrender oneself to God in humility and with thanks.

In "The Fourth Dwelling Places," the metaphor of the fount of water flowing from a spring depicts spiritual delight or "The Prayer of Quiet," which the soul receives from God. At the same time, the metaphor of the Good Shepherd attracts the individual to receive the God-given gift of seeking God within oneself, "The Prayer of Recollection" (Kavanaugh and Rodriguez, 1980, 323–324, IV.2, nos. 2–4; 327–328, IV.3, no. 2).

In "The Fifth Dwelling Places," God wants to be enjoyed deep within the center of the person who is in prayer. All of the faculties are asleep to the things of the world and to oneself; one is left as if without one's senses and without the power to think. One does not understand how one loves.

One prepares to receive God through the sacraments, spiritual reading, prayer, penance, surrender to God, and efforts to grow in love of God and neighbor. The person experiences the subtle nuances of God's presence; he or she understands without understanding. One should ask God for sustenance and for grace to grow in self-knowledge and in love for others. After being in the fifth dwelling place, there is certainty that one's experience was of God.

In "The Fifth Dwelling Places," the metaphor of the silkworm/butterfly suggests "The Prayer of Union." Just as the silkworm enters the cocoon, dies, and emerges as a beautiful butterfly, so the soul enters darkness where it dies to temptations and distractions, and assumes a new life more cen-tered upon God than ever before (Kavanaugh and Rodriguez, 1980, 341–345, V.2, nos. 2–9; 348, V.3, no. 1; 350, V.3, no. 5).

In "The Sixth Dwelling Places," God wants to deepen the individual's desire for Godself. One suffers misunderstanding, illness, or the absence of an adequate confessor or spiritual guide. One grows in the realization of one's own nothingness, practices good works, and hopes in God.

God brings about delicate impulses in order to strengthen and purify the desire for deep union with God. There is a delightful and satisfying sense of being wounded by God, and the accompanying desire to suffer for God and to withdraw from earthly satisfactions.

Sometimes locutions, raptures, the rapture of the flight of the spirit, longings for God, fears of sin, or growth in self-knowledge occur. One should pray to Jesus Christ in his most sacred humanity; and one should unite oneself with the liturgy of the Church.

If one cannot pray discursively, one might let the intellect represent, for example, Jesus in his passion, in such a way that the impression of the passion is stamped upon the memory. One looks with a simple gaze upon Jesus and the will responds to him. The Lord may or may not suspend the faculties; it is important to continue to pray to Our Lord Jesus Christ.

When the Lord gives an intellectual vision, one feels Jesus' presence with certitude but one does not see him. When the vision recedes, one feels alone. In another kind of intellectual vision, the Lord grants suspen-sion in prayer; one sees God in all things and all things in God. This very brief vision engraves itself upon the soul.

Sometimes the Lord gives an imaginative vision in which he manifests his sacred humanity. The Lord seems truly alive to one's inner eye. An imaginative vision comes suddenly, stirs the faculties, and then places them in peace.

As one comes to know God more fully, one longs for an increasingly deeper experience of God. As this longing deepens, one experiences a deep, interior, intimate wound which seems to have come from some mysterious source. The body may be weakened at this point, and one is in solitude. The experience may be of brief duration or it may last for three or four hours.

In "The Sixth Dwelling Places," the metaphor of the desire experi-enced in betrothal suggests "spiritual betrothal" between God and the soul.

God permits the person to experience new kinds of suffering and, at the same time, God bestows visions and raptures (Kavanaugh and Rodriguez, 1980, VI.2, no. 4).

The Lord brings the soul into "The Seventh Dwelling Places" before "The Spiritual Marriage" is consummated. There is a place in the center of the soul where only His Majesty dwells. When God is united with the person in this place, the person has no understanding of what is happening; the faculties are "lost" in God. This experience differs from that of rapture or union because God is dwelling in the center of the soul; it is not as if the soul were above itself or outside itself, as may occur in rapture or union. The three Persons of the Trinity are revealed in an intellectual vision. There is an enkindling of spirit (Kavanaugh and Rodriguez, 1980, 430, VII.1, no. 6).

In "The Spiritual Marriage," the Lord is also revealed in his sacred humanity in the form of an imaginative vision, one significantly different from any previous gifts of God. In addition, union with God occurs deep in the center of one's soul through a delicate intellectual vision; then one continues with God at one's center. The soul is at peace, although the faculties, senses, and passions may be caught up in the trials, sufferings, and temptations of daily life. One becomes concerned to please God and to express love for God. Thus, prayer and the practice of virtue become the foundation for good works done in his service. From one's center where he resides, God gives strong desires to serve him; one should do what one can with great love.

The effects of "The Spiritual Marriage" include: forgetfulness of self, the desire to suffer, joy in suffering, the desire to serve God, an awareness of God's presence, an abiding state of quiet, and amazement at God's continuing presence and work.

"The Epilogue" states that the "castle" holds many more dwelling places than those described. One is encouraged to enter the "castle" for refreshment and renewal and to spend time in the "castle" in praise of God, in whose image she is created.

These metaphors serve to elucidate some of Teresa's more important teachings about contemplative prayer. She develops additional metaphors—such as a fiery brazier, the phoenix, a precious jewel in a reliquary, fine Dutch linen, the dove (which is very much the same figure as the silkworm/butterfly), a fiery arrow, and the divine breasts—to further delineate the nuances of her teaching on prayer. Perhaps the metaphors depicted above will entice the reader to seek and reflect upon other metaphors found within *The Interior Castle*.

Teresian Metaphor as Transition from "Unknowing" to "Being Known"

The Cloud of Unknowing and *The Interior Castle* offer valuable instruction in contemplative prayer. Each work presents its author's respective analysis of what can happen during the experience of contemplative prayer. Such analysis is well appreciated in view of the fact that when one truly engages in contemplative prayer, one becomes completely taken up in it; analysis after the fact is difficult to accomplish. Such analysis is also difficult for the twenty-first-century practitioner of contemplative prayer due to the rapid pace and sensory overload of contemporary culture. In addition, the culture does little to foster reflection upon one's inner realities. Furthermore, one may be hard pressed to identify one's own experience in prayer as "unknowing" or "quiet."

While the Author of *The Cloud of Unknowing* does offer some metaphors, such as "the keen shaft of love," Teresa of Avila in *The Interior Castle* offers a series of metaphors that serve to illumine the search for validation of the experience of the present-day practitioner of contemplative prayer.

Teresa's metaphors were significant in their day—and they are so now. They were linked to life, literally, as in the case of the fount of water or the silkworm/butterfly, and symbolically, as in the case of the castle or the King. People of Teresa's day and ours can relate to these metaphors in themselves because they connect with life. Furthermore, and this is the point of this chapter, when one reflects upon a specific experience in prayer in the light of a particular Teresian metaphor, it may be possible to situate oneself more firmly where one is and where one is called to be in prayer.

For example, one may reflect upon one's own experience of contemplative prayer and upon Teresa's metaphor of the silkworm/butterfly. As one identifies likenesses and differences between one's own prayer experience and Teresa's metaphor, one can come to the realization that perhaps one's own experience is like "The Prayer of Union." Or one might reflect upon a recent period of contemplative prayer and upon Teresa's metaphor of the desire; then one might identify one's own experience as resembling "spiritual betrothal."

The act of reflection upon one's experiences in prayer in conjunction with reflection upon the metaphors of *The Interior Castle* is integral not only to the fullness of one's prayer (Fleming, 1978, 52–53, n. 77;) but also to understanding the message of Teresa of Avila. One's prayer experience should be reflected upon with the aid of Teresa'a metaphors in order to possibly attain further insight into the workings of the Spirit of God in one's prayer. Thus, the life inherent within the metaphors can enable the individual to become more deeply aware of the dynamic content of the life that is one's prayer.

It may be argued, with good reason, that the situation should be reversed, that one's experience in contemplative prayer should be evocative of metaphor, and not the other way around as is suggested here. After all, Teresa herself appears to have derived the metaphors from her own experience in prayer and then linked them to images in life.

At the same time, one must bear in mind that the images derived from Teresa's experience in prayer are accessible to the contemporary contemplative as means of enabling the contemplative to situate one's experience in prayer within the framework of the Western tradition. A word of caution is in order here. One need not know—in fact, it is preferable not to know—with great clarity and certainty, the precise "stage" of prayer one is experiencing.

No one can fully portray the implications of a metaphor for another person. It is each one's responsibility to draw these metaphors close to her or his prayer experience, which may be more "intuitive" than "rational." One's prayer experience should be the measure of the metaphor and not the other way around. While placing primary emphasis upon one's experience in prayer, one might ask, "How does this metaphor help me to find God in my recent experience of prayer?" and "How does this metaphor enable me to experience 'being known' by God?"

Through reflection upon one's prayer with the aid of Teresa's metaphors, it is possible, and it can be helpful, to derive a sense of the context within which one is praying and thereby experience oneself in solitude, but not alone. At the same time, such reflection can enable an individual to experience the satisfying joy of "being known" by God.

In the midst of an experience of "unknowing," one can derive an intuitive glimmer of "being known" by God who dwells deep within the center of one's being. The metaphors of Teresa of Avila respond to the needs for validation presented by the critically formed consciousness of the twenty-first-century contemplative.

RESOURCES

Fleming, David. *The Spiritual Exercises of St. Ignatius: A Literal Translation and A Contemporary Reading* (St. Louis: Institute of Jesuit Sources, 1978).

Johnston, William, ed. *The Cloud of Unknowing and the Book of Privy Counselling* (New York: Doubleday, 1973).

Kavanaugh, Kieran and Rodriguez, Otilio. *The Collected Works of St. Teresa of Avila, Volume One, The Book of Her Life* (Washington, D.C.: ICS Publications, 1987).

_____. *The Collected Works of St. Teresa of Avila, Volume Two, The Interior Castle.* Second edition (Washington, D.C.: ICS Publications, 1980).

Turner, Denys. *The Darkness of God: Negativity in Christian Mysticism* (Cambridge: University Press, 1995).

9

THE VIRGIN MARY IN THE VISIONS OF HILDEGARD OF BINGEN (1098–1179)[1]

SHARON ELKINS

*H*ildegard's appeal today rivals her impact in her own times.[2] Orchestras and ensembles perform and record her music, both in versions that aim at historical accuracy and in ones freely adapted for modern tastes. In her native Germany, her herbal remedies are readily available in pharmacies. The manuscript illuminations from her visionary books are frequently reproduced. Her discussions of gender and her attitude toward nature impress serious scholars as well as New Age devotees. Hildegard claimed that her creative ideas were primarily the result of her visionary revelations, so the relevance today of her mystical experiences is unquestionable.

While many of Hildegard's creations are admired, some of her ideas are more problematic for us today. She wrote her mystical revelations to benefit her own contemporaries, especially the other Benedictine nuns with whom she lived. Like other religious figures of the twelfth century, she praised the monastic life more than marriage. Her high regard for lifelong virginity can alienate modern readers who feel virginity, especially for women, was over-valued in Christian history. However, while it is tempting to take from Hildegard only what one likes and ignore the rest, her visions form a complex whole.

Hildegard's steadfast commitment to her visionary experiences was not only useful for her nuns; it also enabled her to describe the foremost virgin of all virgins—the Virgin Mary—in ways that are still helpful today. Extracts from two of Hildegard's mystical works help focus some of her presentation of the Virgin Mary. The first is her earliest book of visions, the *Scivias*, short for *Know the Ways of the Lord*, written between 1141 and 1151. The second is her collection of songs, the *Symphonia*, probably begun after the *Scivias* and largely finished by 1158. In Hildegard's own day, the *Scivias* was the most renowned of her writings. Two influential churchmen were the impetus for this renown—Pope Eugenius III and the monastic leader Bernard of Clairvaux—who read part of it and encouraged her to make it public. Such an endorsement of a woman's writings was unprecedented. In our day, the *Symphonia* is probably the best known of her visionary works because of the splendid performances of it by musical ensembles like "Sequentia" and the "Anonymous Four."

Hildegard did not set out to be inventive in her ideas about Mary. Indeed, she did not even want to record her visions and make them public. Already as a young child, Hildegard had visionary experiences, but she learned to keep them secret so that she would not appear to be strange. She lived a religious life from at least the age of twelve, when her parents sent her to the anchoress, Jutta, at the monastery of Disibod. But Hildegard continued to keep her mystical experiences private, sharing them with only a few people. At the age of thirty-eight, after the death of Jutta, Hildegard became the leader (*magistra*) of the community of women with whom she lived. But even then, she did not publicize her mystical experiences.

Five years later, in 1141, when Hildegard was forty-three years old, the Voice of her visions told her to "say and write" what she saw and heard. For a while, she resisted the command of the Voice, who usually identified itself as the Living Light or as God the Father. Her reluctance is understandable; we do not know of any Christian women who previously publicized her visionary experiences.[3] Only after Hildegard was incapacitated with illness and confined to her sickbed was she persuaded to obey the Voice and to "cry out" and "write" (*Scivias*, "Declaration").[4]

Once Hildegard began recounting her visions, a flood of creativity was unleashed. She wrote three volumes of prose visions, more than seventy songs she mystically heard, and numerous letters that contain her visionary predictions. In addition to these accounts of her mystical experiences, she composed medical and scientific treatises, a secret language, and sermons.[5] In 1148, the visions led her to establish a new monastery, Rupertsberg, near Bingen, for her nuns, despite the opposition of the monks at Disibod where they had lived. Rupertsberg became so successful that Hildegard began a daughter house at Eibingen on the other side of the

Rhine, where nuns still keep alive her memory. Her popularity caused church leaders to invite her on several preaching tours, where she addressed crowds, including one in the cathedral of Cologne. Following the commands of the Voice helped Hildegard have an influence unparalleled among women of her day and, indeed, the echo of her work is still very much heard, and needed, in our own day.

Mary's Appearances in Scivias

Unlike most female mystics who would come after her, Hildegard did not personally participate in the visions she witnessed. Rather, she watched them unfold, in her waking state, as she heard "with fear and trembling" the Voice speaking to her, explaining what she saw and heard ("Declaration"). In general, Hildegard's visionary world was the inverse of what one might expect: she rarely saw people who had lived but, instead, she saw abstract concepts that assumed human or quasi-human forms. Instead of seeing saints in heaven or people from the historical life of Jesus, Hildegard saw virtues personified or architectural details of buildings—walls, pillars, towers—that represented things like the Zeal of God, God's Will, and Salvation.

This visionary world was filled with female characters, some of whom Hildegard described in terms similar to those often used for Mary. For instance, Hildegard saw a woman who "had a perfect human form in her womb." While this might bring to mind the pregnant Mary, the woman was, instead, Mother Zion, and the perfect child she bore was a daughter (I.iv.1, 16). Hildegard also saw a woman identified as "the mother of the Incarnation of the Son of God." But this woman was not Mary; rather, she was the Synagogue (I.v.1). Several of the women Hildegard saw were both virginal and procreative, the traits often reserved for Mary alone. Indeed, the portrayal of Mother Zion, Synagogue, Virginity, Mercy, and the Church are reminiscent of the way Hildegard's contemporary and patron, Bernard of Clairvaux, described Mary.

Relative to these other female figures, Mary played a minor role in Hildegard's visionary world. Yet Mary did appear and, in contrast to the other female characters, Mary was an actual historical individual. While the personified symbols spoke to Hildegard, Mary never actually spoke or appeared in a human form.[6] Hildegard saw Mary as the dawn, the early light of the new day. For centuries, Mary had been compared poetically to the aurora, but Hildegard said she actually saw Mary as the dawn.

In a number of visions, the Voice told Hildegard that Mary was like the dawn (I.vi.8, II.vi.11, III.i. 9). When Hildegard saw Mary as the dawn, however, the imagery was rich and complex. In one vision, Hildegard noticed something glowing red on the breast of a woman identified as the Church. The Voice then told her that the virginity of Mary was "a red glow like the dawn" on the breast of the Church because of "the most ardent devotion in the hearts of the faithful." The Voice added, "And you hear a sound of all kinds of music singing around her, 'like the dawn, greatly sparkling.'" The music indicated that "all believers should join with their whole wills in celebrating the virginity of that spotless Virgin in the Church" (II.ix.9.). According to this vision, faithful believers play a role in Mary's appearance as the dawn.

Equally complex is a second vision of Mary in which the Voice described Sanctity: "On her breast is the sign of the cross, about which a great radiance shines on her breast like the dawn." Hildegard learned that Sanctity "awakens, in the minds of believers who lovingly embrace her, the repeated remembrance of the Passion of Christ Jesus" who "was born without stain of sin from the beautiful dawn, the Virgin Mary" (III.ix.29). Another vision also linked Jesus with Mary's appearance as the dawn. Hildegard saw on a pillar, that represented Jesus' humanity, that "another radiance shines forth like the dawn." This meant that "God displays in His secret places the purity of the dawn, which is to say the Virgin Mary" (III.viii.12). When she saw Mary as the aurora, Hildegard clearly did not see the typical dawn.

Hildegard had one other type of vision of Mary in the *Scivias*. She was being shown several things when suddenly there appeared before her eyes "as if in a mirror the symbols of the Nativity, Passion and burial, Resurrection and Ascension of our Savior." The heavenly Voice explained to Hildegard that she was seeing "in a true vision (*manifestation*), the mysteries of Him Who came to earth to save humanity—His birth from the Virgin, suffering on the cross, burial in the tomb, rising again from the dead and ascension into heaven." The Voice then told Hildegard that "these mysteries shine before Me in the heavenly places; for I have not forgotten them, but they will appear before Me in great brightness like the dawn until the end of the world" (II.vi.17).

What exactly did Hildegard see in this multifaceted vision? It seems that she saw, as if in a mirror, symbols of mysteries that God sees. The reference to the "great brightness like the dawn" in which these symbols appear might have brought Mary to Hildegard's mind. But only once did the Voice mention Mary, in the reference to Jesus' "birth from the Virgin." Does this mean that Hildegard saw the birth of Jesus taking place before her eyes, as will happen in the visions of later women like Birgitta of Sweden (1303–1373)? Probably not, for Hildegard saw, through multiple layers of vision, a mystery reflected in a great brightness, not a historical recreation.[7] Even in this vision, the Mary that Hildegard saw was more a symbol than a person.

Mary as "the Virgin" in Scivias

When Hildegard saw Mary, she usually saw the glowing light of the dawn. But the Voice usually called Mary "the Virgin." Rarely referred to as "Mary" or "the Virgin Mary" or even "Mother," Mary is ubiquitous as "the Virgin." Sometimes the title "the Virgin" was unadorned: "I, the Father, sent My Son into the world, physically born of the Virgin," or "the mystery of the shining dawn, the Incarnation of the Son of God in the Virgin" (II.vi.9, 11). Other times, the Voice described "the sweet Virgin," "the chaste Virgin," or "the Blessed Virgin" (II.vi.15, 27, 28; III.viii.9).

Although Hildegard's visions usually omitted the Virgin's proper name, her womb (*uterus*) was a frequent topic of conversation (II.v.1; vi.12, 23). Hers was the womb that "was not wounded or corrupted but remained whole" (II.iv.7). The Virgin was intact, whole, and unbroken (*integritas*) (II.iv.8; III.vii.7, 8). The Virgin was "an unplowed field" in which Christ arose (II.vi.24; III.x.7). Indeed, Hildegard usually heard about the most sweet, pure, chaste Virgin when the Voice was making a point about Jesus' conception and sinlessness. Jesus, "miraculously born of the chaste Virgin, lacked all contamination of sin" (II.vi.20).

The basic point remained the same: whether or not the Virgin was chaste, pure, sweet, whole, a womb, or an unplowed field, what mattered was that she was the uncontaminated place of the Incarnation. Barbara Newman rightly noted that for Hildegard, the Incarnation, not the crucifixion, was the "center and final cause of creation" ([1987] 1997: 45). Mary's role in the Incarnation was the virginal conception and birth, and this is her function throughout the *Scivias*. Described poetically, Mary was the pure light in which the sun arose. In biblical terms, she was the Virgin who conceived and gave birth.

It is hard to identify active virtues in Hildegard's Virgin, for her purity, intactness, wholeness, and sweetness all refer to her inviolate nature. She rarely refers even to the Virgin's humility (I.ii.33). Given the variety of stories about Mary that Hildegard knew, the sharp focus of her visions is striking. The Voice does not mention Mary's role in the visitation, the presentation, the crucifixion, or Pentecost. Although the Voice refers repeatedly to the Virgin conceiving and giving birth, it does not narrate the stories of the annunciation and nativity. Had Hildegard seen an image of the human Mary or scenes from her life, she might have thought of other characteristics of Mary. It is hard to view a person and think only of one of her traits. But when Hildegard was shown Mary as the pure light in whom the sun arose, the visions reinforced the emphasis on the Virgin's conception and giving birth.

In the *Scivias*, the full implications of this sharp focus are not yet developed. However, Hildegard does recount two ways that the Virgin had ongoing significance. One had special relevance for her own community. Since Mary was defined ontologically, as being "the Virgin," with scant attention to her other virtues, Hildegard and her nuns were *ipso facto* like Mary. Hildegard learned in a vision that even the widows who joined her community imitated Mary's virginity (I.ii.24).[8] Priests also imitated Mary when they celebrated Mass: "For as the body of My Son came about in the womb of the Virgin, so now the body of My Only-Begotten arises from the sanctification of the altar" (II.vi.14, cf. 26, 34).

Only in the final vision of the *Scivias* does Hildegard begin to consider other ramifications of the virginal conception and birth. After all the instructions of the prose visions, she at last hears a series of songs to Mary, the saints, and the virtues (III.xiii.1).[9] Or, more accurately, the song visions, which Hildegard has already begun to record for her *Symphonia*, break into the prose *Scivias*, which she is finishing at the same time. New images for Mary emerge. Since this final vision has more in common with the songs in Hildegard's *Symphonia* than with the rest of the *Scivias*, I will treat it with the other songs.[10]

Nature Symbols for the Virgin in Hildegard's Songs[11]

The imagery for Mary is so rich in the Hildegard's songs that someone unfamiliar with the *Scivias* might miss the songs' focus. Even though the poetic song texts use additional symbols for Mary, they remained preoccupied with the virginal conception and birth. The consistency is not surprising, for Hildegard said that the songs also came to her in a visionary way. The main difference seems to be that visual images accompanied the words she heard in the *Scivias* while music accompanied the words of the songs.

As in the *Scivias*, the songs often call Mary "the Virgin": "most sweet and blessed" virgin; "O how precious is the virginity of this virgin" (116–117, 134–135). In the songs, Hildegard describes the Virgin's womb: "your womb held joy when all the harmony of heaven resounded from you"; "her womb the holy Godhead flooded with his warmth so a flower grew within her" (122–125, 134–135). The Virgin is the "matrix (*materia*) of sanctity," a "golden matrix" (122–123, 128–131). Like the *Scivias*, the songs omit narratives involving Mary. The virginal conception and birth remain central.

Hildegard saw Mary as the light of the dawn in the *Scivias*; the songs continue to use light imagery for her. She is "the aurora" (129–131, 264–265) as well as "luminous matter (*lucida materia*)" (114–115). The Virgin is "radiant (*illustrata*)" and "illumined by divine radiance" (136–137). Often the references to the Virgin as light occur as part of a sequence that Hildegard hears as a melodic line: "from your womb, O Dawn, came forth a new sun"; "the Son of God came forth from her secret chamber like the dawn" (128–131, 134–135). The songs tell the Virgin that the "unclouded beauty of the sun poured into you" (114–115). Even the Virgin's mind was illuminated (132–133; *Scivias* III.xiii.1). Radiant, sparkling with light, the Virgin is a resplendent jewel (112–115). The examples of these light images are far too many to enumerate.

Although twelfth-century prayers often sought Mary's intercession with her Son, Hildegard rarely did. One song refrain asks, "Pray for us to your child, Mary, star of the sea," referring to Mary in a familiar way (112–113). But the two other songs that asked Mary for her help made unusual requests. One wanted the Virgin to "deign to set us frail ones free from our bad habits" (120–121); instead of interceding with her Son,

Mary was asked to reform the petitioners. The other song asked her to "gather the members of your Son into celestial harmony" (128–131), a fitting plea for singers to make.

In the songs, an image occurs frequently that is only prominent in the last vision of the *Scivias*: Mary is a "sweet green branch" (III.xiii.1), "a leafy branch (*frodens virga*)" (120–121) or "the greenest branch (*viridissima virga*)" (126–131). The appropriateness of the image is striking: *virga*/ branch sounds much like *virgine*/virgin. This branch buds from the stock of Jesse, as did the Jesse trees that had recently become popular visual symbols of Mary's genealogy. From this *virgine*/*virga* comes a wondrously bright flower that opens on the branch (124–125, 132–133, 134–135). Like the sun that rises in the dawn, a flower opening is another striking symbol for virginal fruitfulness.

Sometimes the songs conflate the images of womb and branch: "her womb brought forth wheat and the birds of heaven made their nests in it"; "the tender shoot that is her Son opened paradise through the cloister of her womb"; "your womb blossomed at the entrance of God's Spirit" (126–129, 134–137). The growth metaphors produced lines suitable for the music that accompanied them: "When the time came for you to blossom in your branches, . . . the heat of the sun distilled in you a fragrance like balsam. For in you bloomed the beautiful flower that gave fragrance to all the spices that had grown dry" (126–129).

In these songs, Hildegard remained more preoccupied with the virginal conception and birth than any other twelfth-century theologian. Having no responsibility to preach on the full liturgical cycle or to expound on all of the Virgin's virtues, Hildegard did not need to narrate the corpus of Marian stories. She did not linger on the image of Mary as the mother who held and nursed her Son nor as the one who uttered the *Magnificat*. Rather than develop these familiar stories, Hildegard used nature images of light and growth that emphasized virginal potentiality and fertility.

Described with these images, the Virgin sounds more like a force in nature than a human being. Hildegard was too orthodox to have been consciously promoting such a radical view of Mary, but one can wonder whether her contemporaries drew any parallels between Mary and the nature goddesses. This Virgin was passive: the green vitality flowed through her; the source of her energy is God the Father, who is pleased with her

(122–125, 129–133). Yet it was "her holy body" that "overcame death" (125). The Virgin contained the life-giving force; she blossomed; she gave birth to the sun.

Except for one time when Mary cries out (see below), the Virgin is silent in Hildegard's songs. People address the Virgin and talk about her, but only in one poem-song without surviving music does the Virgin speak (260–261). The poetic language that Mary uses in this address to her Son builds on the now familiar themes:

> O beloved Son, whom I bore in my womb by the might of the circling wheel of the holy Godhead who created me and arranged all my limbs and laid in my womb all manner of music in all the flowers of the tones: Now a great flock of virgins follows me and you, O sweetest Son. Deign by your help to save them.

While Hildegard never recorded musical notes for the Virgin's words, she heard music, perhaps like the music in the Virgin's womb. And like the light dawning, music comes to birth in a virginal way.

Mary and Eve in Hildegard's Songs

Although the songs are filled with nature images for the Virgin like those in the *Scivias*, there is one important difference: in most of the Marian songs, she is also contrasted with Eve or Adam. The *Scivias* was organized chronologically; it told the history of creation, the fall, and salvation. Hence, it treated the story of Eve and Adam long before it dealt with Mary's virginal conception and birth.[12] Lacking a similar organizational principle, the songs often described Mary as being the one who countered the sin of the first humans.[13] While contrasting Eve and Mary was a traditional practice begun in the second-century, when Mary became known as the "Second Eve," Hildegard's visions refer to only a few components of this comparison.

Often the songs' juxtaposition of Mary and Eve again highlights the virginal conception and birth, for the Virgin's way of reproducing contrasted with Eve's. But in the comparisons with Eve, Mary is also portrayed as an active human being. Mary is called "O saving lady (*O Salvatrix*)" (129–131); Mary crushes and tramples the serpent that tempted Eve (110–111); Mary "poured ointments on the sobbing wounds of death that

Eve built into torments for the souls" (112–113). After tearing down the house of death that Eve had built, the Virgin rebuilt salvation (112–113, 116–117). Mary even has a voice: "While the unhappy parents were blushing at their offspring . . . , then you [Mary] cry out with a clear voice, lifting humankind in this way from that malicious fall" (118–119).

The only times Hildegard portrays an active Mary are in the songs with Eve. Usually Mary and Eve counter each other's actions. One woman blots out the malice that flowed from the other; one woman beautifies heaven more than the former marred the earth. "Because a woman constructed death, a bright virgin demolished it. Therefore the supreme blessing comes in the form of a woman beyond all creation" (116–117). But in one song, their common identity as women (*feminae*) seems more important than their differences. This song moves without a break from praising the woman produced from the side of man, the "mirror of all God's beauty," to praising Mary, greatly loved of God (128–131). It is as if only reflecting on the woman Eve stirred Hildegard from her preoccupation with Mary as fecundity, light, potentiality, and luminous matter.

In repairing the damage that Eve brought, Mary became active in a way Hildegard and her nuns could imitate. Just as Mary poured healing ointment on the wound of sin, Hildegard used and wrote about medicinal herbs. She was like Mary the builder, for she herself oversaw the construction of Rupertsberg and its daughter house at Eibingen. And like Mary who cried out with a clear voice, Hildegard began recording her visions when the Voice told her to "cry out" and write.

Conclusion

By the time Hildegard finished the *Scivias* and *Symphonia*, she had fully developed her idea of Mary. Space does not permit extending this detailed analysis into Hildegard's two major later visionary works—*The Book of the Rewards of Life* (1158–1163) and *The Book of Divine Works* (1163–1173)—but they contain no significant changes in their treatment of Mary. Hildegard still does not see Mary in a human form; rather, she continues to refer to Mary as "the Virgin," to stress the virginal conception, and to credit Mary with establishing the Order of Virginity. There are only a few new images for Mary in these books.[14] *The Book of the Rewards of Life* compares the Virgin to a white cloud through which the sun shines

(IV.xxiii.440; trans. Hozeski 1994: 187).[15] *The Book of Divine Works* says she is like the slumbering (*dormientem*) earth which came uncontaminated from Abraham (I.i.17), perhaps a reference to her Immaculate Conception. Nature imagery for the Virgin remains prominent.

Hildegard's treatment of Mary shows how a visionary could be innovative while staying within orthodox parameters. Focusing on the virginal conception and birth, Hildegard's visions dealt with a traditional theme. But focusing so exclusively on this one topic, ignoring virtually everything else about the Virgin, the visions presented a novel view of Mary. Instead of being the intercessor with her Son, Mary was the dawn, a budding branch, luminous matter. Fertility and radiance were her main characteristics.

For Hildegard and her community, the virginal potentiality of Mary affirmed their nature. As part of the new Order of Virginity that Mary had helped to initiate, these women were like Mary in their very being. But Mary was also like the early morning light, the budding branch, and even the earth itself. By describing Mary in images from nature, Hildegard presents a Mary who is an archetype, a symbol of fecundity and new life.

If Christians thought of budding trees and the dawn's early light as Mary, then they might have a greater appreciation of the natural world. Hildegard's Mary could aid ecofeminists and others who want new images that better integrate God and the world.[16] Mystics like Hildegard help us understand the tradition in new ways. But another significance of Hildegard for us is not related to the specifics of what she said and did. She shows the wisdom of trusting one's visions, accepting one's inspirations. Maybe her example will encourage others also to share their visionary insights.

NOTES

1. I wish to thank Mark Burrows for his helpful comments on the version of this paper that I presented at the American Society of Church History Spring Meeting in April 2000.

2. The best books about Hildegard include Newman (1987) 1997, Newman 1998, Flanagan (1989) 1998, and Burnett and Dronke 1998.

3. Perpetua is the only woman one might consider a precursor, yet her situation was radically different. In Carthage at the beginning of the third century, Perpetua recorded four brief dream-visions she had while in jail awaiting martyrdom. After her death, the redactor of her martyrdom publicized these four visions.

4. Although I have utilized the critical Latin edition of Hildegard's *Scivias* by Führkötter and Carlevaris (1978), I have cited the English translation by Hart and Bishop (1990).

5. For bibliography, see Newman (1987) 1997: 281–282.

6. Hildegard also saw Eve, whom she considered to be a historical figure, in a symbolic way, as a white cloud containing "within itself many and many stars" (I.ii.10, 11).

7. The manuscript illuminations that accompany the *Scivias* portray Mary in a human form only twice in order to illustrate this vision and the final one in the book. Instead of showing the birth of Jesus from the Virgin, the illumination shows Mary seated beside the baby Jesus, who is in a tomb-like manger. Whether Hildegard was responsible for the illuminations for *Scivias* is much debated: see Madeline Caviness in Newman 1998: 110–124 and in Burnett and Dronke 1998: 29–42. Caviness argues that deviations between the text of the visions and its illumination indicate that Hildegard was the painter; since Hildegard was alive when these illuminations were made, she alone would have dared to depart from her prose text. Others contend that the deviations suggest that some-one other than Hildegard conceived the illuminations, for Hildegard would have strictly reproduced in both prose and art what she had seen in her visions. In either case, looking at the illumination, one would not know that the ways of seeing in this vision were as multilayered as Hildegard describes in the text.

8. The nuns' virginity also meant they were like Christ, for, along with Mary, the virgin Christ instituted the new Order of Virginity and made it glorious (I.iii.5; II.v. 7, 9). Speaking as God the Father, the Voice further endorsed virginity, saying, "Virginity was made by Me, for My Son was born of a virgin" (I.ii.24). Although Hildegard repeatedly commented on the nuns' virginity, she only rarely referred to them as brides of Christ (II.vi.76; III.viii.16). Beer argues that Hildegard eschews nuptial imagery because she saw herself as the faithful warrior and "the nurturing mother, not the ecstatic lover. So, on those occasions that she does use sexual imagery to explain her relation to God, she emphasizes that it is procreative, rather than erotic, in nature" (1992: 52, 54).

9. The second time Mary is represented as a woman in the manuscript illuminations for *Scivias* is in the illustration that accompanies this Vision 13 of Book III. However, from what is said in the vision itself, there is no indication that Hildegard saw Mary in a human form.

10. In general, this final vision in *Scivias* seems to be an earlier version of Hildegard's morality play *Ordo Virtutum*. However, the imagery for Mary in this final vision in *Scivias* is more extensive than in the antiphon that begins *Ordo Virtutum*.

11. All song references are to the final vision of the *Scivias* or to Newman [1988] 1998. I utilize Newman's literal translations.

12. For rare contrasts between Mary and Eve in the *Scivias*, see III.viii.15.

13. The contrast between Eve and Mary encouraged great melodic variations. On Hildegard's music, see Stevens in Burnett and Dronke 1998: 163–187.

14. Because it is a visionary interpretation of Scripture, *The Book of Divine Works* includes traditional biblical metaphors for and stories about Mary that were not in the earlier books of visions (III.ii.3, iv.12, v.8). See also Derolez and Dronke 1996: lxxi.

15. In *Scivias*, Eve was described as a radiant cloud; see endnote 6 above. Perhaps this image also links the two women.

16. See for instance Sallie McFague (1993).

RESOURCES

Beer, Francis. *Women and Mystical Experience in the Middle Ages* (Rochester, NY: Boydell Press, 1992).

Burnett, Charles and Peter Dronke, eds. *Hildegard of Bingen: The Context of Her Thought and Art* (London: Warburg Institute, 1998).

Flanagan, Sabina. *Hildegard of Bingen: A Visionary Life* (London and New York: Routledge, 1989, 1998).

Hildegard of Bingen (Hildegardis Bingensis). *The Book of the Rewards of Life* (Liber Vitae Meritorum) [1158–1163], trans. Bruce W. Hozeski (New York and Oxford: Oxford University Press, 1994).

_____. *Liber Divinorvm Opervm* [1163–1173], eds. Albert Derolez and Peter Dronke. CCCM 96 (Turnhout: Brepols, 1996).

_____. *Liber Vite Meritorvm* [1158–1163], ed. Angela Carlevaris. CCCM 90 (Turnhout: Brepols, 1995).

_____. *Ordo virtutum* [1141–1151], ed. and trans. Peter Dronke in Nine Medieval Latin Plays. (Cambridge: Cambridge University Press, 1994).

_____. *Scivias* [1141–1151], eds. Adelgundis Führkötter and Angela Carlevaris. CCCM 43-43a (Turnhout: Brepols, 1978).

_____. *Scivias* [1141–1151], trans. Mother Columba Hart and Jane Bishop (New York: Paulist, 1990).

_____. *Symphonia* [mid-twelfth century], ed. and trans. Barbara Newman (Ithaca and London: Cornell University Press, 1988, 1998).

McFague, Sallie. *The Body of God: An Ecological Theology* (Minneapolis: Fortress Press, 1993).

Newman, Barbara. *Sister of Wisdom: St. Hildegard's Theology of the Feminine* (Berkeley and Los Angeles: University of California Press, 1987, 1997).

_____. ed. *Voice of the Living Light: Hildegard of Bingen and Her World* (Berkeley, Los Angeles, and London: University of California Press, 1998).

10

CHRISTIAN MYSTICISM IN POSTMODERNITY: THÉRÈSE OF LISIEUX AS A CASE STUDY

MARY FROHLICH

*T*hérèse of Lisieux died of tuberculosis in 1897 at the young age of twenty-four, having spent the last nine years of her life as a cloistered Carmelite nun. She very quickly became, and continues to be, an astonishingly popular saint. Canonized in 1925, she was named a Doctor of the Church in 1997, on the hundredth anniversary of her death. Throughout the world, most parish churches include a shrine to Thérèse, and often it is the most visited spot in the church. A recent global tour of her relics drew crowds in the tens of thousands at every stop. Millions of people of every race and nation profess deep affection for her, and place their trust in her prayers.

Was Thérèse a "mystic"? Obviously, one's answer depends on the understanding of mysticism from which one is operating. The question is of particular interest because Thérèse appeared on the scene just as modernity gave way to postmodernity, and one of the characteristics of this postmodern era is an increasingly widespread interest in mysticism. At the same time, the variety and divergence of positions on what mysticism is and does is also exploding. An exploration of how a mutually critical conversation among a variety of contemporary perspectives on mysticism is necessary if we are to respond adequately to the question of whether Thérèse may rightly be called a "mystic."

In this exploration, two distinct sets of concerns are interwoven. One is the interest of scholars from the field of religious studies in finding a basically secular and explanatory theory of mysticism; the other is the interest of Christian theologians in defining a specifically Christian mysticism. Thérèse makes a particularly interesting case study for an inquiry into mysticism exactly because there is such a discrepancy between her revered status within the believing community and the general poverty of interest in her on the part of secular scholars.

In the context of postmodernity, both theologians and secular scholars *need* to engage in serious conversation with one another in order to make sense out of mysticism. An exploration of Thérèse's story using both types of perspectives shows how such a dialogue raises new questions—and offers new possibilities—for those focused on each set of concerns.

Mysticism: From Ancient Greece to Postmodernity

Recent studies have demonstrated quite decisively that "mystical" is not a univocal term; that is, it has had quite different meanings in different eras, and the way it is commonly used today is actually quite novel in relation to the longer history. Grace Jantzen's *Power, Gender, and Christian Mysticism* traces the origins of the term in the mystery religions, for which the *mystikoi* were those who had been initiated into the secret rites which were not to be revealed to noninitiates. Next came a Platonic usage, in which the "mystery" is that which is known only when one moves as far as possible beyond the realm of ordinary bodily life and perception, into the realm of the immaterial spirit. This basic understanding of the mystical as "something hidden yet revealed to some" remains foundational for Western philosophical and theological traditions.

In Greek translations of the Hebrew Scriptures, the term appeared in a story context: the king, facing a crisis, devises a *mysterium* or "secret plan" that he shares only with a few trusted advisors (Judith 2:2; Tobit 12:7). In the early Christian context, the "mystery" was the hidden-and-revealed Christ discovered when one gains true insight into Scripture. Later, this meaning was applied to the sacraments: here, too, there is a literal presence within whose depths is hidden the living presence of Christ. Christian theologians have continued to emphasize that the essential meaning of the mystical is simply the gift of divine life that God freely shares with human beings; hence, all Christians share in the mystical life even though some may receive special or more intensely manifested gifts.

The idea of mysticism as direct, experiential communication from God began to emerge only in the later Middle Ages. Many of the most studied mystics are from this period, when many dramatic visions and ecstasies were recorded in textual form. Yet, the modern understanding of the mystical, which has held sway from the Enlightenment until fairly recently, has a very different kind of focus on "experience" than did these medieval mystics. The medievals, it seems, did not view recounting their experiences as a matter of describing past events of the inner life. Rather, they saw themselves as living in a communal drama of shared life with God, within which the act of recounting their visions or insights was equally a part of the drama (Suydam and Ziegler). As Jantzen spells out, the modern view emerged as a reaction to the Cartesian and Kantian problematic of ultimate disjunction between the knowing mind and the known reality. In various ways, the "mystical" is proposed as an antidote: here is a unique kind of "experience" that transcends this alienating dichotomy. Much interest develops in defining the exact character of such an experience, and in claiming it as a proof or way of access to what is most real (whether that is defined as "God" or in nontheistic terms).

Although we are now said to be within a postmodern era, the postmodern still operates within the modern problematic of the disjunction between human consciousness and reality. It is characteristic of postmodernity, however, to assert that there can never be a single "grand theory" or "grand narrative" that resolves this problem; rather, human consciousness is by nature fragmentary, transient, and incapable of root self-knowledge. One response to this may be to celebrate mysticism as a kind of orgiastic letting-go to the ever-changing flow of the Now (Cupitt). By first delineating a rough typology of four presently operative explanatory approaches to mysticism, the case of Thérèse of Lisieux can then be discussed in relation to each of them. The "postmodern" element of this is that on the one hand each different stance may appear to deconstruct or undermine the others while, on the other hand, the interplay of perspectives opens up insight on levels not possible through any one of them alone. The question of a Christian faith perspective continually plays among the explanatory views, and needs to be explicitly addressed.

Four Explanatory Approaches to Mysticism

I. *Mysticism as intense, extraordinary spiritual experiences.* Here the "mystical" is identified with unusual experiential phenomena such as visions, ecstasies, paranormal insight, etc. Even among those who are theologically well educated, this is more often than not the first meaning of the term when it is used within ordinary conversation. A presumption that is not always stated is that "experience" is intentional—that is, it involves a subject attending to an object (the object, in this case, being a vision, an ecstatic feeling, etc). Many contemporary studies of mysticism implicitly or explicitly take this definition as a starting point, searching spiritual texts for accounts and descriptions of unusual experiences in order to analyze them. Often, the approach taken is a "constructivist" one, which presumes that mystical experiences are necessarily specific to an era, a religion, a culture, and even to the psychosocial history of an individual person. Constructivists presume that there is no essence, no common core, no crosscultural common denominator of mysticism (Katz; Jantzen).

II. *Mysticism as availability to a transcendent, nonintentional core dimension.* This approach goes to the opposite extreme, stripping away all attributes from the "experience" that is defined as mystical. Or, it may deny that mysticism has anything at all to do with experience. An example of the redefinition of experience is the argument that mystics transcend intentionality, and that the core of mysticism is no longer definable in terms of subject and object. These scholars argue against constructivism by asserting that we can discover within the mystics' accounts references to occasions ("experiences") when they entered into a state of pure, unlimited consciousness and thus transcended anything definable by culturally specific terms and categories (Forman). Other scholars—for example, Denys Turner—deny that this central apophatic moment is in any sense an "experience"; rather, it is better defined as a faith conviction that God is active in a dimension that one does *not* know.

III. *Mysticism as a language-event evoking mystery.* In his *Mystical Languages of Unsaying*, Michael Sells takes the argument against defining mysticism in terms of experience to another level. After all, he says, we can never really have access to whatever experiences the mystics may have had. All we actually have are texts; and these he brilliantly analyzes to show how five mystics from different cultural and religious settings use remarkably similar linguistic strategies to create an "anarchic" moment of meaning that breaks apart ordinary categories and thus evokes "mystery." Sells concludes that we simply have to prescind from the question of whether there is a common mystical experience, or even whether we can define any particular experience as mystical. What remains is mystical language and its potential to evoke in us something of high value.

IV. *Mysticism as performance of a mystical drama.* A number of recent studies, especially of medieval mystics, have explored mystical phenomena as communally enacted dramatizations of the root religious story of the culture (Suydam and Ziegler). A newly emerging position, represented by Mark McIntosh and Frederick Christian Bauerschmidt, unites the postmodern insights into language and performance with an explicit Christian theological commitment. The "mystical," then, is what is enacted in the liturgical anamnesis of Jesus' bodily self-giving into community. Thus, the "mystical body politic of Christ" is "an actualized practice of compassion and forgiveness . . . a visible sign of an alternative to other visions of human community" (Bauerschmidt, 197).

Thérèse of Lisieux as a Case Study

Thérèse Martin grew up as the youngest of five daughters in a deeply pious French family of the late nineteenth century. When she was nine years old, her favorite older sister (Pauline) entered the Carmel of Lisieux; four years later, a second sister (Marie) did the same. On Christmas Eve of 1886, just before she turned fourteen, Thérèse experienced a radical conversion and became determined to enter Carmel herself as soon as possible. Refused by the local chaplain and the bishop, she took her case to the pope and, although he did not directly give the permission, she did in fact enter Carmel at the age of fifteen.

In most regards, Thérèse's life there was quite mundane, although despite her youth she was very quickly made assistant to the novice mistress. Among the novices with whom she was charged were another Martin sister (Céline) and a cousin (Marie Guérin). On the eve of Good Friday, 1896, Thérèse coughed up blood—a sign of serious tubercular illness. Shortly thereafter, she found herself in a deep state of interior darkness, which apparently continued until her death eighteen months later on September 30, 1897.

The main vehicle of Thérèse's popularity has been her autobiographical

Story of a Soul (1898), although the critical edition of her complete works runs to eight volumes and includes letters, plays, poems, transcribed conversations, and prayers. Shortly after she died, her sister Pauline (now Mother Agnes) edited Thérèse's manuscript so that it better fit the preconceptions of popular spirituality of that era. It was then published, and the sisters took promotion of Thérèse as the task of the remainder of their lives (into the 1960s). In 1956, the unedited version of her basic text finally became available to scholars and, eventually, to the public.

An examination of the incidents and texts from *Story of a Soul* supports a further exploration into the case for Thérèse as mystic according to each of the four positions sketched above. (Numbers in parentheses refer to pages in the 1996 Institute of Carmelite Studies translation of *Story of a Soul*.)

I. *Mysticism as intense, extraordinary spiritual experiences.* If this is taken as one's primary understanding of mysticism, it is somewhat difficult—but not impossible—to make a case for Thérèse as mystic. A careful reading of her texts reveals at least two or three events that could perhaps be accounted as "visions," as well as a number of references to other intense experiences of God.

The first "visionary" experience is the most ambiguous. When Thérèse was six or seven years old, she was gazing out an upper-story window of her home, when she was terrified by the sight of a veiled figure passing through the garden below. The figure looked like her father, walking stooped over with an apron over his face (45–46), but her father was out of town at the time, and it was very unlikely that anyone had, in fact, walked through the garden. The interpretation of this as a prophetic vision came much later, when Thérèse's father endured a humiliating illness that cast a "veil" over his mental faculties.

When Thérèse was ten years old, she herself became extremely ill. For several months she was attacked by waves of incapacitating paralysis and hallucinations. Then, on Pentecost Sunday, while two of her sisters wept and prayed beside her, Thérèse looked up at a nearby statue of Mary and was moved to the core of her being by the Virgin's radiantly tender smile. She was instantly cured of her malady (65–66). This incident has been much discussed, since it is not clear whether her illness was a hysterical reaction to stress, the first effect of infection by the tuberculosis pathogen, or some other form of pathology. Nevertheless, the character and content of her healing experience do seem to qualify as "visionary"—regardless of what additional explanation one may wish to propose.

On May 9, 1896—a month after Thérèse had entered into her final spiritual darkness, which would last until her death one and a half years later—she had a remarkable dream of being visited by Venerable Anne of Jesus (one of the companions of St. Teresa of Avila, sixteenth-century foundress of Thérèse's branch of the Carmelite Order). She had never previously had any interest in Anne, but now experienced the most profound consolation as Anne embraced her with sisterly love and reassured her that God was "very content" with her. This dream-vision left Thérèse with the felt conviction that "there was a heaven, and that this heaven is peopled with souls who actually love me" (191).

One can also find references to Thérèse's experience of the infinity of God's love. She speaks of "the rivers or rather the oceans of grace that flooded my Soul" (181); of "the shoreless ocean of [God's] love" (254); and of the "abyss [of God's love] whose depths I cannot fathom" (256). Yet, much more prominent in her writings is her repeated insistence that her path is *not* characterized by the extraordinary. A typical statement is, "Do not believe I am swimming in consolations; oh, no, my consolation is to have none on earth" (187). She explicitly states that her retreats, including the one before her profession, were arid and without consolation (165). Her final months were a time of "thickest darkness" (211). If one studies Thérèse's life with a balanced perspective, it is evident that, for her, ordinariness, smallness, and obscurity were far more predominant than the occasional burst of dazzling light.

In short, Thérèse is not likely to be chosen as an outstanding example of the mystic if one's definition rests largely on a notion of extraordinary experiences. This, as well as the fact that she neither presents a schema of degrees of progress in the spiritual life nor offers a developed doctrine of a traditional mystical state such as "transforming union," excludes her from most contemporary anthologies of mystical texts. Yet, her life also offers an implicit critique of this first way of understanding mysticism; for what is "extraordinary" about Thérèse simply does not come to the fore if one looks for it only on the level of the unusual and paranormal forms of experience.

II. *Mysticism as availability to a transcendent, non-intentional core dimension.* Denys Turner's *The Darkness of God* presents perhaps the best-developed argument against definitions of mysticism that focus on extraordinary experience. His main point is that any positive or negative experiences are only "feedback" from the activity of God, which is fundamentally beyond the sensing capacity of the human psyche. The most profound mysticism, then, is not that which is manifested in extraordinary experiences but, rather, that which radically accepts God's "unknown" activity as the core of one's being and then organizes the practice of ordinary life on that basis.

It is much easier to recognize Thérèse as a mystic with this approach. For example, when she describes her preprofession retreat as characterized by "the most absolute aridity and almost total abandonment," she goes on to say that this is because "Jesus was sleeping as usual in my little boat." She then speaks of how she learns "the way to please Him and to practice the most sublime virtues" as "He nourishes me at each moment with a totally new food; I find it within me without my knowing how it is there." When she states that for seven years she has "slept" during her hours of prayer, like a child asleep in her parent's arms, she adds that, after all, doctors put their patients to sleep when they wish to perform operations; thus she signals her awareness that it is in this sleepy, totally surrendered "unknowing" that God is most powerfully at work (165). Another typical text says, "Never have I heard [Jesus] speak, but I feel that He is within me at each moment; He is guiding and inspiring me with what I must say and do" (179).

In these and many other texts we see Thérèse affirming a radical sense that she lives in God and God lives in her, even though more often than not her psychological experience is of an absence rather than a presence. Thérèse was deeply formed in the teaching of her Carmelite mentor St. John of the Cross, for whom it is in the "dark night" that God is most truly discovered. Her most foundational image, the Holy Face, expresses this paradox on the psychological level: the Face of Jesus, the most intimate expression of God's presence, appears to her as humiliated, abused, veiled, unresponsive. The eighteen-month "night of faith" that culminated her life can be read as the fruit of her complete surrender to the God who is known only in unknowing. If a mystic is one who totally opens her life to a divine dimension completely beyond the capacity of the human person to grasp, comprehend, or control, Thérèse gives evidence of qualifying.

An advantage of this approach to mysticism is its clear acknowledgment that what is "hidden and revealed" in the mystical life is genuinely transcendent. A disadvantage, however, is that a rigorous insistence that the transcendent dimension can be neither actually experienced nor truly named may lead to an inarticulateness about the criteria that qualify a person or phenomenon as mystical. We find evidence that Thérèse lived a virtuous life, and that it was rooted in faith rather than in a felt sense of God's presence; but can this not be said of millions of others as well? To democratize mysticism by saying that every genuinely virtuous person has, *prima facie*, surrendered her or himself to the God of mystery is, perhaps, a half-truth. Something more needs to be said about how the fullness of mystical life manifests itself.

III. *Mysticism as a language-event evoking mystery.* One approach is that of Michael Sells, who shifts the focus entirely from experience to language. What the mystic experienced is inaccessible, and is perhaps no longer of interest even to the mystics—who often seem more intent on subverting the subject and object of experience than in positing them. But mystical language can be analyzed, with the discovery that it typically strives to create a meaning event that "does not describe or refer to mystical union but effects a semantic union that re-creates or imitates the mystical union" (Sells, 9). That is, by strategies of saying and unsaying—by "wild" propositions" and seemingly contradictory anti-propositions—the reader's insight is broken open to what is beyond saying.

Sells chooses for analysis five of the most profoundly apophatic and philosophical Western mystics: Plotinus, John Scotus Eriugena, Ibn 'Arabi, Marguerite Porete, and Meister Eckhart. At first glance, Thérèse does not seem to fit in their company. Most of her discourse is simple, conversational, devotional. Yet, an occasional turn of phrase catches our attention as, indeed, enacting the apophatic "turn." One of the best known is her statement: "Yes, in order that Love be fully satisfied, it is necessary that It lower Itself, and that It lower Itself to nothingness and transform this nothingness into fire" (195). This fulfills all three of Sells' characteristics of classical Western apophatic language: an underlying metaphor of outflow or overflow; an "unsaying" that identifies the fullness of being (Love) with nonbeing (nothingness); and a revealing of the utterly transcendent within the utterly immanent (Sells, 6). Using these characteristics as a guide, one can locate a deep apophatic undercurrent in Thérèse's use of language.

Yet, this undercurrent rarely surfaces with the intensity that one finds in the much more dramatic writings of many others. Once again, it is unlikely that Thérèse will attract a great deal of attention from those for whom this approach is definitive. That very fact reveals a weakness of this approach: it appears to limit mysticism to those with the gifts and inclination to employ language in a very particular, intense, and sophisticated manner.

IV. *Mysticism as performance of a mystical drama.* Mary Suydam is one of a number of scholars who have developed the idea of mystical spirituality as "interactive and performance-oriented." Suydam defines performance as "any action, done in public before an audience, that is in some way transformative for both actor and audience" (Suydam and Ziegler, 173). Studying the medieval Beguines, she finds that these women typically produced their texts in a process of active engagement with companions, scribes, and fellow-actors. Their spirituality was expressed as a "sacred performance" in which a community created both individual and group identities through the enacting of a creative variant on the culture's sacred story.

Even though Thérèse's era is a long way from the Middle Ages, the internal culture of the Carmel of Lisieux may have shared some of the characteristics of medieval oral culture. In the Carmel, a small group of women were acutely engaged with one another within a highly ritualized life structure. In a sense, the cloistered contemplative way of life is consciously designed to be an all-absorbing communal enactment of the Christian story. In the Carmel of Lisieux, this was further intensified by the presence of four sisters and a cousin, all from a family that even outside the monastery had dedicated itself to such an enactment. In this context, Thérèse's life and writings can be interpreted as a "sacred performance" on two levels. It can be read as a rather ostentatious effort on the part of Thérèse and her sisters to "make a saint" and to create a public drama around this image of sanctity; or, more sympathetically, as a very real theological drama of self-giving, self-loss, and heroic faith.

The primary exponent of the first, more psychological reading is Jean

François Six. He focuses on how the Martin sisters were trained from infancy to egg one another on in the public performance of exemplary Christian identity. In this family drama, the sisters cast themselves as saints and martyrs, existing in their own near-heavenly realm far from the immorality and clamor of the world. They learned to observe and criticize one another closely, extravagantly praising the smallest act of virtue while agonizing over their own or another's smallest perceived fault. Even in childhood, the four who later entered Lisieux Carmel ostracized their middle sister, Léonie, because she was unable or unwilling to play this game according to their expectations.

Thérèse, the baby of the family, had a stubborn streak but eventually charmed them all with her head-over-heels commitment to the game of virtue. At some point after the four sisters were ensconced in Carmel, the idea that Thérèse was a potential saint began to take hold of their imaginations—perhaps especially that of Pauline (in Carmel, Mother Agnes). It was she who ordered Thérèse to write the first part of her *Story*, and proposed to Mother Marie de Gonzague that she have her write the last part (the middle section was written at the request of another Martin sister, Marie). After Thérèse's death, Agnes edited the text to better fit the image of virtue and sanctity that she believed Thérèse represented, and all the Martin sisters dedicated the rest of their lives to promoting the persona of the "little saint," which their family drama had spawned.

There may well be a dimension of truth in this rather cynical portrait of Thérèse's "sainthood" as a carefully manicured performance that is as much a product of her sisters' imagination as of her own actual virtue. Yet, there can be little doubt that there was a deep sincerity in the actions of the sisters; they genuinely believed themselves to be participants in a grand drama modeled on the archetypal story of Christ's passion, death, and resurrection. For theologians Mark McIntosh and Frederick Christian Bauerschmidt, it is quite possible to find a genuine mystical dimension in such a performance. They suggest that if the mystical self is, like the Trinity, relational in its core, then its active participation in performative give and take is not an afterthought. The true mystic does not "transcend" the interactive drama of human ethical and political life, but rather gives himself or herself into it so radically that the lives and actions of others in the drama are drawn into new configurations. In the case of the Christian mystic, the authenticity of this performance is discerned according to how it enfleshes the dramatic structures and fruits of Christ's eucharistic and paschal self-giving.

It is interesting to analyze Thérèse's "Christmas conversion" of 1886 in view of this theory. Thérèse, although almost fourteen years old, was still expecting to partake of the childhood custom of receiving gifts in her shoes after Midnight Mass. Her father, tired and annoyed, made a cutting remark about her childishness; but instead of making a tearful scene, as she previously would have done, Thérèse suddenly discovered the will and the strength to respond cheerfully. She later wrote, "I felt charity enter my soul, and the need to forget myself and to please others; since then I've been happy!" (99)

The incident is very small, and yet, even many years later, Thérèse regarded it as the key turning point in the story of her life. It is a "mystical" event in the sense that the moving force of the conversion came from the hidden dimension of grace; Thérèse wrote, "The work I had been unable to do in ten years was done by Jesus in one instant" (98). Yet, it is also very concretely performative. In that moment of grace, Thérèse behaved differently, thus eliciting different behavior from her father and others present. More importantly, in the larger drama of her life, this incident opens a new "act" in which the action is shaped by Thérèse's passionate desire to participate in Christ's self-giving on behalf of sinners. The next scene is the famous story of her prayer for the conversion of the murderer Pranzini, followed quickly by the recounting of her strenuous efforts to enter Carmel at age fourteen.

Thérèse's most complete expression of her mature self-understanding was her "Act of Oblation to Merciful Love," which she wrote on the feast of the Holy Trinity in 1895 and ritually enacted a few days later. This statement is expressed very explicitly in terms of a drama of eucharistic self-giving. She says:

> O My God! Most Blessed Trinity, I desire to Love You and make You Loved, to work for the glory of Holy Church by saving souls on earth and liberating those suffering in purgatory. . . . In order to live in one single act of perfect Love, I offer myself as a victim of holocaust to your merciful love, asking You to consume me incessantly. . . . May this martyrdom, after having prepared me to appear before You, finally cause me to die and may my soul take its flight without any delay into the eternal embrace of Your Merciful Love . . . (276–277).

To understand this text as a performative act, rather than as simply a beautiful prayer, requires placing it back into the full context of Thérèse's life. Her enactment of love was by no means limited to her contemplative prayer; rather, she understood it as requiring active care for others in large and small ways, often against her natural inclinations. Among her well-known stories of charity is that of a sister who displeased Thérèse in every regard, but who was so impressed by Thérèse's kind behavior toward her that the sister thought herself to be Thérèse's favorite (222–223). Another is that of the elderly, crotchety sister whom Thérèse patiently helped day in and day out, despite often receiving verbal abuse for her troubles (247–248). Stories such as these make up a large portion of Manuscript C, written in June and July of 1897, only months before her death. These months were ones of terrible physical and spiritual agony for Thérèse, as she underwent the horrors of tubercular disintegration and asphyxiation without painkillers while apparently lacking spiritual consolation as well. Her beautiful words about being a "martyr" and a "victim of holocaust" were thoroughly tested in the mundane, little trials of life as well as in the ultimate crucible of pain, darkness, and death.

Yet, once again, one may ask how this makes Thérèse a "mystic" rather than simply a holy woman. According to this approach, the only answer is in observing how her performance (including her written texts as well as all the other reverberations of her life) has, in fact, drawn forth new and more authentic performances of the paschal mystery in the lives of others. In the hundred years since her death, Thérèse's story has inspired literally millions of other conversion stories, large and small. For those so inclined, this can be taken as evidence that, indeed, something of the hidden God has been powerfully made manifest in this life.

Conclusion

It has been said that postmodernity is a vision that can open upon either nihilism or mystical faith. Each of the four positions examined here—those focused on extraordinary experiences, on "unknowing," on the anarchical potential of language, and on performance of mystery—attracts a significant constituency within the postmodern context. Yet, it is also "postmodern" to affirm none of them as definitive, and to focus instead on the sparks (of insight) and gaps (of the unknown) revealed in the interplay of perspectives. After a study such as this, some may conclude that, since nothing can be proven, all this attention to Thérèse's life really is "much ado about nothing." Others, however, may begin to catch a glimpse—in a spark, or through a gap—of how her life was organized from its core by something that was, indeed, "mysterious."

Thérèse's own understanding of this was, of course, shaped by a radical Christian faith. The Book of Hebrews states, "Faith is the assurance of things hoped for, conviction of things not seen. . . . By faith we understand that the worlds were prepared by the word of God, so that what is seen was made from things that are not visible" (Hebrews 11:1, 3). Not all share the Christian's conviction that faith in the mystery of Christ is more significant than any other aspect of a person's witness. Yet, by examining Thérèse's life through the prism of these various contemporary insights into mysticism, even those who do not share her faith interpretation may be struck by the potency of her testimony to the power of "things not seen." And this, after all, is the fundamental meaning of mysticism.

RESOURCES

Bauerschmidt, Frederick Christian. *Julian of Norwich and the Mystical Body Politic of Christ* (Notre Dame: University of Notre Dame, 1999).

Cupitt, Don. *Mysticism After Modernity* (Malden, MA: Blackwell, 1998).

Forman, Robert K. C., ed. *The Problem of Pure Consciousness: Mysticism and Philosophy* (New York: Oxford University, 1990).

Furlong, Monica. *Thérèse of Lisieux* (New York: Pantheon, 1987).

Jantzen, Grace M. *Power, Gender, and Christian Mysticism* (Cambridge, MA: Cambridge University, 1995).

Katz, Steven T., ed. *Mysticism and Philosophical Analysis* (New York: Oxford University, 1978).

McIntosh, Mark A. *Mystical Theology: The Integrity of Spirituality and Theology* (Malden, MA: Blackwell, 1998).

Sells, Michael A. *Mystical Languages of Unsaying* (Chicago: University of Chicago, 1994).

Six, Jean François. *La véritable enfance de Thérèse de Lisieux* (Paris: Le Seuil, 1972).

Suydam, Mary A., and Joanna E. Ziegler. *Performance and Transformation: New Approaches to Late Medieval Spirituality* (New York: St. Martin's, 1999).

Thérèse of Lisieux. *The Story of a Soul: The Autobiography of Saint Thérèse of Lisieux*, third edition. Trans., J. Clarke (Washington, DC: Institute of Carmelite Studies, 1996).

Turner, Denys. *The Darkness of God: Negativity in Christian Mysticism* (Cambridge, MA: Cambridge University, 1995).

11

ELIZABETH ANN SETON: "ACQUIESCENCE TO THE DIVINE WILL"

WENDY M. WRIGHT

ccording to one of her biographers, it was a prayer she loved. Pope Pius VII had composed it and Elizabeth Ann Bayley Seton adopted it as her own, reciting it over and over through the years.

> May the most just, the most high and the most amiable Will of God be accomplished forever (Kelly, 1987, 255; 443, n. 60).

The practice known as "acquiescence to the Will of God" was a foundational part of the spiritual life of this early American-born saint and mystic. The discipline of recasting all life's experiences into a framework of ultimate meaning, which can be seen in germ in Elizabeth Ann's youthful journals, deepened in her widowhood and later flowered under the influence of her mentors, the French Sulpicians. Exploring Elizabeth Ann Setan's appropriation of this practice can help us assess its value for contemporary use through the lenses of feminist reflections on "writing women's lives" and contemporary theories of virtue ethics.

Life

Elizabeth Bayley Seton (1774–1821) is not usually a figure who springs to mind when Christian mysticism becomes the topic of conversation. Indeed, the often contentious scholarly study of mysticism in its Christian forms generally focuses on figures living before the eighteenth century. Mother Seton is known primarily as the patroness of the parochial school system in the United States, and as the first American-born individual to be canonically proclaimed a saint by the Roman Catholic Church.

Yet, if mysticism is defined as "the experience of the deeply felt presence of the transcendent other" (Perrin, 48–49), then Elizabeth Seton, as shall be shown, certainly qualifies as a mystic. It was in part through her consistent spiritual disciplines, including her habitual and intentional practice of "acquiescence to the Will of God," that she cultivated the deeply felt presence of God.

Her remarkable life itinerary may be summarized as follows. Elizabeth Ann was the second child born to a prominent New York physician, Richard Bayley, and Catherine Charlton (d. 1777). When Elizabeth was only three years old, her mother and infant sister died, a loss that was to set a subsequent pattern of search for intimacy which would later characterize her relationships with others and with God (Thorgren, 1997). When her father, to whom she was devoted, remarried, she and her older sister were sent to live with relatives in New Rochelle. This painful itinerancy continued for much of her childhood. The refined, education young Elizabeth received befitted the daughter of one of the new American nation's upper class. Her religious formation in the Episcopalian Church was thorough and devout, and for the rest of her life, practices cultivated in her Episcopal youth would be foundational: reliance on Scripture as a guide for daily living, emphasis on the sermon in the Sunday liturgy, and an eagerness to be guided by clergy in matters of church doctrine and law.

At the age of nineteen, Elizabeth married William Magee Seton, a member of a prominent mercantile family. The first years of their marriage were prosperous, both in financial and familial ways. She bore her husband five children and threw herself into the busy rounds of affluent domesticity. In these years, she also grew in religious depth under the tutelage of her Episcopal pastor, Henry Hobart, who guided her spiritual reading. She found she came to need the solace of religion as the family business soon began to flounder and forced them into bankruptcy. With his business losses, William's health declined. Soon he was so ill that the young wife, accompanied by their eldest daughter, set sail for Italy, hoping the Mediterranean air would restore her husband's vitality. But upon arrival at Leghorn in October 1803, the ship was quarantined due to an outbreak of yellow fever, and the family was incarcerated in a damp lazaretto, where William languished and, after their release, died in December.

The Filicchi family, Italian business associates of Elizabeth's husband, took in Mrs. Seton and her daughter. The two remained with the family for several months in Leghorn, and it was there that they were introduced to the Roman Catholic faith—a pivotal moment in Elizabeth Seton's life. When she returned to New York, she took with her a compelling sense that the Church of Rome was the true faith, especially as it affirmed the real presence in the Eucharist. But her leanings were met with horror at home. Not only did her pastors and friends seek to reassert the truths of Protestant Christianity to the widow; they recoiled at the face of Catholicism in early America. It was the Church of the poor, of a small disreputable group of immigrants, a Church without real standing or recognition.

As months of intellectual and spiritual struggle followed, Elizabeth was torn between the faith of her upbringing and the new faith to which her losses and her heart had brought her. She was received into the Catholic Church in 1805, attended by Antonio Filicchi, her Italian mentor. The matter of providing for her five children now occupied her and she opened a boarding school, but her Catholicism proved an obstacle to acquiring boarders. She was rescued from her plight by Fr. Dubourg, president of a Catholic college in Baltimore. At his suggestion and with his help, she moved to Maryland, a more congenial location for Catholics, with the intentions of opening a school for girls. In Baltimore she did just that. She also took her first vows in a newly formed religious congregation, the Sisters of Charity of St. Joseph, and, as "Mother," welcomed several other recruits. The community was placed under the supervision of the Sulpician Order of priests. Frs. DuBourg, first superior of the Sisters and later Bishop of Louisiana, Pierre Babade, of St. Mary's Seminary, John Dubois, third superior of the community and later Bishop of New York, and Simon Bruté, of St. Mary's, later Bishop of Vincennes, were to profoundly shape the spirituality of their American charge.

In 1809 the community moved inland to the more rural location of Emmitsburg, where teaching was the work of the Sisters of Charity. Although their primary income derived from borders from wealthy families, they also established a free school for the children of the poor. For all of them, it was a challenging life. Providing for the physical, spiritual, and intellectual needs of their charges, as well as developing the religious and practical routines of a new community was a formidable task. Within the first few years, Mother Seton ran into considerable difficulties with administration, both within the community and from superiors without. At one point, in fact, it was not clear whether she would remain as "Mother." Physical conditions were primitive and many of the early sisters fell ill; not a few died. Among the casualties were Elizabeth's dear friend and sister-in-law, Cecilia Seton, and two of Elizabeth's own children, her youngest and eldest daughters. The latter's death was the occasion of Mother Seton's agonizing struggle with despair.

Elizabeth Seton remained in Emmitsburg until her death in 1821, at the age of forty-seven. By that time the Sisters of Charity were duly established in Maryland and had made foundations in Philadelphia and New York.

Spiritual Practice

The foundations of Elizabeth Bayley Seton's spiritual life were established during her Protestant girlhood. This included a love of Scripture and a habit of familiar conversation with God. Commentators have pointed out the extent to which Elizabeth's early loss of her mother and her father's subsequent frequent absences laid the groundwork for the divine intimacy that would later grow to an extraordinary degree.

> In the year 1789 *when my father was in England* one morning in May in the lightness of a cheerful heart I jumped in the waggon [sic] that was driving to the woods for brush . . . [with] a heart as innocent as a *human heart* could be filed with the even enthusiastic love to God and admiration of his works—still I can feel every sensation that passed through my soul—I thought at that time my father did not care for me—well God was my Father—my All. I prayed—sung hymns—cryed [sic]—laughed in talking to myself of how far *He* could place me above all sorrow—Then layed [sic] still to enjoy the Heavenly Peace that came over my Soul; and I am sure in the two hours so enjoyed grew ten years in my spiritual life . . . (*Collected Writings*, 264–5/Kelly, 1987, 115).[1]

Mrs. Seton remembered this girlhood incident years later when she was incarcerated on the Italian Coast in the dank lazaretto prison with her failing husband, William, and ailing daughter. In that critical period, when her once joyful and prosperous life as wife and helpmate was moment by moment dying before her, Elizabeth turned with renewed trust to the protective Fatherhood of God. In her Italian journal she wrote:

O my God, imprint it on my Soul with the strength of thy Holy Spirit that by his grace supported and defended I may never more forget that Thou art *my all,* and that I cannot be recieved [sic] in thy Heavenly Kingdom without a pure and faithful Heart Supremely devoted to thy Holy Will—*O keep me for the sake of Jesus Christ* (*Collected Writings,* 247/Kelly, 1987, 102).

Awoke with the same rest and comfort with which I had laid down— gave my W. his warm milk and began to consider our situation tho' so unfavorable to his complaint as one of the Steps in the dispensation of that Almighty Will which alone could choose aright for us . . . (*Collected Writings,* 256/Kelly, 1987, 107).

My William often asked me if I felt assured that he would be accepted and pardoned, and I always tried to convince him that where the soul was so humble and sincere as his, and submission to God's will so uniform as he had been throughout his trial, that it became sinful to doubt one moment of his reception through the merits of his Redeemer . . . (*Collected Writings,* 275/Kelly, 1987, 125).

Elizabeth's acceptance of the protective Fatherhood of God implied her unquestioning acceptance of the Divine Will, understood as those events in life that one cannot change. Thus, in her grieving, she transposed what might have been anger or bitterness or a sense of abandonment into a sense of being paternally protected, even in this most desolate of moments. The concept of the "Will of God" is central to this practice of hers.

The concept is, of course, as old as Christianity itself in the form of the Lord's Prayer, which the New Testament records as taught by Jesus: "Our Father which art in heaven, Hallowed be thy name. Thy kingdom come. Thy will be done in earth, as it is in heaven" (see Matthew 6:9–10). Thus reads the King James English that Elizabeth would have memorized as a little girl. The early church associated the Will of God not only with this anticipatory prayer of Jesus' but also with his paradigmatic actions. Thus St. Paul could write, ". . . who gave himself for our sins to set us free from the present evil age, according to the will of our God and Father" (Galatians 1:4). For the early church, Jesus, the Son, conformed to his Father's will by his obedient response. "And being found in human form, he humbled himself and became obedient to the point of death—even death on a cross" (Philippians 2:8).

Over the centuries, the notion of obedient acquiescence to God's will certainly flourished in Christian spiritual teaching, especially in the western Church. Whatever the "will of God" might have meant for Paul or other early Christians, obedience to it came, by Elizabeth Seton's century, to be a central category in the patterning of an ideal Christian life. In her Italian correspondence, one can see the extent to which she relied for comfort on the concept that a loving Father knew better than she what was to be the shape of her life. The painful events of William's bankruptcy and death were part of a larger benevolent plan and, as a Christian, the young wife's embrace of these realities was necessarily mantled by the protective shelter of God's loving paternal Will.

After her conversion to Roman Catholicism, Elizabeth Seton continued to live vigorously into the spiritual practice of acquiescing to the Divine Will as she understood it to be manifest in the particular, often difficult circumstances of her life. In fact, her practice seems to have been intensified and enhanced through her adopted faith. Her conversion, it is a matter of public record, was an agonizing one in which the polemical apologetics of both denominations, on top of family pressure, alternately swayed and confused her. She finally surrendered to the faith she had first encountered in Italy. Its intense sacramentality drew her, especially its teaching of the real presence in the Eucharist. For the rest of her life, Elizabeth Seton would hunger for and be filled with Eucharist as an experience of embodied intimacy with God (Wright, 1997).

With this life-changing conversion, the widowed mother began to deepen her practice of acquiescing to God's Will. This was encouraged, in the first place, by the spiritual tradition of her new faith. Catholic piety had long been profoundly participative. Not only was Jesus met as founder, savior, and model, a Catholic participated in the reality of God-with-us in a visceral way: through Communion and through a radical participation in his life, suffering, death, and resurrection, both in the liturgical seasons of the church year and in devotional practices. Indeed, the Catholic tradition stressed a lively identification with the suffering and dying of Jesus the Christ as the motive and dynamic of the spiritual life.

Seventeenth- and eighteenth-century Catholic spirituality, especially in its French forms, emphasized not only offering up one's own suffering as a participation in the suffering of Christ but also surrender to the inevitabilities of one's life and one's situation as part of this participation. The great spiritual guide of the laity, St. Francis de Sales (1567–1622), a copy of whose *Introduction to the Devout Life* Mrs. Seton was given by her Italian hosts and which she read with fervor, recommended that persons in varying "states of life" adapt their devotion to their circumstances and that marriage, parenthood, widowhood, as well as religious life are vocations. God's Will was manifest to one primarily through the responsibilities of one's state in life.

Other examples of this spiritual teaching can be seen in *Abandonment to Divine Providence*, attributed to French Jesuit Pierre de Caussade as well as in the French or Berullian school of spirituality. Take for instance the spiritual teachings of John Eudes (1601–1680) of this school. Eudes preached that one should give oneself to Jesus and act in his dispositions and in his intentions. He not only preached this doctrine but also put it into practice. He repeatedly gave himself to Jesus and Mary in order to "fulfill the will of the father" in union with them.[2]

Thus, by the eighteenth century, Catholic spiritual teaching had drawn a close connection between the faithful following of Jesus and acquiescence to God's Will as manifested in the conditions of one's life. If those conditions were painful, and if they were offered up in love, they could be understood as a participation in the Christ life. As Jesus surrendered to the Divine Will, so those who lead the Christ life must also.

Perhaps most germane to Elizabeth Seton's experience were the teachings of Jean-Jacques Olier (1608–1657), the founder of the Sulpicians, the order of priests that became in the new world the overseers of the Sisters of Charity of St. Joseph. Olier, like others in the spiritual current known as the French school, had stressed identification with Jesus through acceptance of the crosses that came with one's state in life.

> While [the French school] were certainly in favor of ascetical practices, their devotion to the cross entailed not the choosing of crosses for oneself, but embracing the crosses that arose from one's state in life. In fact, Fr. Olier warns against choosing particular acts of mortification as potential sources of pride and self-love. Instead, devotion to the cross entails . . . that existential condition that defines who we are and what we do. Unlike the crosses we choose, and to which we become accustomed, which we put down at will, the crosses of our state in life are realities, sufferings, humiliations, to which we never grow accustomed, which we can never abandon and still claim to be who we are . . . we make sense out of these crosses . . . only by joining them to the one saving cross of the Lord Jesus. There our sufferings are transformed, find meaning, become salvific (Thayer, 1999, 8–9).

Olier's priests, including those who came to the new world in the wake of the French Revolution, like the Sulpicians who guided Mother Seton's new congregation, were steeped in the disciplines of their founder. The identification with Jesus that Olier espoused involved an interior discipline, a submission of all the powers of the soul to God in complete dependence. This was first and foremost for him a matter of the submission of the will. As the personal will decreased, the Will of God could increase in the soul.

> Let us study how to renounce our inner core, how to condemn it and how to surrender it to God, so that he can imprint in us what he wants and insert in us his inclinations, his sentiments and even his dispositions. . . . Our will is more affected by sin than the rest of us. Therefore it is more haughty and arrogant. It is always ready to give orders and rarely disposed to obey. It takes great effort and continuous attention to keep it in subjection and submission. . . . Therefore true and perfect interior humility consists in the submission of the will to God, along with our understanding, which should act as if it were dead and wait very faithfully, submitting itself to the divine impressions and to those lights that God promises to his children (Deville, 1987, 103).

Olier's approach was clearly echoed in the words of one of Elizabeth's Sulpician advisors in 1809, when the unexpected death of her young sister-in-law Harriet Seton, who had come as a new convert to Catholicism to join the little band, left Elizabeth grief stricken.

> Let us adore the unsearchable, and always wise and merciful ways of Providence; and let us more than ever convince ourselves, that Jesus wishes to be the sole possessor of our hearts, to abandon ourselves with perfect resignation into his hands . . . having no other thought, in troublesome and painful encounters, than to submit lovingly to whatever God will be pleased to ordain (Melville, 1951, 227).

Mother Seton learned from her French-born advisors. Her early instinct to shelter her most painful losses under the protective mantle of a loving Father, transposing her grief into a sense of accepting the Will of God, became in her later years an intentional spiritual discipline. Thus she could write for her "daughters" in the Sisters of Charity a series of reflections on the spiritual life, which included a section on ways to honor the will of God. [3]

1ˢᵗ. We are not to be satisfied with having high ideas of the will of God considered *in itself* which is but as a *first step* toward our union with him. We must try to learn what his divine will is in regard to ourselves as a *second step*, about which the first would avail but little—our Saviour came from heaven only to do the will of his father and when the bitter chalice was presented to him, bathed in his bloody sweat he cried, *Thy Will* O my Father, thy will, not mine be done—He knew his Father's Will, but for we must beg earnestly that he will send his light from above to enlighten that night in which our *SENSES, MIND* and *will* are lost, and so lost in the ignorance and corruption of our Nature that we have no possible means of finding our road to heaven but by a persevering attention to the path our Saviour himself has trodden—in this path we will find many enemies to combat, trials to endure, and obligations to fulfil, but he has not only traced it out with his blood, but he even goes on before us, pours on us the abundance of his graces for our Strength and comfort and holds out the eternal crown which he prepares for us— But as we know from our first set out in our Pilgrimage of this world towards our Eternity, that we have always *good* on the one hand and *evil* on the other our third step towards God must be to have great Confidence in his Providence with regard to the good and evil which he permits or sends to us, recieving [sic] them *equally* and in the order of Grace, and *from his own hand* this *third step* is most essential to lead us towards the main object of doing *his will*, one only *evil* can happen to us which is sin, all other trails, *whatever they may be,* are meant only to try us, to purify us, and draw us to that region we are called to by detaching us from this earth where we would gather roses though we know they are covered with piercing thorns. We must let this world go round us with all its changes and *wait in Peace* for that eternal day in which we will see the *goodness* of our God in everything that has happened in it.

These three first steps of *honoring the will of God, embracing the will of God, and confiding in the will of God,* all raise us up towards him . . . (*Elizabeth Seton's Notebook,* 67–69).

The Mother Superior continued her admonition with a description of the fourth, fifth, sixth, and seventh steps in this spiritual discipline designed to lead toward union with God: knowledge of human corruption and weakness, the habitual practice of purity of intention, peace of soul, and the exercise of holy love. These steps, she assured her daughters in religion, will assure as close a union with God as is possible in this life. In the end:

I no longer live says St. Paul—it is Christ who *lives in me* the *fire* of this love, the waters of tribulation cannot quench. St. Augustin says the heavens, the earth, all creation cryeth to me, LOVE—a soul in this happy state may be surrounded by duties, it passes through all in Simplicity and peace, conversing interiorly with God while exteriorly attentive to the objects of its duty, adoring and offering all to him, no affectation in its humility, or harshness in its mortifications, or constraint in its modesty, God is seen in every one around it, and all its actions are directed to his will, no trails or sufferings of life can surprise it—its eye is ever raised towards Calvary from whence it draws its sure strength and Consolation—(*Elizabeth Seton's Notebook*, 72).

That Elizabeth Seton made acquiescence to the Divine Will a pillar of her spiritual practice cannot be doubted. She, along with her Sulpician mentors, accepted the concept that God's paternal beneficence sustained human life and that there was great wisdom, indeed divinely sanctioned wisdom, in surrendering one's own will. This surrender was traditionally both a habitual and an occasional practice. It was habituated especially in religious life, in which surrender of one's own will to the will of the superior was virtually equated with surrender to the Will of God. One can see this equation enshrined in the rule that Elizabeth's Sisters of Charity followed. This was a modified version of the rule written for the French Daughters of Charity founded by Vincent de Paul (1581–1660) and Louise de Marillac (1591–1660). Within limits, the superior, who encouraged spiritual formation through the observance of a community's rule, was seen functionally as the one who aided the religious in practicing curbing of the personal will. The rule did encourage surrender in obedience to religious superiors. But it was not chiefly through the Vincentian heritage that Elizabeth was grounded in acquiescence as a more generalized practice. It was her personal Sulpician guides, especially in later life her most trusted soul friend Fr. Simon de Bruté, who encouraged her in such surrender when painful, irreversible circumstances occurred.

The latter, occasional, practice was one at which Mother Seton excelled, having been schooled by life's painful losses early on to trust in a greater, if hidden, providence at work. Only occasionally in her life it seems did her trust in a loving if inscrutable Divine Will elude her. She faltered in 1812, when her eldest child, Anna, died at the age of sixteen. An anguished letter to her spiritual advisor, Fr. Bruté, revealed her uncharacteristic doubt, as she struggled to transpose her despair into a transcendent vision.

On the grave of poor Anina—begging crying to Mary to behold her Son and plead for us and to Jesus to behold his Mother—so uncertain of reunion—then the Soul quieted even by the desolation of the falling leaves around began to cry out form Eternity to Eternity thou art God – all shall perish and pass away—but thou remainest forever—then the thought of our dearest stretched on the cross and his last words coming powerfully, stood up with hands and eyes lifted to the pure heavens crying out forgive they know not What they do—did She? Adored, did she know?—and all the death bed scene appeared—in this moment in the silence of all around a rattling sound rushing towards—along Anina's grave a snake stretched itself on the dry grass—so large and ugly and the little gate tied—but Nature was able to drag to the place and tie and untie, saying inwardly my darling shall not be rooted by the hogs for you—then put up the bars and softly walked away—oh my dear ones companions of worms and reptiles!—and the beautiful Soul *Where?* (Kelly, 1987, 304–305).

The acquiescence of the will in the exercise of the religious life became for Elizabeth a habitual practice, one that encouraged its practice in times of extremity. Typical is a letter written in 1819 to Cecilia O'Conway, the first young woman to join Elizabeth in the Sisters of Charity. Cecilia had originally hoped to join a cloistered Spanish contemplative order but lacked funds, so was advised to join the new American foundation. But the desire for more retired life never left her. Mother Seton counseled her thus:

My own loved Cecil –
It is a dark gloomy morning so I take it to say the little painful word to her my Soul loves, who it appears is *very sick* of the *old sickness* she and I so often nursed before—but say beloved Soul how many times did we agree, that if there could remain a *doubt* about the *present situation*, the *fears* that would follow a *change* brought about by our own *Will*, and against the will of all those who are answerable, after a clear statement of the doubts has so often been made—how often did we agree that all this considered it was better to go on, and take the abundant sweet heavenly graces *day* by *day*, only seeking and *seeing him* in all our little duties (so small an offering)—and taking from the hands of all around us every daily cross and trial *as if he gave it himself*—(Kelly, 1987, 303).

Interestingly, it was precisely the habitual practice of acquiescence in community, especially the conflation of the instructions of the superior with the Will of God, that was the cause of one of Elizabeth Seton's own

pivotal spiritual crises (the others were occasioned by her conversion and
Anna's death). The years were 1809–1811, the period of the founding of
both her school and her little band. Her baptism into the role of foundress
under the supervision of the Sulpician fathers was a rude one. She and
several of the sisters had enjoyed a warm and fruitful relationship with one
Fr. Babade, whom Elizabeth hoped would be their founding advisor.
Instead, three other priests were assigned to the new community over the
course of the first years. At first, the fledgling mother resisted the spiritual
authority of the assigned overseer, insisting that Fr. Babade was essential to
her spiritual progress. When her new superior requested that she give up
even her correspondence with her former advisor, she struggled. She fared
even worse under the second assigned priest. She wrote imploringly to
their mutual superior, Archbishop John Carroll:

> Sincerely I promised you and really *I have endeavored to do everything* in
> my power to bend myself to meet the last appointed *Superior* in every
> way but after continual reflection on the *necessity of absolute conformity
> with him,* and *constant prayer* to our Lord to help me, yet the heart is
> closed . . . An unconquerable reluctance and diffidence takes the place
> of those dispositions which ought to influence every action, and with
> every desire to serve God and those excellent beings who surround me I
> remain motionless and inactive (Kelly, 1987, 33).

This second superior apparently had equal misgivings about Mother
Seton, for he planned to replace her as head of the Sisters of Charity with
another woman to whom he had given spiritual direction in the past. By
the time this man was replaced with a third superior to whose authority
she was to acquiesce, Elizabeth Ann had begun to perceive the spiritual
lesson in these difficult events. She wrote to Fr. Babade that "I shall be
gathering the honey and dispensing it—the peace and safety of a mortified
spirit is my daily lesson." Her hope was that God would not turn away her
"humble broken heart—broken of its perverse and obstinate resistance to
his will" (Kelly,1987, 34).

Late in her life, by this time steeped in the spirituality of her most
cherished director Sulpician Fr. Bruté, she would write a series of Good
Friday reflections.

> The good Friday of Death and Life! The death of our Jesus—the Eternal
> Life of our Souls . . . Out of the depths I cry to thee O Lord—Lord hear

my voice . . . My Soul is Sorrowful—my spirit weighed down even to the dust . . . in thy good time—when it shall please the Lord—then will my bonds be loosed and my soul be set at liberty. O what ever is thy good pleasure—thy blessed will be done—if my time is short—let me have only one wish—to please thee—but one fear—that of offending thee (Kelly, 1987, 330).

The practice of acquiescence to the Divine Will was thus a central spiritual practice for Elizabeth Ann Seton, one that matured through the years and one she taught to her daughters in religion. It was a practice that she understood to be central to intimate union with God, a practice that mirrored and conformed her to Christ. Through this acquiescence, she continually and profoundly experienced the presence of God.

Contemporary Considerations

Reading through the extant writings of a woman like Elizabeth Seton is fascinating time travel for a contemporary academic. Her words have a spontaneity and freshness that collapses the more than two centuries that have elapsed since they were written. Yet she did live in a very different era, both culturally and spiritually, and the question remains: To what extent might Elizabeth Ann Seton's practices and teachings, which led her to an extraordinary intimacy with God, have significance for those of us who live in the twentieth century?

I have written elsewhere about the delicate task of appropriating the spiritual wisdom of the past, arguing that the present-day reader must live with the language of classic texts in two distinct ways. First, he or she must be aware of the values, images, and assumptions that are so specific to an author's time that they do not translate well. Second, he or she must be alert for language or teachings that, while foreign or distasteful, might well be lived with and lovingly contemplated in order that the universal religious meaning might be hulled from the husk of historical appearance (Wright, 1993, 17–28). Mother Seton's practice of acquiescence to the Divine Will deserves careful consideration. Of the many lenses I might choose to evaluate her practice, I will settle on two: feminist reflections on writing a woman's life and contemporary virtue ethics. Both perspectives will of necessity only be briefly explored.

Writing a Woman's Life

One aspect of the contemporary woman's movement, in its religious as well as its secular forms, has been the recovery of woman's stories from the past. Since "herstory" has not always been recorded, scholars have been actively retrieving and interpreting the stories of notable women of previous generations. Often, these stories have been chosen to demonstrate the autonomy, agency, and valuable works these foremothers have accomplished. Christian women in religious life have frequently been noted because of the extent to which their lifestyle, circumventing as it did the typical female fate of marriage and motherhood, afforded them opportunities to express themselves and contribute to their cultures. The great women mystics of the Christian past have thus become spiritual mothers in the present day; their sayings anthologized, their stories held up as inspiration, their prayers become the stuff of present-day devotion.

Considering her accomplishments, Elizabeth Ann Seton is certainly a woman to elicit our admiration. With extraordinary courage and imagination, she navigated the varied and sometimes treacherous currents of life into which she was led. Wife, mother, foundress, spiritual mentor: she did it all. Yet, the question remains: To what extent do the specifics of her own spiritual practices translate helpfully into the present day and to what extent might they be life-giving for contemporary women? Taking a cue from feminist literature, an interesting picture emerges.

Several years ago, Carolyn G. Heilbrun published an extended essay entitled *Writing A Woman's Life*, a piece that intelligently assessed the narratives of women's lives as they have come down to us in the canon of Western literature. Heilbrun suggested that not until the 1970s did a narrative begin to emerge that could adequately express the fullness of real women's lives. She located the turning point in a generation of American poets: Levertov, Cooper, Kizer, Kumin, Sexton, Rich, Plath. Heilbrun contends that before these groundbreaking wordsmiths began to write boldly of their genuine experience, the sanctioned narrative that was available to a woman forbid anger and the open admission of the desire for power and control over life. Rather, the old genre of female autobiography tended to "find beauty even in pain and to transform rage into spiritual acceptance" (Heilbrun, 1988, 12). An appropriate story for a woman was one that celebrated docile acceptance of what is. It was nostalgic, sentimental, and romantic, with safety and closure, not adventure or experience, being its chief values. Always a woman's story was cast primarily in terms of relationship with husband, father, or children. "What does it mean to be unambiguously a woman? It means to put a man at the center of one's life and to allow only what honors his prime position. Occasionally women have put God or Christ in the place of a man: the results are the same: one's own desires and quests are always secondary (Heilbrun, 1988, 20–21)." It should be noted that in making this statement, Heilbrun places herself in the camp of "equality feminists" (who emphasize male and female equality) rather than "difference feminists" (who emphasize female distinctiveness, especially their capacity for relationality). According to this former analysis, these female narratives are born of oppression. Women in patriarchal cultures are dependent utterly on men—legally as well as by convention. They thus create the only narrative available to them, one from which "unwomanly" thoughts, actions, and ideals are expunged. This is not a matter of simply fictionalizing their own stories but of understanding their own lives solely within the confines of the female narrative.

From the vantagepoint of this critique, Mother Seton's story might be seen anew. Her practice of acquiescing to the Will of God especially suggests itself for reexamination. Now, clearly, this is neither a simple matter nor one that can be handled fully here. It also does not represent the only possible feminist perspective. But a few words are in order. First, one might well raise a question about the narrative that shaped Elizabeth's life. She was a woman who understood herself chiefly in terms of her relationships to others and the others who dominated her life were male. Deeply attached to her father in her youth, in his frequent absences she transferred her affection and dependence to God conceived as paternal protector. Devoted to her husband during her married years, she transferred her devotion, at her husband death, to her Italian mentor, Antonio Filicchi. Always in matters spiritual, men in authority were her revered advisors: the Protestant pastor, Henry Hobart, Catholics Archbishop John Carroll, Frs. Babade and Bruté. These were the persons on whom she most relied, despite the fact that she functioned primarily in a female world and cultivated deep and lasting friendships with women.[4]

It could be argued that Elizabeth had little choice but to rely on male advisors, but her reliance, with few exceptions (the difficulty with the third Sulpician superior is a case in point), was unquestioning. She raised no proto-feminist objections to male headship, nor did she pray with androgynous images of God. Her choice of religious life was not a rejection of the patriarchal version of marriage but a life that emerged out of the ashes of a marriage she had found fulfilling. She did not reject marriage as such but, in rejecting her Protestant past and through force of circumstance, the Catholic celibate option opened up for the young widow.

Despite her remarkable achievements, Elizabeth Ann Seton remains a less than satisfactory model if one wishes to see in her self-styled life evidence of a story that breaks out of the old genre of female narrative. Certainly, it needs to be recognized that Mother Seton *did* live in the eighteenth and not the twenty-first century and thus could not be expected to promote a vision of female autonomy that her century could not imagine.

Through the same lens of feminist critique, one might also want to question Elizabeth Seton's practice of acquiescing to the Will of God. This practice, as described, was not solely a spiritual practice enjoined for women. Rather, it was a practice deeply embedded in the Christian narrative by the eighteenth century and highlighted by the French Sulpicians who were Mother Seton's most formative spiritual advisors. It was a narrative that arose parallel to the rise of the French monarchy. Although it is difficult to chart causal connections, it is interesting to note that in the Grand Siècle—that age of political and social absolutism during which surrender to the prerogatives of royal power and a relinquishment of personal power was required of all citizens—a parallel spirituality emphasizing surrender to the prerogatives of divine power emerged. This is, of course, patriarchy writ large on the historical canvas. A citizen was asked to see the social structure, with its hierarchies and privileges, as ordained by a greater wisdom. Acceptance of what was, fitting into one's prescribed place, these were necessary virtues in such a social and political situation. Acquiescence to the Divine Will might, from a feminist perspective, seem a fitting spiritual practice to keep all those who were oppressed by an unjust system neatly in their prescribed places. What is, is the Will of God.

The questions the feminist critique raises about Elizabeth Ann Seton run along these lines. Feminist thought of the sort Heilbrun reflects rejects both the structures and ideas that support the domination of some groups and the subordination of others. It seeks liberating stories that allow the full expression of diverse experiences into the human community. It wants to allow all persons access to narratives that empower rather than disempower. It seeks as well stories about divine life itself that do not subordinate human beings to a deity described as arbitrarily subjecting the created order to "life as it is." Feminist religious thought focuses on liberating images of the Divine that call forth human cooperation and compassion for the afflicted. Moreover, it subverts ecclesiastical language that casts human beings as groveling subjects, rejects patriarchal images, and prefers more egalitarian models of divine-human relationship such as friendship. Does Mother Seton's example and her teachings allow us, especially women, in an era very different from hers, to construct authentic narratives about our lives and our relationship to ultimate reality? Given the way that many twenty-first-century women now frame their stories, it might be difficult for some to pray as she did and genuinely achieve intimacy with the Divine.

Contemporary Virtue Ethics

One might well critique the static conception of society and the divine action in the world that supported Elizabeth's practice of acquiescing to the Divine Will. But from another perspective, her teaching might be seen as a rich resource for the present day. In the past several decades, ethicists in the fields of philosophy and theology have turned attention to the development of character and the cultivation of virtue. In addition, developmental, moral, and educational psychologists have contributed to our collective thinking by studying the human life cycle. Together, these fields have contributed to a renaissance in "virtue theory" (Crossin, 1985).

Oversimplified, contemporary virtue theory locates morality not in specific acts but in the formation of character or the cultivation of qualities or virtues that create a moral perspective from which specific acts emerge. It also gives attention to the communal, social nature of the formation of character and virtue. It is concerned with the life well lived in a society that seems to be at a moral impasse.[5] Of course, mysticism or spiritual practice is not reducible to morality but, in a Christian context, the moral and spiritual lives are intimately intertwined. The assumption is that growth in love of God implies a growth in love of neighbor. And the cultivation of virtues traditionally relates not only to ethical action but also to growth in holiness. Persons seen as authentic mystics in the Christian tradition are persons who manifest an exemplary holiness as a result of their profound intimacy with God. They are, in their manifold variousness, "other Christ's." As such they exemplify the virtues defined by the Christian spiritual tradition.[6]

Elizabeth Ann Seton was one who quite self-consciously cultivated the Christian virtues. When one reads her surviving writing, one is struck with the extraordinary strength of her character, the extent to which she was able to negotiate with grace and resilience the often terrible challenges that life offered her. This was in part due to a naturally buoyant temperament. But it was even more a result of her conscious practice of framing her experience with a wide, beneficent lens. In her day, acquiescence to the Will of God, understood as the acceptance of what is as part of a greater divine plan, was a formative spiritual practice, one that built character and aided in the acquisition of virtue. When considered in the light of recent virtue ethics, these observations emerge.

Some virtue ethicists have attempted to name virtues, which seem relevant to the contemporary world. Italian theologian Romano Guardini enumerates acceptance as the virtue that undergirds all effective moral action. It is intriguing to consider Elizabeth Seton's practice of acquiescing to the Will of God as one reads of Guardini on the virtue of acceptance.

> This is not a weak submissiveness, but a clear-eyed view of the truth upon which a person can build by decisive action. Such is needed because human desires often exceed human being . . . Acceptance means first of all that a person must accept himself or herself as an individual with definite character, temperament, possibilities and limitations. Each person has both strengths and weaknesses. Thus, each must learn to accept the self just as it is and build on the available material . . . Moving beyond . . . the person must learn to accept the situation and circumstances of life. One's destiny is a determination of outer events and inner character . . . One's destiny is ultimately in the hands of Divine Providence and so can be accepted. In this light, misfortunes which cannot be avoided cannot only be endured, but even be accepted in their bitterness (Crossin, 1985, 22–23).

Karl Rahner is content to explore virtue in more traditional terms. He sees virtue as the fully developed power of the human soul, especially the "power to realize the moral good." For Rahner, hope, the second of the traditional theological virtues, is the virtue that draws a person out of himself or herself. It is the virtue, thus seen, that might most apply to Elizabeth Seton. Hope propels the person outward into an unseen future.

> Hope . . . is the process of constantly eliminating the provisional in order to make room for the radical and pure uncontrollability of God . . . Hope is also that virtue which actually convinces the believer that God's grace is effective for him or her individually (Crossin, 1985, 26).

Protestant theologian Stanley Hauerwas has described the moral life of the Christian as a way of seeing the world that is attained through discipline. Character, for him, is more than the possession of specific virtues. Character, rather, is the basic moral determination of the self that can and should grow progressively into conformity with Christ. This growth is facilitated by the articulation of a coherent narrative that embeds the formation of self in the greater Christian narrative. From a Hauerwasian perspective, Mother Seton was, in her prayer, journals, and letters, thus engaged in constructing a meaningful narrative of her life that also provided the foundation of her strong, virtuous character.

These reflections on both feminist theory and virtue ethics are clearly suggestive and partial, but they allow us to begin creatively turning over the legacy that Elizabeth Bayley Seton has left us. Feminist thought, however, provides us with a certain caution: it is not enough to follow a mystical exemplar without first discerning the extent to which her thought is embedded in ideas suited best to another era. The view of women as necessarily subordinate assumed in the eighteenth century has changed radically in much of Western Christian thought. One might ask if Elizabeth Seton's spirituality, especially her practice of acquiescence to the Divine Will, is so embedded in a patriarchal vision that it cannot speak to the twenty-first century. However, if one should choose to adopt such a practice, care should be taken to ensure that it does not degenerate into the simplistic belief that God directly causes all things to occur and that the religious response must be one of acquiescence. Western culture, and the Christian churches for the most part, have come to accept the idea that human choice, rather than the Divine Will, is responsible for many of the ills of the world. Sin is now seen not only as personal but also as social and structural. It is considered a legitimate religious response to struggle against injustices such as racism, sexism, and the oppression of the poor. One might ask in the present context whether the outmoded genre of female autobiography with which Elizabeth understood her life, which transforms pain into beauty and rage into docile acceptance, allows for the sort of transformative social vision called for in contemporary Christian circles.

On the other hand, her practice of acquiescence might be favorably evaluated in light of contemporary virtue ethics. Rage against unjust structures, for example, must be distinguished from the sort of hopeless rage or depression that results from a failure to accept the unalterable pains and obstacles of life. Acceptance can be the clear-eyed realism that allows for untoward events to be embraced, not merely endured, allowing the person to remain supple and responsive to life rather than braced against its inevitable disappointments. Death, illness, failure, irrevocable events: these may embitter and paralyze if they are not incorporated in an overarching narrative of hope.

Virtue ethics suggests that Elizabeth Seton's spiritual practice does, indeed, provide a template for the formation of character through narrative. She was engaged in the process of constructing a self whose ultimate meaning derived not from her personal stories of loss but from the hope supplied by the overarching Christian story. She looked deeper than the provisional hopefulness supplied by life's joy—and she made room for God. Her practice of acquiescing to the Will of God can suggest to us a subtle, yet radical spiritual path that, if followed faithfully, might lead to a deep and abiding, indeed mystical, sense of the presence of God.

NOTES

1. Elizabeth Seton emphasized her thoughts by underlining, sometimes multiple times. In the quotations these words and phrases have been italicized. Her frequent use of long dashes in place of ordinary punctuation is represented by the use of em and en dashes. The quotes also retain the original spelling and punctuation or lack thereof. Her collected works have yet to be fully published in a critical edition, thus the citations in this article come from a variety of sources, some printed, some in manuscript. Only the first volume of her *Collected Writings* is presently available. Where applicable, I have included the page numbers from that volume as well as from the Kelly *Selected Writings,* which at present allows the best printed access to a chronologically inclusive selection of Seton writings. See bibliography.

2. This practice of assigning to divine volition all the events of life was prominent in these centuries. Not all spiritual writers underemphasized the importance of the human will, however. Francis de Sales and Vincent de Paul, drawing on the current of Christian humanism, stressed human initiative and volition alongside the practice of surrendering to all circumstances as the Will of God (Wright, 1993, 148–150).

3. This notebook, presently in manuscript form in the archives of the Sisters of Charity of Cincinnati, is undated. Elizabeth assumed her responsibilities as superior in 1809 and died in 1821.

4. Elizabeth's long correspondences with Julia Scott and Cecilia and Rebecca Seton are especially telling in this regard. See Celeste, 1989.

5. Thinkers as diverse as Catholics Josef Pieper, Romano Guardini, Karl Rahner, and Bernard Häring, and Protestants Jergen Moltmann, Stanley Hauerwas, and Craig Dykstra have laid the modern theological foundations of virtue theory. Alasdair MacIntyre has led the philosophical investigation. The premodern roots of the philosophical-theological enterprise are both classical (Aristotle) and medieval (Aquinas). The psychological theories of Erik Erikson, Lawrence Kohlberg, and James Fowler among others have provided insight from the social sciences.

6. Faith, hope, and love were enumerated as the chief three. Temperance, prudence, justice, and fortitude make up the official list of seven. Of course, models of holiness have changed over the centuries, even in the Christian tradition. The wonderworker of the early Middle Ages and the virtuous religious founder of the high Middle Ages are not the favorites of the modern world. Today the martyr has come back into favor, especially the martyr for the cause of the poor and of justice.

Resources

Marie Celeste, S.C. *The Intimate Friendships of Elizabeth Ann Bayley Seton* (New York: Alba House, 1989).

Crossin, John W. *What Are They Saying About Virtue?* (Mahwah, NJ: Paulist Press, 1985).

Dirvin, Joseph I. *Mrs. Seton: Foundress of the American Sisters of Charity* (New York: Farrar, Straus and Giroux, 1975).

Deville, Raymond. *The French School of Spirituality: An Introduction and a Reader.* Trans. Agnes Cunningham, S.S.C.M. (Pittsburgh: Duquesne University Press, 1987).

Elizabeth Seton's Notebook. n.d. Manuscript AMSJ. A11 074. Archives of Sisters of Charity of Cincinnati, Mount St. Joseph's, OH.

Heilbrun, Carolyn G. *Writing A Woman's Life* (New York/ London: W. W. Norton Co., 1988).

Kelly, Ellin and Annabelle Melville, eds. *Elizabeth Seton: Selected Writings* (New York/ Mahwah: Paulist Press, 1987).

Kelly, Ellin M. *Numerous Choirs: A Chronicle of Elizabeth Bayley Seton and Her Daughters* (Evansville, IN: Mater Dei Provinciatate, 1981).

Melville, Anabelle M. *Elizabeth Bayley Seton: 1774–1821* (New York: Charles Scribner's Sons, 1985).

Perrin, David. "Mysticism and Art: The Importance of Affective Reception." *Église et Théologie* 27, 47–70 (1996).

Seton, Elizabeth Bayley. *Collected Writings. Volume I: Correspondance and Journals 1793–1808*. Eds. Regina Bectle, S.C. and Judith Metz, C.S. (Canada: New City Press, 2000).

Thayer, David D., S.S. "Living the Spirit of Jesus: Major Themes in the French School of Spirituality." *Alive in the Spirit: Prayer in the French School of Spirituality: Proceedings of the 1998 Conference* (West Seneca, New York), 1–13 (1999).

Thorgren, Vie. "Relationships: Gift for Elizabeth, Gift for Us." Papers from the Symposium, Seton Legacy 1996–97. *Vincentian Heritage* 18/2: 239–248 (1997).

Vermaelen, Elizabeth A., S.C. "Decision Making in the Life of Elizabeth Ann Seton." Papers from the Symposium, Seton Legacy 1996–97. *Vincentian Heritage* 18/2: 213–222 (1997).

Wright, Wendy M. "Elizabeth Ann Bayley Seton and the Art of Embodied Presence." Papers from the Symposium, Seton Legacy 1996–97. *Vincentian Heritage* 18/2:249–260 (1997).

Wright, Wendy M. *Francis de Sales: Introduction to the Devout Life and Treatise on the Love of God* (New York: Crossroad, 1993).

GLOSSARY

absorption: Consists of a close attachment to God accompanied by a deep love for God so that one is "absorbed" in God (Tanquerey 1930, n. 1454).

anchoress: The term applied to a woman who withdrew from the world to live a life of silence, prayer, and self-denial. In the Middle Ages, women adopting this lifestyle did so with the bishop's permission and were confined by him to the walls of their cells. These cells were often attached to churches, but they were also found at convents and in city gates. Men who lived in a similar manner were known as anchorites.

Angela of Foligno (ca. 1248–1309): Born in Foligno, Italy, married a wealthy man, and had several sons. In 1285 Angela had a vision that changed her life, after which she dedicated herself to helping the sick and the poor. Soon after her conversion, her husband, sons, and mother all died. She became a Franciscan tertiary and continued to have mystical visions of Christ and his passion. Angela described her experiences in her *Memorial* and *Instructions*, both of which she dictated to her scribe, Brother A. She was popularly venerated after her death and officially received the title of "Blessed" in 1701.

apocalyptic: Refers to the reflection in those parts of the Bible that concern themselves with the final period of world history often referred to as the "end times." These sections of the Bible are usually referred to as apocalyptic literature. They depict the final confrontation between the powers of evil (the devil) and the powers of good (God) in this world. The Book of Daniel and the Book of Revelation are examples of apocalyptic texts in the Christian Bible.

apophatic: A spirituality that practices the "negative way," a stripping away of all words and images to be open to the sheer transcendence of God, because God is infinitely beyond the human capacity to know. It is the opposite of cataphatic spirituality, which emphasizes knowing God through concrete images and analogies.

ascetical practices: Voluntary practices that enable a person to achieve self-discipline. They are usually adopted for religious reasons and understood to combat vices and develop virtue. Ascetical practices may involve the renunciation of ordinary social goods such as marriage or property. Other practices may be more severe and grow from a penitential attitude or the desire to follow the crucified Christ. Asceticism may be exterior (i.e., fasting) and/or interior (i.e., subduing the passions).

asceticism: Derived from the Greek *ascesis*, meaning exercise. Asceticism is the practice of setting limits to one's choices (such as fasting or service to one's neighbor) for the sake of the gain of some other good for oneself or the community.

Avignon: A French town where presiding popes preferred to live away from the turmoil in Rome between 1309 and 1377.

Beguines: A movement beginning in the twelfth century in Northern Europe that consisted of women who practiced a lifestyle of Christian service, communal living, celibacy, and dedication to prayer, but did not make religious vows. They were sometimes at odds with church authorities because of their independence. Some Beguines became well-known mystics; for example, Hadewijch of Antwerp and Mechtild of Magdeburg. In their own time the Beguines, as they are called later, were often simply called *pious* or *holy women.* They were women who not only desired a life of holiness but also had to earn their living (e.g., with the spindle). In doing this, they presented a new form of female devotion and prayer whose core was the emotional and spiritual "action of the heart" versus a mere, superficial or passive belief in the teachings of the Church.

Benedictines: The Order of Saint Benedict (O.S.B.), the oldest order of monks in the Christian West. Saint Benedict lived from 480–457 in Italy. Each Benedictine monastery, unlike most other religious orders, is not consolidated into a central organization. Instead, each monastery is independent with its own leadership. However, the various monasteries are linked together to form a confederation at the head of which is the abbot primate. The Benedictines live a simple life focused on a rhythm of prayer and work.

beneficed clergy: Clergy who held ecclesiastical offices and were awarded revenues in exchange for fulfilling the duties of the office. The term *benefice* was originally used for a grant of land for life (*beneficium*) given as a reward for services.

brigandage: Describes the activities of military companies in the Middle Ages who formed around captains. Their members frequently worked for hire and became masters at plundering and pillaging the countryside. Companies could grow to contain as many as two to three thousand members, including exiles, outlaws, and landless or bankrupt adventurers. They fomented violence and destruction and were said by Shakespeare in *Richard II* to "write sorrow on the bosom of the earth."

Caroline Walker Bynum: A specialist in medieval religion and has written several highly influential works on the topic of medieval women's mysticism. Her books include *Jesus as Mother; Holy Feast, Holy Fast; Fragmentation and Redemption;* and *The Resurrection of the Body.* Bynum received a MacArthur Fellowship in 1986 and currently holds the Morris A. and Alma Schapiro Chair in History at Columbia University.

Cartesian: An adjective referring to the ideas of René Descartes (1596–1650). This French philosopher taught that the thinking mind is a substance that we can know with certainty, and that it is really distinct from any physical body. This doctrine is the foundation of the modern form of dualism.

Cathars/Catharism: Medieval lay reform movement defined by teachings on the fight between God and devil, and between the body and the spirit, on asceticism, and with faith in special sacraments to be administered close to death. Especially influential in Southern France, and eventually declared to be heretical. The Cathars (Greek: the pure ones) were one of the largest religious movements in the Middle Ages who disseminated in the twelfth and thirteenth centuries, especially over the Rhineland, in England, and in North and Southern France. Critique of the Clergy and call for a poor church as well as a truly apostolic life motivated them. Thereby they only accepted the New Testament (especially the Gospel of John and the Apocalypses) as well as the Psalms and few Old Testament prophets. Also they just accepted one sacrament, the *consolamentum,* a kind of spiritual baptism that combined baptism, ordination, confession, and penance and obliged to a life of sexual chastity. This practice, as well as their (Manicheic) teaching of a dualism between God and Satan and their belief that Christ was not truly human (but an angel sent in human appearance for humankind's recognition of the good), was offensive to traditional

Catholic teaching. The battle against the heretical Cathars in Southern France found a highlight in the Albinguensian Crusade (1209). Nevertheless, the fall of this movment in the fourteenth century is due to the rise of the mendicant movements, e.g., the Beguines and the Franciscans.

Catherine of Siena (1347–1380): The youngest of twenty-five children, born to a dyer in Siena, Italy. Catherine began having mystical experiences at the age of six and became a tertiary of the Dominican Order at the age of sixteen. Late in life she became active in public affairs and was an ardent supporter of the Crusades against the Turks. She was influential in helping to bring Pope Gregory XI back from Avignon to Rome. Her *Dialogue* and over four hundred letters are still extant. She was canonized in 1461 and declared a Doctor of the Roman Catholic Church in 1970.

Cistercian Order: Medieval monastic reform movement that stresses asceticism, solitude, obedience, and work, but also the cultivation of contemplation, the *cognitio experimentalis Dei*, through study of sacred texts. The Cistercian Order produced outstanding spiritual works by both male and female members.

cloud of forgetting: That state in which one lets go of all thoughts and images and rests in an awareness of God in God's naked existence (Johnston 1973, 53–54).

constructivism: The belief that every human experience is fundamentally shaped by contingent factors such as memory, language, culture, setting, etc. In this view, there is no possibility of universal or pan-cultural forms of experience, even at the level of mysticism.

co-redemptrix: A title given to Mary that emphasizes her instrumental participation in Christ's work of redemption through her "yes" to be the mother of Jesus, through her moral union with Jesus throughout his life, and through her compassion with Jesus on Calvary. The title "co-redemptrix" characterized Mary as the New Eve at the side of Christ, the New Adam. Because Mary had been pre-redeemed by Christ in the Immaculate Conception, she could be his helpmate and co-redemptrix during the sacrifice on the cross.

cosmology: The study of the origin, structure, and evolution of the universe (frequently referred to as the "cosmos"). Various cosmologies exist. Depending on which cosmology or "model" of the universe we accept, we will draw different conclusions about how we are to treat the natural world.

Dominican Order: Medieval Christian order founded by St. Dominic (d. 1221) with an emphasis on the preaching apostolate; hence the importance of the itinerant lifestyle of its male members. Other characteristics include voluntary poverty and a high regard for scholastic learning.

dualist/-ism: A remnant of ancient Greek philosophy perceiving the reality as a hierarchy of spiritual and material, higher and lower realms of being.

economy of salvation: The process by which God brought humanity redemption, that is, humanity is redeemed from the condition of sinfulness and brought into a condition free of sin. Often this term refers to the major events that have brought about this redemptive process, for example, the birth, life, and death of Jesus Christ. Other events involved in the salvation process include the raising up of the prophets or the formation of the twelve tribes of Abraham into the people of Israel.

embodied prayer: A spiritual attitude expressed through a physical posture such as out-stretched arms, folded hands, kneeling, prostration, standing, or sitting. It may also be expressed through a bodily condition such as fasting, abstinence, eating, or keeping night vigils. Practices of embodied prayer make it clear that the whole person participates in the act of praying.

Enlightenment: A cultural and philosophical movement that spread throughout the Western world in the eighteenth century. Its adherents believed ardently in intellectual reason and unlimited progress. Many saw Christianity as an opponent of both. This movement shaped much of the character of what is now termed "modernity."

eschatology: The doctrine of the last things. The term is applied particularly to that part of systematic theology that deals with the final destiny of the individual soul, in particular, and with humankind, in general.

faculties: The imagination, the memory, and the intellect. Teresa of Avila uses the term "faculties" rather freely, and is not always precise or consistent; one can assume this definition from a nearby reference in the text (Kavanaugh and Rodriguez 1980, 336–337, V.1, no. 5).

Freud/Freudian psychoanalysis (Sigmund Freud, 1856–1939): Considered the father of psychoanalysis, a field of study that looks to unconscious factors in order to help explain confusing or self-contradictory human behavior. Foundational to Freud's theory is a notion that sexual instincts or drives are critical to the formation of human psychological development. While Freud himself did not offer a fully developed theory of female masochism, he did believe that female sexuality was fundamentally passive; it was left to his female students such as Helene Deutsch to argue that it was also fundamentally masochistic. Deutsch based this theory on the belief that sexual intercourse was inherently painful for a woman and that women have a deep-seated need to be overpowered in order to experience sexual pleasure. Freudian psychoanalytic theory remains influential today although many of its tenets, including female masochism, have been strongly criticized.

Hadewijch of Antwerp: While scholars are not certain of the details of Hadewijch's life, the style of her works suggests that she was a woman of the higher class who most probably lived in the middle of the thirteenth century. Hadewijch was a Beguine and is thought to have either founded or been a "mistress" of a Beguine community. In her writings she implements the imagery and rhetoric of courtly love and, as such, she often uses the metaphor of the Knight and his Lady to describe the relationship between God and the soul. For this reason, God/Love is often referred to as a feminine figure in her works.

Hauerwasian perspective: The angle of ethical vision of contemporary theologian Stanley Hauerwas. He emphasizes the importance of the virtues in understanding the Christian life. Growth in virtue, which he sees as growing conformity to Christ, is facilitated by the construction of both a personal and communal narrative. The individual story is thus meaningfully formed in the context of the overarching Christian story.

imaginative vision: Produced in the imagination by God or by an angel during sleep or when one is awake (Tanquerey 1930, n. 1492).

Imitatio Christi: Identifying oneself with the suffering of Christ, often in a very physical sense (e.g., fasting, bleeding, stigmatization, etc.). As the desire for a life in poverty that would follow Christ in a mendicant life was denied to them, medieval women tried to identify with his life and death within the limitations of their female lives and bodies. Out of that sprang the rather emotional and physical veneration of the *Corpus Christi*, the body of Christ in the holy sacrament of Eucharist, and the new female forms of spirituality that the Beguines, for example, practiced.

incarnation: The embodiment of some divine being in human form. In the Christian tradition, the Incarnation refers to the taking on of human flesh by the Second Person of the Trinity, which is celebrated in the event of the birth of Jesus Christ. The doctrine that Jesus Christ has two natures, both divine and human, was proclaimed by the Council of Chalcedon in 451.

intellectual vision: Occurs when the mind perceives spiritual truths without sensible impressions. Sometimes they are obscure; at other times they are clear and momentary. Intellectual visions resemble intuitions, which leave a deep impression (Tanquerey 1930, n. 1493).

intentionality: Psychological beings' (such as humans and animals) normal way of knowing by directing their intention toward an object that is in some way mentally envisioned. Scholars of mysticism debate whether a form of knowledge that is not structured in this way, but is a kind of sheer self-presence without an object, may be possible.

intratrinitarian life: Refers to the life that the three Persons of the Trinity share with one another. The Trinity is defined as three separate Persons, usually referred to as God the Father, God the Son, and God the Holy Spirit. These three Persons enjoy a community of life in which human beings participate as they grow in intimacy with God.

Jean-Paul Sartre (1905–1980): A French philosopher, political commentator, novelist, and major figure in the philosophical movement of existentialism. In one of his major existentialist works, *Being and Nothingness* (1943), Sartre outlined his convictions concerning the human fear and avoidance of the radical freedom and responsibility of the self. Sartre was a leader of the French resistance to German occupation during WW II and won the Nobel Prize for Literature in 1964. Sartre was a lifelong companion of Simone de Beauvoir.

Kantian: An adjective referring to the ideas of Immanuel Kant (1774–1804), a German philosopher who taught that the human mind can know with certitude only certain principles that are intrinsic to the mind itself. The mind knows things in the world only as "phenomena," or appearances, rather than as the things-in-themselves.

locution: A manifestation of the divine thought to the exterior senses (auricular locution), to the interior senses (imaginative locution), or to the intelligence (intellectual locution) (Tanquerey 1930, n. 1494).

Low Countries: A cultural region with unstable political boundaries during the Middle Ages. The Low Countries included parts of Luxembourg, the Netherlands, Belgium, and France. Characterized by great wealth due to cloth manufacturing, shared Low German dialects, and the rise of urban and ecclesiastical centers such as Liege and Bruges.

Mechthild of Magdeburg (ca. 1208–ca. 1282/94): Although little is known of Mechthild's life, it is generally accepted that she was born into a noble German family and wrote her one mystical text, *The Flowing Light of the Godhead*, over several decades. Mechthild was a member of the Beguine movement, a movement in which women lived communally and devoted their lives to poverty, chastity, service, and religious devotion but did not join an official religious order. Her writing reveals a familiarity with Christian mystical traditions and is thought to anticipate some of the classical mystical teachings of Meister Eckhart.

metaphor: An implied comparison. Since the comparison is implied rather than stated directly, the responsibility for reflecting, intuitively as well as rationally, upon the significance and nuances of the metaphor rests with the reader.

Middle Ages (ca. 500 to 1450): Imprecise and contested term that denotes the millennium between the fall of the Roman Empire and the rise of the Renaissance in European history.

New Age: Imprecise and contested term that denotes the rise of the so-called "Aquarian Age" during the sixties in Northern Atlantic cultures. Characterised by intense interest in mysticism, alternative lifestyles, and utopianism.

nihilism: The philosophical belief that life is meaningless, and that there are no possible foundations for taking any particular moral or intellectual stance.

passing bells: The bells rung by church sextons to announce deaths in the medieval period. The ringing of these bells was restricted in many cities during the plague to reduce the fear associated with the sharp increase in death.

patriarchal cultures: Cultures that are structured according to patterns of domination and subordination thus disallowing the full flourishing of the subordinate groups. The classic example of patriarchy is found in unequal male-female relationships in which femaleness is denigrated, female narratives are marginalized, and female authority is suppressed.

patrician class: Sociological term for a new wealthy class of Christians in European medieval history, whose power was linked to the emergence of urban centers and the increasing importance of money and trade rather than to the ownership of land. Often allied to the kings rather than the regional land-owning nobility.

perichoretic: Refers to the dynamic and vibrant interaction between persons and things. In the present context it refers to the relationship between persons. A rhythmic, active, non-static relationship is described here, one that could be depicted as a "dance" as two or more people get to know each other intimately.

pettifogging: The use of unethical or petty methods by attorneys in conducting trumped-up cases.

postmodernity: Modernity, with its optimistic belief in reason, science, universal principles, continuity, and progress, is said to have begun breaking down in the early twentieth century. The postmodern era is characterized by radical pluralism, eclecticism, discontinuity, and impermanence.

prayer of quiet: Occurs when God takes possession of the most delicate point of the soul, the intellect, and will; God gives gentle repose and joy and leaves the understanding, memory, and imagination free to exercise their natural activity (Tanquerey 1930, n. 1419, 1438). Teresa of Avila explains the prayer of quiet in *The Interior Castle, IV.*

prayer of recollection or passive recollection: A gentle, affectionate absorption of the mind and heart in God, a grace given by the Holy Spirit (Tanquerey 1930, n. 1436).

prayer of union: A most intimate union of the soul with God, accompanied by the suspension of all the interior faculties (intellect, will, understanding, imagination, memory) and by certitude of God's presence within the soul (Tanquerey 1930, n. 1449). Teresa of Avila explains the prayer of union more fully in *The Interior Castle, V.*

rapture: An experience of ecstasy, sometimes a result of mystical exercises, that takes an impetuous hold on the soul as if one were carried by an eagle; it may conclude spiritual betrothal (Tanquerey 1930, n. 1459).

rapture of the flight of the spirit: May follow rapture; it is so impetuous that the soul seems to be severed from the body (Tanquerey 1930, n. 1460).

recluse: Men and women in the middle and late middle ages who vowed to live a life of withdrawal from the world. They sometimes lived in little cells attached to churches.

religious life: A lifestyle involving community living, engaging in a life of prayer, and (frequently) being committed to particular works or services, such as teaching or caring for the poor. Religious orders or religious congregations, as these groups are frequently called, are most often associated with the Roman Catholic Church. Members of religious orders usually commit themselves by vows of poverty, chastity, and obedience for life after an initial period of several years in temporary commitment. Examples include the Benedictines, Ursulines, Jesuits, and Oblates of Mary Immaculate.

revelation: A supernatural or mysterious experience of seeing, hearing, or feeling spiritual insights.

seven deadly sins: Include pride, covetousness, lust, envy, gluttony, anger, and sloth. They are referred to by Gregory the Great and Thomas Aquinas, among other medieval theologians. They are also called "capital" sins and are understood as foundations for other sins.

Simone de Beauvoir (1908–1986): A French philosopher, novelist, and socialist closely connected with the philosophical movement of existentialism, a philosophy predicated on the radical freedom and responsibility of the human person. Her groundbreaking work, *The Second Sex,* was published in French in 1949 and translated into English in 1952. In this work she uses literary, historical, and religious materials to uncover the sources of women's oppression. Asserting that "one is not born, but rather becomes a woman," de Beauvoir argues that women are consistently objectified and made the "other" of men, a condition that leads to their systematic loss of self and identity. De Beauvoir was a close companion of the existentialist philosopher Jean-Paul Sartre from the 1930s until his death in 1980.

sleep of the faculties: Completes the prayer of quiet and prepares one for the prayer of union (Tanquerey 1930, n. 1446).

Spanish inquisitors: Members of the sixteenth-century Spanish Inquisition, a Counter-Reformation movement and legal body established by church officials to investigate and punish Protestant reformers who were viewed as heretics; often civil leaders executed the assigned punishments (Cory and Landry 2000, 292–293, 393).

spiritual betrothal: Comprises the elements of the prayer of quiet and the prayer of union; in addition, the soul becomes absorbed in God and, as a result, there is a slowing of physical functions (such as breathing) and a sense of immobility. Spiritual betrothal may include rapture and rapture of the flight of the spirit (Tanquerey 1930, n. 1454–1456, 1458). Teresa of Avila explains spiritual betrothal in *The Interior Castle, VI.*

Spiritual Marriage: Occurs when God takes possession of the most delicate point of the soul, the interior faculties, and the exterior senses in a stable and permanent fashion. Spiritual Marriage is characterized by intimacy, serenity, and indissolubility (Tanquerey 1930, n. 1419 and 1470). Teresa of Avila explains Spiritual Marriage in *The Interior Castle, VII.*

spiritual/spirituality: Intentional expression and appropriation of religious beliefs and practices, an ongoing search for authenticity, connectedness, peace, and meaning.

survivor psychology: The work of the psychiatrist, Robert Jay Lifton. Lifton has studied extensively survivors of wartime trauma and natural disasters. His subjects have included Vietnam War veterans, survivors of the bombings at Hiroshima and the Buffalo creek flood, and Nazi war doctors. On the basis of his research, Lifton has identified five psychological characteristics that survivors share. They include such traits as death guilt, a death imprint, and psychic numbing.

suspension of the faculties: The intellect, will, understanding, imagination, and memory are suspended in their functions; God occupies the interior of one's soul (Tanquerey 1930, n. 1449).

theological virtues: The virtues of faith, hope, and charity enumerated by St. Paul as the foundation of the Christian life. Along with the four "cardinal" virtues—temperance, prudence, fortitude, and justice—derived from ancient philosophy, they form the basic elements of Christian thought on virtue or moral character.

tropological: A particular way of reading the Bible that takes seriously the various metaphors, analogies, and similes contained in it. Once a more technical and narrowly defined term, it now refers to a reading of Scripture that takes into serious consideration the symbolic value of the text as it is configured in these various literary devices.

unknowing: Occurs when one experiences a kind of darkness of mind in which one knows and feels nothing but a "naked intent" toward God (Johnston 1973, 48–49).

urban centers: A comparatively late historical phenomenon of the European West that led to new forms of self-government by city communes (also see *patrician class*). Urban centers appeared during the Middle Ages along centrally located trading routes. They attracted socially diverse groups, including the new monastic reform orders, but also created uncared-for groups of urban poor, including children, women, and the elderly. Jewish ghettoes are another distinctly urban phenomenon of the European Middle Ages.

vita (plural vitae): Latin term for the written story of a saint's life; a genre for "biographies" of men and women in the process of becoming canonized as the official saints of the Church. A *vita* is not the same as a modern biography that attempts to account data of the exterior life of a person; its intention, rather, is to testify to the spiritual life of a saint or a holy person. Cistercian hagiographers in the twelfth century started to write *mystical* *vitae* that were not chronological, but stressed one *virtus*, one spiritual gift of a holy man or woman in order to present this life as an *exemplum*, an example of a holy life. The *vita* of Marie d'Oignies written by Jacques de Vitry (1160/70–1240) stresses one *virtus*, one spiritual gift of the holy woman, and is written as a sequence of *exempla* in which many of her *virtues* shall be shown. Listening to her *vita* as "an example of a life to whom God gives the fullness of virtues" (Geyer 1992) has challenged "the faithful" in the time of the crusades.

vows: serious promises of poverty, chastity, and obedience given by men and women who have joined a religious order, usually given as a life commitment in order to realize the goals of the particular religious order or community. (Also see *religious life*.)

Waldensians: Medieval Christian reform movement eventually declared to be heretical. Founded by a wealthy merchant, Peter Waldo, at the end of the twelfth century. Waldensians propagated many of the ideals of Protestantism, for example antipapalism and a return to the Bible as sole religious authority, but also stressed voluntary poverty in imitation of Christ and his followers.

witches: Contested term that, from a Christian point of view, denotes men and women who have entered a pact with the devil and engage in evil magic (*maleficum*) to harm animals, personal property, and human beings. Witchcraft thus defined constitutes a form of heresy. From a New Age perspective, witches today engage only in life-enhancing magic and are followers of pre-Christian pagan teachings.

INDEX

CONTRIBUTORS

ANN W. ASTELL received her Ph.D. from the University of Wisconsin-Madison in 1987. A medievalist, she is Professor of English at Purdue University. Her publications include four books from Cornell University Press: *The Song of Songs in the Middle Ages* (1990), *Job, Boethius, and Epic Truth* (1994), *Chaucer and the Universe of Learning* (1996), and *Political Allegory in Late Medieval England* (1999). She is the editor of *Divine Representations: Postmodernism and Spirituality* (Paulist, 1994) and *Lay Sanctity, Medieval and Modern* (University of Notre Dame Press, 2000).

SHARON ELKINS is Professor of Religion at Wellesley College, Wellesley, Massachusettes, where she teaches courses on historical and contemporary Christianity. She is also Adjunct Professor of Church History at Pope John XXIII National Seminary in Weston, Massachusettes. After publishing *Holy Women of Twelfth-Century England* (1988) she turned her attention to female visionaries and the Virgin Mary, the main topic of her current research and writing. She also is preparing for publication her journal from a thirty-day silent retreat, *Adventures in Prayer: Doing Ignatius of Loyola's Spiritual Exercises Today.*

ANNETTE ESSER is a teacher of Catholic theology in Germany. Born in Cologne in 1957, she holds an M.A, from Münster University, Germany, and an S.T.M. from Union Theological Seminary, New York. Currently she is working on her Ph.D. thesis on ecumenical aspects of women's spirituality at the Catholic University of Nijmegen, the Netherlands. Annette Esser is co-editor of *Feminist Theology in European Perspectives* (KOK Pharos, 1993) and of *Re-Visioning Our Sources: Women's Spiritualities in European Perspectives* (KOK Pharos, 1997).

MARY FROHLICH is Associate Professor of Spirituality at Catholic Theological Union in Chicago. Special areas of interest include the spiritual classics, mysticism, psychospiritual development, and the spirituality of place. Her articles on Thérèse of Lisieux have appeared in the annual volume of the *College Theology Society* (1999) and in *Theological Studies* (2000). Other publications include *Praying with Scripture* (Center for Learning, 1993), *The Lay Contemplative* (St. Anthony Messenger, 1999), and *The Intersubjectivity of the Mystic* (Scholars, 1993).

JANE MAYNARD is the Director of Field Education and Instructor in Pastoral Theology at the Church Divinity School of the Pacific in Berkeley, California. Jane has studied Psychology at the University of Pennsylvania and the University of Illinois in Urbana. She holds an M. Div. from the Church Divinity School and a Ph.D. in Theology and Personality from Claremont School of Theology. Jane is an Episcopal priest who has worked as a hospital chaplain and pastoral counselor in addition to her work as a seminary professor.

JANE MCAVOY is Associate Professor of Theology at Lexington Theological Seminary. She is an ordained minister with ministerial standing in the Christian Church (Disciples of Christ) and a member of the Forrest Moss Institute of Disciples Women Scholars. She writes in areas that intersect concerns of feminist theology, worship, and spirituality. Her books include *The Satisfied Life: Women Mystics on Atonement* (2000) and *Communion with the Friends of God: Prayers and Meditations* (2001).

ROSEANNE MCDOUGALL, S.H.C.J., is interested in linking Christian spirituality and the Christian tradition with implications for daily living. She has also begun to explore some interdisciplinary relationships between religion and literature, and between religion and psychology. Currently serving as adjunct professor of religion at LaSalle University and lecturer in theology at St. Joseph's University, both in Philadelphia, she is a coordinator and teacher in "Theology for Ministry," an educational program sponsored by the Society of the Holy Child Jesus in Nigeria. She has taught at Immaculata College, Chestnut Hill College, and Rosemont College, as well as at the University of Portland. Roseanne received the Ed.D. in religion and education from Teachers College, Columbia University, the M.A.T. in religion from the University of San Francisco, and a professional diploma from the Graduate School of Religion and Religious Education at Fordham University. She has been a professed member of the Society of the Holy Child Jesus for forty years.

DAVID B. PERRIN, O.M.I., grew up in a family of seven children on a small farm in Petawawa, not far from Ottawa, Canada's capital city. He obtained a B.Sc. in chemistry from the University of Western Ontario in 1978. After a two-year teaching sojourn in Haiti, and then philosophy studies, his career path led him to the Institute of Spirituality at the Pontifical Gregorian University in Rome, Italy. He returned to Canada to do a Ph.D. in theology at Saint Paul University (1995), where he is currently Associate Professor and Dean of the Faculty of Theology. He has published two scholarly books on John of the Cross: *Canciones entre el alma y el esposo* (1996) and *For Love of the World* (1997), as well as *The Sacrament of Reconciliation: An Existential Approach* (1998). He has also published popular and scholarly articles on mysticism, asceticism, spiritual direction, the spirituality of reconciliation, and an article in the area of men's studies.

ELLEN ROSS IS Associate Professor of Religion at Swarthmore College in Swarthmore, Pennsylvania. She is the author of *The Grief of God: Images of the Suffering Jesus in Late Medieval England* (Oxford, 1997), and of numerous articles on late medieval Christian spirituality and contemporary thought. She teaches courses on comparative mysticism, medieval spiritual life and thought, images of Jesus in history, literature, and theology, and religion and literature. She leads retreats on Christian spirituality that celebrate traditional and contemporary religious reflection.

KIRSI STJERNA is Assistant Professor of Reformation Church History at Lutheran Theological Seminary at Gettysburg, Pennsylvania. A native of Finland, she has Master of Theology degree from Helsinki University (1988) and a Ph.D. from Boston University (1995). She writes on Medieval and Reformation spirituality, theology, and women, St. Birgitta of Sweden, and Martin and Katie Luther.

ULRIKE WIETHAUS is the author of numerous articles and books on medieval Christian mysticism, including *Ecstatic Transformation* (1995), *Maps and Flesh and Light* (ed., 1993), and *Dear Sister* (with Karen Cherewatuk, 1993). She combines her interest in women's spirituality with crosscultural and interdisciplinary work on the arts, film, and cultural respresentations of the sacred. She is currently completing a monograph on issues of diversity in medieval Christian mysticism.

WENDY M. WRIGHT holds a Ph.D. from the University of California at Santa Barbara and is currently Professor of Theology at Creighton University and director of the Center for the Study of Catholicism. She also teaches regularly in several graduate ministerial programs including Seattle University's ITM program, Creighton's Christian Spirituality Master's program and the National Methodist Academy for Spiritual Formation. Her expertise falls in the areas of history of spirituality, family spirituality, spiritual direction, and women and spirituality. Her academic work has focused on the Salesian spiritual tradition founded by Francis de Sales and Jane de Chantal. Listed among her books are *Bond of Perfection: Jeanne de Chantal and François de Sales* (Paulist), *Francis de Sales and Jane de Chantal: Letters of Spiritual Direction* (Paulist Press Classics of Western Spirituality Series), *Francis de Sales: Introduction to the Devout Life and Treatise on the Love of God* (Crossroad Spiritual Legacy Series), *Sacred Dwelling: A Spirituality of Family Life* (Forest of Peace), *The Vigil: Keeping Watch in the Season of Christ's Coming* (Upper Room), and *The Rising: Living the Mysteries of Lent, Easter and Pentecost* (Upper Room). She is a frequent contributor to *Weavings* and *Family Ministry*. She and her husband, Roger Bergman, are the parents of three young adults.